Truth Behold

Chris Barry

Raider Publishing International

New York   London   Swansea

© 2007 Chris Barry

All rights reserved. No part of this book may be reproduced stored in a retrieval system or transmitted in any form by any means with out the prior written permission of the publisher, except by a reviewer who may quote brief passages in a review to be printed in a newspaper, magazine or journal.

First Printing

The views, content and descriptions in this book do not represent the views of Raider Publishing International. Some of the content may be offensive to some readers and they are to be advised. Objections to the content in this book should be directed towards the author and owner of the intellectual property rights as registered with their local government.

ISBN: 1-934360-52-X
Published By Raider Publishing International
www.RaiderPublishing.com
New York   London   Swansea

Printed in the United States of America and the United Kingdom
By Lightning Source Ltd.

I dedicate this book to the memory of my father.
To my children, Sheena, Barry & Natasha and to all of you
who challenge injustices that deprive us of the essence of life!

Truth Behold

Chris Barry

Chapter One

Jim Finds Himself On The Edge Of A Cliff

With the letter grasped tightly in his fist, the future seems so dim.

"Ohhhh Holy God, I'm so hearty sorry for offendin' thee and with ya'r help I'll not sin again. Please forgive me for what I'm about to do and grant me soul eternal rest..." muttered Jim as he stumbled his way into the harsh, cold November winds, "Jaysus Christ, why has this happened to me? How can I provide? Maybe the life insurance will provide a future for Peg and wee Johnny. Hopefully she'll forgive me and come to terms with me actions. Please God, make this ayeze..." sobbed Jim as he crouched at the edge of the cliff looking out yonder to sea.

The gale force wind howls around the cliffs off Doulus Head and the waves lash in anger against the rocks below. As Jim edges forward, the rocks seem clouded, near, yet so far away. His heart thuds while his mind willingly chooses to take a back seat to his senses of reality. His legs now deeply rooted on the soggy grass grasped to the cliff top by its shallow roots. His head tells him to jump, his frustrated spirit whispers, "hold on." However, his heart wishes to remain neutral.

As the rain now blankets his life earned tears, his sobs of justification to end his turmoil are heard no more as the howling November winds circle around his wet clad body in an ironic way as if to say, "jump and get it over, what're ya holding on for? With a little nudge from us, it'll be all over. Go on, wan more step is all it'll take..."

Jim covers his eyes with his cold trembling hands hoping that maybe if he doesn't see the way down the landing will feel less traumatic. His eyes force a glimpse through his grasped fingers as if to ask for one last peek at the world. A voice deep from within calls out, "take a recheck, take a recheck. What God has put together, no man shall pull asunder."

Suddenly, his body is lifted from the ground and flung backwards by a whirlwind and as Jim's face hits the ground, the taste of soil on his lips sends tremors up his spine at the very thought of his intentions. As he gently but cowardly glides his semi-lifeless body to the edge of the cliff and looks at the future of his family and loved ones. He quivers at the thought of its very existence. A life without him would be a life robbed of love, respect and happiness for those that needed him.

"How could I've even thought of such a way out?" he sobbed to himself, wiping the tears from his eyes and looking around with a clearer vision into the world that needed him.

The guilt and shock of his actions instilled energy into the reality of the here and now. There is a blast of thunder and for some unknown reason it reminds him of an old folklore omen, "winter's thunder, a summer's wonder." Was this a sign that things would be okay?

The evening is fast closing in and the strong winds are dying down but the rain is still persistent to make its presence known as if to teach him a lesson and show him the way. As his attention is now drawn to the evening sky, past scenes of his life flash before him. Some happy, some sad, but none that he was unable to challenge, overcome or aspire to. These few moments of reflection and reconciliation with himself give him the strength to get his confused guilty lifeless body to its feet and with his head huddled into his shoulder pits he slowly stumbles his way back to his car. Jim finds it strange but relieved to fit into his surrounds and the journey home seems much longer. He keeps a watchful eye out for the drivers and passers by, and wonders if they look at him in a suspicious manner.

Ironically, other then the odd nod they seem oblivious of his existence.

"Maybe me guilty insecure self doesn't show, hopefully not. I've always been good at coverin' up me insecurities and emotional pain. Maybe I can continue foolin' the world around me but somehow I fear not. Somethin' happened to me today on that cliff. I got a wake up call from life and I can't go back to livin' the life of that man I allowed meself to be. The man I desperately wanted everywan to like but disliked so much meself. The man that needed to be wanted and wanted so desperately to be needed, always afraid to say NO, just in case people might reject me. The man that put family and loved wans on the long-finger, 'cause I convinced meself that I was needed to work those extra hours, 'cause others were too selfish or lazy to take responsibility for their own workload...." were the thoughts that flooded his mind as the tightness in his throat forced his suppressed tears to flow.

Jim pulls the car into a laneway just off Darby's Bridge as his vision of the road ahead becomes blurred from his floodgate of tears. With his face embedded into his cupped trembling hands, his inner voice speaks words of wisdom from within, "Jim, my dear man, I guess if we're to be truthful with ourselves, many of us have become the person you allowed yourself to be. I guess, as we get suffocated in the insufficient things in life, many of us ignore the basic ABC's of living, which are common sense and that success is about happiness and contentment with oneself. But, more importantly, it's love and happiness that empowers people. How could you ever find success in life when you dropped off your true self and the little child within you somewhere along the pathway of life? Jim, my dear man, where're your childhood dreams, they're your future. They're the miracles of life that'll come true if you allow them. You were a happy child, content with simple joys. But look at you now. You're a stranger to yourself. A people pleaser you've become, who in time will become a pest, not only to yourself but also to others if you don't take a good honest look at yourself and start taking responsibility for your own life. But to be willing to do so, you'll have to stop living life in the shadows and footsteps of others. You'll need to live at the helm of your own life and only take a back seat when fate wills you to do so. This will allow you to take responsibilities for your own mistakes and look upon them as a learning process. A learning process that'll help you to grow and mature while searching out personal excellence...."

"Jaysus Christ, where did it all go wrong?" Jim cries aloud banging his fist on the dashboard, "Was it really that letter that stated, as from Monday ya'r services are no longer required or was it just simply I took life for granted and ignored the most important people of all. The people that surrounded me with love when I was to busy to notice and in doin' so I lost sight of who I really am?"

As Jim sits there, aimlessly gazing into the evening sky, he confronts his past, present and future and wonders why so much energy in his boyhood rearing and education was founded on not how to be a man but more so, on how not to become a woman! And for that reason alone, he had always had difficulty with his feelings and emotions. In fact, he had become emotionally constipated from years of suppressed feelings. The tears in their own strange way released the airlock in his emotions and as he turns the key in the ignition, he promises to grant himself the right to reclaim his own life.

His body, mind and spirit together now face a rebirth in life, a life that is to be lived and not endured while walking in the footprints and shadows of others. As he drove out of the laneway, an old grey donkey in the field nearby looks over the ditch with ears erect and head turned to the side, brays as if to say, "I'll never understand ye humans."

As Jim drives up the tree-lined boreen to his home, the evening seems much brighter and a warm glow surrounds the moon. The curtains from the sitting room window edged apart and a familiar bobbing smiling face greets the lights of the car. Once again, his son Johnny didn't let him down. He is the miracle of life that would help Jim to rediscover and reclaim his life. Johnny is Jim's Down's syndrome miracle who has developed an impish sense of humour over the years and who faces each day with a smile. He had just turned nine on his last birthday but people would have you know that he is much older in spirit.

On entering the house Peg, Jim's wife calls out, "Supper's ready and get out of those wet clothes before the hand of death grabs a hold of ya. Why didn't ya wear ya'r donkey jacket? It'd keep ya warm and dry. Although in the next day or so, I'd say the weather is due to change. I can tell, there's frost and plenty of snow on the way, 'cause the robins are startin' to hop around the doorway in search of food."

As he gently kisses her on the cheek, the moment suddenly darts him into reality, "The note....ohhhh-Holy-God....the note," he thought to himself.

Rushing up the narrow pine staircase to the bedroom, he grabs the note from the bedside locker and in that clumsy moment, he knocks over the vase of dried bog cotton. With an unconscious reflex reaction, he slips the note into his trouser pocket. As the vase hits the floor with a thud, Peg shouts up from kitchen, "Jim, everythin' ok?"

Jim calls back, "Yep.....grand......just grand."

And really, it was, because for the first time in his life he is ever so grateful that fate had granted him a second chance at living life.

Jim's life wasn't meant to be over that day for he was only confronted with another one of life's corner stones. Corner stones that we bump into on our pathway through life and have difficulty in encountering them as we haven't got the time or inclination to file down the sharp edges to smooth the journey around them. Little did Jim know that the ghost of times past would visit him over the next twelve months and get Peg and himself to confront the truth, conquer their demons and swim their emotional oceans while climbing their spiritual mountains. These moments were to become the stepping-stones to regaining their true-selves, understanding their identities while reclaiming Peg's stolen childhood dignity.

    Peg and Jim live in an old country cottage that they inherited from Jim's uncle. The boreen that leads up to the cottage is planted with brambles, wild roses, fuchsia, the odd holly bush together with a few beech and oak trees growing in between. At the end of the boreen, an ash and an oak stand side-by-side. Peg in her own wisdom is able to tell the forecast of spring from the theory, "if the oak buds before the ash, then we'll only get a splash. But if the ash buds before the oak, then we'll surely expect a soak." She is also of the belief that if the May blossom is brought into the house in the first week of May, "bad luck it'd bring to all who visit." Along the boreen, wild primroses and daffodils bloom in springtime while foxgloves graced with buttercups and daisies take over at summertime. No matter what time of the year you had, it's a welcoming boreen to take a short stroll down. The front of the house is overgrown with creeping red and white roses mingling in the ivy, honeysuckle and pink clematis, Peg would have it no other way. Many a time Jim threatened to cut back the overgrowth but he was stopped on his tracks by Peg's persistent personality.

    At the front kitchen window is an old railway sleeper and it's here Jim loves to sit during the summer with the newspaper and a mug of tea on a Sunday morning after Mass, relaxing in the isolation and peacefulness of his surrounds, yet alerted to the aroma of frying lamb chops and mint sauce coming from the kitchen. It's a great position to sit in if you wanted full view of the local comings and goings, for in the distance you can see the main road on route to the Ring of Kerry. Most of all, it's heavenly to sit there in the evening time coming into late spring listening to the different breeds of birds as they out chirp each other singing their mating calls. But what was truly delightful, was to watch a bird nurse a young gearrceach in the nest in early summer and to listen to the little chirps of excitement when she would bring it a worm or two. Peg found it very therapeutic to sit by the kitchen window listening to the dawn chorus in late spring and early summer. She found sharing those precious hours with the birds helped her make sense of challenging moments.

There are two main rooms downstairs with a small bathroom out the back. The kitchen has a flagstone floor that comes to light with the whiteness of the whitewashed stonewalls. All the furniture is made from old floorboards that Jim reclaimed from an old mill nearby. And the porcelain cream colour sink that stands proudly under the back kitchen window is Peg's pride and joy for she found it in an old house nearby and restored it back to its former glory. She took great pride in helping Jim plumb it in while building the marble wash-stab that surrounds it. In the centre of the kitchen is an old country pine table covered with a red check tablecloth that matches the curtains on the front and back windows. The windowsills are brought to life with pink and white potted geraniums that are in full bloom for more than ten months of the year. The kitchen is always warm and welcoming and the smell of fresh baked bread and scones that comes from the old Stanley cooker is a sure sign to any visitor that a cuppa is on the way.

The sitting room is just off the kitchen and Peg polishes its wooden pitch pine floor once a week. The large open fire that is lit every night without fail keeps the bedrooms warm and cosy as the heat from the fire travels up the stairway leading to the landing from which two small bedrooms lead off. The room is decorated with soft furnishings that Peg made herself in the local ICA craft classes that are held once a year in the village hall. Photos of the family and friends and President John F Kennedy hang on the walls and over the fireplace is a picture of the Sacred Heart. This is Peg's special room and just beside the fireside, she has her own rocking chair. Beside it stands her most cherished possession, her spinning wheel. She had bought it in the flea market in England and over the years, she had learned to spin. She would sit there in the evening time and often late into the night, knitting or sowing or simply spinning out yarns of wool that she got from the local farmers. She would hand dye the wool with dyes that she made from seaweed, lichen, leaves, bark, beetroot, onions and other vegetables. As she did so, she would hum and sing country western songs. Jim often just stood at the doorway staring at her, engrossed at the peacefulness she found in the simple joys of life. When it came to overcoming illness, tiredness or just her simply run down days she would find great healing power in music or going to the nearby strand for long reflective strolls.

Just under the front sitting room window Jim had made a little wooden trunk for Johnny's toys. But Johnny is more in favour of using it to stand on to view the outside world on rainy days. You were sure to find him standing on it looking out the window, evening after evening waiting for Jim to come home from work.

The bedrooms are decorated in pastel shades and each bed is covered with a patchwork quilt that Peg had made from clothes from parcels from America. According to Peg, each patch could tell a story as she could tell you from whose pants, dress or shirt each patch came from. Over the long winter evening, while she was sewing them she would have Johnny help her remove the pins. Repeatedly she would recite the nursery rhyme to him,
"See a pin and pick it up.
All day ya'll have good luck.
See a pin but let it lie.
Luck will surely pass ya by."

Throughout the house are pieces of antique furniture that Peg had restored and brought back to life with a polish mixture that she had seen the nuns make in the Industrial School from linseed oil, petroleum jelly and the white of an egg. The scent of mint and lavender is to be found throughout the house in wintertime to keep the moths away as Peg is of the belief that it would keep them out.

On the landing windowsill, a candle flickers well into the night. Peg lights this candle each night and says a little prayer while looking up into the night sky. The light from the candle holds a deep and haunting secret that Peg has held in her heart for years. Over the candle is a small framed pressed rose that Peg picked when she left the Magdalen Laundry in Cork and has kept it in memory of her little secret. Underneath the pressed rose is a poem…

The Rose

The essences of life is reflected within a Rose
Each petal reveals a year of life just lived
Its bud reflects a woman's womb
Embracing a miracle of life within

Its various colours resemble the Human Race
Each graced with a beauty of its own
Its tender scent enlightens our senses
To the uniqueness of Humanity alone

The leaves are the friends that care
Protecting us from stormy times
The thorns are there to remind us
Of challenges we encounter as life unfolds

The stem resembles the pathway of Life
We're destined to take on route to Eternity
While the roots reflect our inner strength
Arising from our glowing Spirituality

Overall, it's a very homely house personalised by Peg's motherly and womanly touch. Peg is a woman who doesn't ask for much in life but takes great pride in doing her best. If there was one thing she learned while in care with the nuns, she would have you believe that it was how to be frugal and capable of making a little go a long way. What fascinates Jim mostly about her is the way she is able to lose herself in deep thought. She could sit amidst a crowd, yet her mind would be lost in deep thought and she could become totally oblivious of the people that surrounded her. Even though she didn't ask for much in life, by nature Peg is a determined soul. To Jim, she is like a rough diamond that when polished sparkles like the rays of the setting sun in late summer. Take Peg out of her apron and curlers and my-o-my, is she able to turn heads as she strolls by dressed in all her beauty. Her womanly disposition gives Jim a true understanding of why the Christian teaching of the three persons in the one God remains a mystery and in his opinion the same could be said about women. She is a great homemaker and a very protective mother. But her hot impulsive temper has often caused many martial arguments, but none that were serious enough to be of any grave concern to Jim. His way of coping was, finding a life for himself outside the home.

Peg strives so hard to have the perfect home and family. Even though she is a loving wife, she has problems expressing her love to Jim. Their sexual life is non-existent and any approach made by Jim to her in the bedroom is met with the reply, "not tonight darlin', I've a headache comin' on," or "Arrrah shur, ain't it the unclean time of the month again." This is her way of referring to her periods, a saying that was instilled into her during her time in care in the Industrial School for Girls in Tralee that was run by the nuns. But Jim often thought who was he to question the workings of Peg's body? She has a knack of turning the simplest of arguments into a hornpipe without music and for a day or two afterwards she is like the television in the local pub, all picture and no sound. Understanding her temperament has taking Jim almost a lifetime.

Jim has worked in the office of the local creamery responsible for the day-to-day orders coming in and going out. Even thought his attire could have been of a casual nature, Peg would insist that he wore a collar and tie each day, clothes that came from parcels they received from America. Time and time again, he would try and convenience her that suits were for condemned men, weddings and funerals. But she would stand firm and insist that he remained loyal to the collar and tie regime.

Throughout their years of marriage, living with Peg made him come to realise that women were on this earth to be loved and not understood. If Jim was to have his full senses and not make life difficult for himself, there were just some things he didn't question about Peg. He had learned over the years that the best way to handle a temperamental woman was not to confront her, but more so, not to give her something to worry or complain about. But regardless of all her faults, he loves her dearly and she is his whole world.

Peg's whole world is wrapped around Johnny, their Down's syndrome son. Since birth he has suffered from asthma and eczema, he also has a speech impediment. The upper part of his tongue was attached to the roof of his mouth at birth. The attending doctor snipped the attaching ligature of skin and this has helped in some way. Peg is very protective of him but insists that he should be treated like any normal child when it came to teaching him manners and courtesy.

The other person that plays an important role in her life is her brother, Sean Og. He works as a farmhand on a neighbouring farm. There is a very close bond between them and they often engross themselves in secretive chats about their past. They are always on the look out for each other and wouldn't have a bad word spoken about each other. Sean Og lives in one of the old thatched buildings at the back of the cottage adjoining the farmyard. It has a little open fireplace, a sink, and an old wrought iron bed and in the corner is an old pine table and chair that he made out of reclaimed floorboards from the old mill. The small windows that look out onto the farmyard are dressed with rose print curtains made by Peg. The red rose creepers and honeysuckles around the front door give a welcoming scent. All in all, it's nice and cosy and for him, it's home-sweet-home. He always keeps it warm and cosy. To him, this is his little palace and with the swallows nesting in the eaves along with the odd field mouse, he believes he is surrounded with good omens. His mother always believed that when a swallow chooses to build its nest in the eaves of a home, happiness, good luck and success come to all who dwell within.

To Sean Og, little Johnny is very special. Some would say that he is the son he never had. Sean Og, himself has many hang-ups from his time in care under the guardianship of the Christian Brothers in St Joseph's Industrial School for young Boys in Tralee. He has carried the shame of his past around with him for years. This umbrella of shame that he lives under is one of the main ingredients of the root to the depression that he is a victim of. The shame of what happened to him in that school made him believe that he was no good and not worthy of kindness or recognition. It hasn't only stolen his childhood but it has broken his confidence and the backbone of his dreams. But despite the tough times he experienced while in care he had learned some very valuable practical skills, like soling a shoe, mending a pocket in a trousers or replacing a missing button not to mention the handyman skills that are needed to keep a home together.

He takes great pride in his willow basket making. Over the years, it has gone from a simple hobby to a nice source of income. The locals as well as the tourist are eager to purchase from him. One could be in no doubt that Peg and himself are brother and sister when they stand shoulder to shoulder. But it's their personalities that pull them apart, Sean Og's placid gentle outlook in life is always out shone by Peg's fiery determined one.

Chapter Two

Peg Finds The Note

The following morning, Jim is busy attending to the cattle and feeding the foul but the events of yesterday are still haunting him. "Could I've really thought of endin' me own life? As long as I'll live, I'll never let Peg know what was goin' on in that stupid impulsive head of mine. But, I'll have to get around to tellin' her about the job ..." he thought to himself.

Work was scarce and what they made on the few rough acres of mountain land wasn't enough to make a decent living on. Up until now, he was able to provide well. Some would say, they were comfortably well off. Unlike many other local families, they had needed nor wanted for nothing.

"Where will I get a job? It might mean that I'd have to go back yonder to England and work for a few months of the year. Maybe I could work on the lump, that'd mean I wouldn't have to pay tax. That'd make me a handy few bob. Ach shur, maybe Sean Og could help out with the heavy jobs around the farm and anyway Peg is an independent woman, I'm sure she'll manage..." he pondered as he tries to reassure himself. With all the troubling thoughts that were going on in his head, he totally forgot about the note in his trouser pocket that he left on the bedroom floor.

Meanwhile, Peg is busy with the housework and while sorting out the bedrooms, she decides to wash Jim's trousers. On clearing out the pockets what does she pull out, the note! Peg, like most women is naturally inquisitive and is curious to search out the contents of this crumbled up piece of paper. As she ponders on the contents word-by-word, she feels a weakness waft through her body.

Sitting on the edge of the bed she starts to reread it aloud as if to convince herself, what she read, was really what she had just read.

My Dearest Peg,

To tell you that I love you seems empty when what I'm about to do may seem so loveless. Over the years, I've tried so hard to be the strong one in the marriage but it was the bones of your perseverance and strength that really saw us through.

I've become a man that can't only provide for my family, but one that's not capable of sharing failures due to my own inadequacy. A waster, I'll not become, much less a burden on you.

The step, I'm about to take isn't one of a copout or of self-pity. The life insurance will see you and Johnny through. It'll provide you with the life you both deserve. A life, I'm unable to provide. A man has to be a man to exist and that I can't simply be. Life without my pride and manhood isn't a life for you or me. I must free my Spirit, as there's no purpose in living without dignity.

My dearest Peg, this note expresses all my love for you. Please pray for me while I'll watch over you and Johnny. Ask God to forgive me for what I'm about to do.

Your loving husband

Jim xxx

"Jaysus Christ, please tell me this can't be. Me Jim would never think of takin' his own life, or would he? Ohhhhhh , what've I done that's so wrong? How could he be feelin' like this, could it be that I was unaware of it all this time? Noooo, this can't be happenin' to us. What am I goin' to do? What'll I say to him? No, I'll put the note back and say nothin', maybe it was just wan of his stupid anxious impulsive moments, maybe he wasn't goin' to do it. Maybe I shouldn't make a fuss. Ohhh…..Christ….what'll I doooo?"

These were just some of the agonising questions that went round and round in her head. At this stage, she could feel her throat tightening up and her jawbones jamming. Her eyes were filled with tears and her knees were quivering. As she focuses on the note, once more she reads it repeatedly in her mind. Her tears now start to flow and the words become blurred from her teardrops as they drop one by one onto the note. Holding it close to her heart and looking up to Heaven she cries aloud, "this can't be happenin' to us. I thought life was so good and me Jim seemed so happy in himself. What can be troublin' him so much that he felt he had to take his own life? Please God, don't do this to me, do ya not think I've suffered enough. I'll try and do me best. I'll be a better person, wife and mother. I'll even go to church a bit more, if that's what ya want of me. I'll do anythin' ya want but please God, don't take Jim from me. How will I cope? What'd happen to Johnny should anythin' happens to me......"

Opening up the note fully to reread it again, in her anguish she continues to gulf back the tears. All this time Johnny was lingering in the hallway and on overhearing his mother's cries he runs to tell his father.

"Da, Da," Johnny yelled anxiously.

"What can the matter be, son?" asked Jim picking up another sod of turf.

"Ma kyin', Ma kyin', kum Da, kum Da," yelled Johnny tugging at his father's shirtsleeve.

"Cryin', where son?"

"In edumm, in edumm."

"Ohhhh Jaysus, the note, Jaysus Christ, she has found the note," mumbled Jim to himself and with that he drops the gabhail of turf and dashes into the house, leaving Johnny in his trail.

He scrambles up the stairway two steps at a time into the bedroom and there he finds Peg hunched up crying with the note clenched in her fist.

"Peg darlin', ohhhh me darlin' Peg, I'm so sorry, I'm... soooo..... sooooo..... sorry."

"Sorry?" gagged Peg.

20

"I never meant to upset or hurt ya. It was all just a stupid mindless moment in time. I got let go at the creamery and didn't know how to tell ya. I didn't know how we were goin' to cope. And Peg, ya see, I don't know, ohhhhh Jaysus, what can I say I didn't know what got into me. I just acted and didn't know why. Peg, believe me when I say, I'm soooo….soooo….sorry," cried Jim standing over Peg with his hands joined together and eyes focused onto the ceiling as if in his heart asking God for forgiveness and clarity for his explanation.

The moment was engulfed with Peg gagging. Then finding her strength, she arises to her feet and with that her anguish turns to anger. Screaming and yelling she belts out at Jim with clinched fists.

"Ya feck'in bastard, ya selfish no good feck'in bastard, how could ya," she sobbed aloud grasping the crumbled up suicide note in her fist.

"Peg….please…Peg," pleaded Jim as he tries to calm her down.

"Ya….. nooooo….. good….damned son of a bitch," she yelled slapping him across the face.

"Ohhhhh Christ….what….a mess…..I've caused," gasped Jim trying to embrace her.

"Ya're a selfish feck'in bastard, ya've everythin' that life could give ya, a good childhood, lovin' parents, a lovely son and a lovin' wife, what could be so bad that ya felt ya had to run out on us and throw in the towel in the arena of life. If ya had a past like mine and memories of it that taunt ya day in and day out maybe then ya'd have a reason to question the cross that destiny left ya to carry. Ya see Jim, Sean Og and I didn't have all the joys in life that a child deserves. Jaysus Christ Almighty, ours were a gruellin' existence where pieces of our childhood Heaven were daily sent to Hell but regardless of our past, we go on trying to live each moment while making the best of it."

All this time, Johnny stood huddled up sucking at the ear of his teddy bear and sniffling back the tears that ran from under his little round-rimmed specs. He had never seen his Mum so angry and it troubled him so. After a few moments Jim and Peg found comfort in each other's arms, sobbing and crying until their tears could flow no more.

For the first time in her life, the secret of Peg's past is revealed as she tells Jim about her horrific childhood. Now, for Jim the jigsaw of the missing parts of their relationship fit together. He now understands why she feels, thinks and reacts to everyday situations.

In 1947, due to their mother illness, Peg at the age of eight and her brother Sean Og who was just five years old at the time were sent into care to the Industrial Schools run by the Religious Orders. They were never told of their mother's death while they were detained at the schools. They waited for her to come and collect them day after day. During their stay at the schools, they were both badly emotionally, physically and sexually abused.

Chapter Three

Adopting A New Approach To Living

That evening while Johnny is tucked up cosy in the land of nod, Jim speaks with Peg about his redundancy and shares his worries with her. She takes it calmly and makes plans for the future but she worries about Christmas and how they will pay the overdue bills.

"Sentimentality will have to go out the front door while practicality finds its way in the window if we're to survive the comin' year," said Peg as she tries to visualise the future.

"If we can get through Christmas and over the month of January we'll have a milk cheque comin' in," said Jim trying to be optimistic about the future. "And then maybe I'd have a job as a farm labourer as there should be some handy jobs around comin' into springtime. Please God, things mightn't be a bad as they seem...."

"We'll just have to tighten our belts Jim, and the first yoke to go will be that new car ya bought a few months back..."

"The car, do ya not think we'll need that?" replied Jim in a reluctant manner, as the new Rover was his pride and joy.

"Shur, why can't ya trade it in for a older model. All we really need is somethin' to get us around and the money that we'll save could go to payin' back the bank loan. We could also sell a few of the cattle and rams to cover any of the outstandin' bills," she said as she bit into her lower lip, something she was accustomed to doing when she was in deep thought.

"Maybe so," replied Jim reluctantly. Silently wishing though, he could reason out why they should keep the car but he knew better than to argue with Peg.

The following day, Peg has a word with the local accountant, Gerry, who drops in for a dozen of fresh eggs that he buys from her every week. She confides in him about their predicament and asks for his guidance on how they might set up some form of budgeting plan that would help them sort out their financial difficulties. Gerry, by nature, is a down to earth, practical, intelligent man who is always ready for a challenge. His energy for living is edged on by the fire in his belly that makes him hungry for tackling problems.

"Well it's as plain as this Peg, when you start to get the feeling that there's too much month at the end of your money. Or put it another way, if you're on a monthly wage and as the second Friday of that month approaches you ache for payday, or if you're on a weekly wage and come Tuesday, there's no jingle of coppers in your pocket and the pounds have all run out, then you'll certainly need to learn the art of budgeting," insisted Gerry unbuttoning his overcoat and shoving his tweed cap into the back pocket of his trousers.

"I think after a year on the unemployment benefits there'll be no more cheques and too many days if we don't strap our belts and batten down the hatches when it comes to our finances," joked Peg as she tries to be light hearted about their worries.

"I myself think that if you can manage a household budget and at the end of the year come out with a profit then you've the ability to manage your own small business," called out Gerry going to his car and taking out a black folder containing information on budgeting for families surviving on tight purse string.

"I see," muttered Jim.

"There's one section here with all the necessary details on how to get the best out of your money," explained Gerry handing the page to Jim. "Monitoring your money isn't about meanness, it's about being sensible and getting your money to work for you."

"This….looks….quite….detailed," said Peg glancing at the page over Jim's left shoulder.

"Yerra, it ain't," shrugged Gerry.

"Emm," nodded Jim looking through the file.

"Once you get started and remain loyal to the daily exercise, it'll fall into place and it'll all make sense. On a daily basis, take account of all your spending and the money you receive that includes the money you pay out for treats for Johnny. You'll be surprised at the amount of money we spend on small treats and never notice it amounting up. You'll need to take account of all the outstanding bills and loans from the bank and so forth. Here are the headings, housing and utilities, groceries and household supplies, car expenses, seasonal expenses, clothing, medical care, personal expenses, emergencies and repairs to house and farm, animal foods and farm veterinary care etc. At the end of each month, amount up all your outgoings and balance it against the money that you received for that month. That'll give you a good indication of where your money is goin'. You'll then have a clearer picture where you should cut back and hopefully sort out your financial problems. Willpower will be needed to keep to the plan at hand and to put a plug in the hole of impulse spending," insisted Gerry as he circled each heading with his pencil.

"Shur that's great, we'll start at the beginnin' of next week and keep it goin'," said Peg. "Are ya happy with that, Jim?"

"Everythin' seems to be in order," nodded Jim taking another glance at the file, "I dare say, anythin' will be a help to get us out of the red in the bank."

"Money is a strange object, it isn't until we're without it, we tend to worry about it," sighed Gerry. "If we were to make money our servant and not our master then maybe we'd have a better understanding of how to manage it…."

"I guess ya're right there," nodded Jim.

"Everyone wants more money. The trouble is, when you've more, it still ain't enough. The more we have the more we spend. The more we spend the more we want. Many of us find ourselves caught up in the rat race of society, skittering around trying to justify penny pinching on our health in order to make an extra pound. Our ancestors would have us believe that money is a good servant, but a bad master. How many times have we heard, the love of money is the root of all evils. Money causes many temptations. We worry about money. People kill for money. People fall by the hand of suicide over money. Women often consider selling their bodies for money. The more we abuse money, the more money seems to abuse us. But there's one thing we all have experienced is that debt always increases stress and worry. Budgeting is something we tend to associate with when we find ourselves deep in debt. But the fact of the matter is that if we budgeted on a weekly basis we wouldn't find ourselves in debt. And as I've said, budgeting isn't about being mean, it's about being sensible. It's about working with your money and in return getting your money to work for you," sighed Gerry taking out his pipe as he relaxes into the rocking chair.

"Money is somethin' we all take for granted when there's a steady flow of it and it's only since I've lost me job at the creamery that I fully realise the power it has over our lives," muttered Jim to himself.

"How people handle money, power and fame often reflects their sense of their own self worth. I often think money can be likened to sex, you think of it when you don't have it. When you have it, your thoughts are directed to something else," giggled Gerry to himself. "Learn to be happy and content with what you've got. If money is a problem for you, please don't give up. They're answers and ways to help you through. Don't go through the worry and the problem alone. Talk to someone that you can trust. Seek help and advice from a financial adviser. Your life is more important than money. But above all, don't let money problems make you throw in the towel in the arena of life."

"How right ya are," sighed Peg and the horrific thought of Jim taking his own life sent a shiver up her spine.

"I've a verse here that says it," chuckled Gerry taking out his wallet and handing a short verse to Peg. "I usually read it as my party piece in the pub after a few noggins of whiskey."

Peg unfolds the small piece of white paper that contains the verse and from the finger marks and dog-ears, she could see that it had been well versed and read. At first, she reads it quietly to herself and then as she walks over to the back kitchen window she reads it aloud,

*"**Money***
It'll buy ya a grand big house but never a home
It'll buy ya a fancy bed but never a peaceful night's sleep
It'll buy ya sex but not true love
It'll buy ya statue but certainly not respect
It'll give ya wealth but not happiness
Money is only relevant to the lifestyle we choose to live by
On ya'r deathbed ya ache not for money but contentment
So why, throughout our lives do we worship it so.
Put it back in its rightful place, manage it but never allow it to control ya.
Make Money ya'r Servant and not ya'r Lord and Master."

"There's a lot of wisdom in that verse," chuckled Jim as he carefully wraps the hen eggs in newspaper and puts them in a basket for Gerry.

"Look, I'll leave the file here with both of you and all you'll have to do is fill it out and I'll have a good glance at it when I'll come back next week," said Gerry tapping Jim on the shoulder. "But in the meanwhile, I'll keep an ear to the ground in the hope of finding some work for you, Jim."

"Now.... that'd be grand Gerry..... so until we meet again...... God bless ya," replied Peg as Gerry makes his way off down the boreen.

That night when Sean Og returns home from work they confide in him about their concerns but he assures them that there's nothing to worry about, as he himself will help out financially and after all that's what families are all about, helping each other out during good times and challenging times. But they did agree that the car and the yearlings that were grazing in the top meadow should be sold and the outstanding bills should be cleared as soon as possible.

Chapter Four

Jim And Peg Seek Out Help

The following week Jim and Peg turn to the local doctor for help regarding their emotional turmoil. The local doctor is a much loved man and is better known to the locals as Doc. Peg is anxious to find out if Jim needs to go on a course of pills, as she fears if the depression engulfs him, he might try to attempt suicide again. Doc ain't too worried and seems to think that pills ain't the answer. He feels that pills may bring about short-term happiness but never inner contentment and it's contentment that helps a person through their struggles in life. Anyway, Doc is not a man to hand out pills too freely. He is a descendant of the old school of medicine. "If castor oil doesn't work, try something else," is the slogan the locals would use to describe his physiology in treating ailments and worries.

Doc lives alone in the local village and his small clinic is attached to his home. A little damp, dark room that is graced with his medial certificates, a picture of Michael Collins and a photo of his wife who tragedy died while giving birth to their first newborn many years ago. Over the fireplace ticks an old oak clock that's always ten minutes early. This is to allow Doc a few minutes to recover with, "chasin' the hair of the dog," recovering from the night before. Doc is a drinking man but only takes enough to allow him the ability to keep a clear head the following morning. The memory of his wife's death has tainted his life and some would have you believe, that's the reason why he escapes from reality on his trips down alcohol lane.

He was the doctor who attended her in labour, fifteen years ago. Just as she was about to give birth to their firstborn she suffered a massive uterine haemorrhage. He was neither able to save his wife nor their firstborn. Not a day goes by that he doesn't talk about her to the locals and this is how he keeps her memory and love alive. He is totally dedicated to his work and the community and it's well known that following the death of his wife he married his profession. And night or day, hail, rain or snow he is always ready and willing to answer that call. One thing for sure, you were in no doubt that Doc was near even before you clapped eyes on him or heard the echoing tone of his Limerick accent, it was that strange scent of the combination of tobacco and antiseptic that impregnated his clothing that alerted you to his presence.

In the surgery, Jim takes a few minutes to recollect his thoughts and explains to Doc why he felt like ending his own life and why he felt so alone in his heart. His tries to describe the feelings and emotions that overtook him on the edge of that cliff and asks Doc why is he feeling like this when he should be strong enough to take the knocks and falls in life.

"After all I'm a man that was reared by the psychology of the schoolin' of hard knocks," he replied when Doc asked him why he thought he should be able to overcome setbacks in his life in the isolation of his aloneness.

"From my experience in helping people who find themselves in a similar situation as yourself Jim, I've come to realise that there's so much dis-ease around a suicidal state of mind. And it's that very state of dis-ease that taunts a person to finally throw in the towel in the arena of life," explained Doc.

"Am I to blame for this dis-ease that's givin' me such a confused state of mind?" asked Jim in a hesitant tone of voice that leaves Doc in no doubt that Jim is very embarrassed and feels uncomfortable about talking openly about his personal feelings and emotions.

"Well Jim, the greater part of your contentment or misery depends on your personal disposition and not on your circumstances. My good man, each day listen to yourself and be honest with what you hear. It's that inner voice inside you that'll help you manage your feelings and not control them," said Doc running his fingers through his hair. "And by simply doing this, you'll allow yourself the privilege to live for the moment while granting yourself permission to shed guilt, self denial, resentment and any other negative beliefs or attitudes that inhibit you from living life to it's utmost. Negative thinking is one of the causes of life's major illnesses and it's the cause of many a troubled wandering mind. We all have the power to turn our negative feelings and emotions into positive ones and by doing so, we don't allow our inner feelings to induce illnesses on ourselves. This is one of the major steps in taking responsibility for our own well-being. Start with giving yourself a smile each morning and then give one to a stranger. A smile is a free gift from God. So treat yourself to one each day...."

"Emm," nodded Jim.

"And Jim, when it comes to honesty, you must be honest with yourself first before you can be honest with others," sighed Doc looking across at the photo of his wife. "After my wife died, I found it very difficult to understand God, but it was good to know that He was always around in case I needed a friend to morose to. So I guess what I'm trying to say is, get in touch with your own spirituality and allow yourself permission to befriend your spirit guide and your guardian angels. They'll see you through tough times if you stay in contact with them. Prayer has it's own medicinal powers. But above all, always remember when people you need can't be there for you, be there for yourself..."

"What would ya tell a child if one of their parents were taken from them by way of suicide?" Peg asked Doc as she glances across at Jim with raised eyebrows.

"What'll I tell the children? Yeah...yeah... what'll... I tell....the children?" sighed Doc standing up and walking to the window that looks out onto a small overgrown garden. "That's the most horrific question that awaits a parent or loved ones when their nearest and dearest are taken from them by way of suicide."

As he stands there looking out the dusty windowpanes, he loosens his tie and takes a moment or two to recollect his thoughts. Stroking his chin, he turns around and responds with a long deep sigh.

"Dear, ohhhhh dear, a suicide is like an earthquake. It vibrates tremors through the hearts of loved ones left behind and rocks the foundation of any community. So many questions are asked, yet answers are so hard to be found to comfort the loved ones while they try and find solace during their bereavement."

Making his way back to his chair, he takes out a match from his jacket pocket and uses it as a toothpick. He then places his specs on the oak desk and continues speaking in his slow deep Limerick accent.

"What'll.....I tell....the children? Yep. That's the shocking reality that a person has to face when children of any age are left without a parent due to suicide? Truth behold, the simple answer is, tell them the truth. Many people feel that in order to protect children and save them for any hurt or pain of the reality of the situation, it's better to guard them from the truth. More than often the opposite is true. If we hide the truth or mislead our children regarding the death of a loved one it can often do more harm than good. Children are very strong human beings and have an open constitution for the truth. If children are confronted with the realities of the death of their loved one from someone else, they may find it difficult to trust you again. Hiding the circumstances of the death is in my opinion, preventing the person who died, the right to die with dignity. Suicide is a shocking, daunting reality that invades all walks of society and no one is immune from the hand of death."

All this time Peg and Jim just sat in silence totally bewildered by what Doc had to say and as they watch him reposition his specs on his nose and walk across the floor they link on his every word.

"How right ya are, Doc," muttered Jim and the intense frown on Jim's brow revealed to Doc that Jim's innermost feelings that had remained dormant for many years were being unravelled.

"Honesty and empathy are the best policy when it comes to explaining to children about the death of their loved one," muttered Doc picking up a small jug of rainwater to water the geranium plant on the dusty windowsill.

"What does suicide emotionally do to a young child, Doc?" asked Peg.

Taking another few moments to think and recollect his thoughts Doc replies in a consoling tone of voice.

"The feelings that children experience during grieving after the death of a close friend or parent aren't unlike that of an adult. They often feel abandoned and alone. They may blame themselves for the death of the parent, afraid that they'll be punished and die a terrible death. It ain't unusual for them to be overcome with feelings of insecurity. They may start to develop a fear of the dark or even begin bed-wetting. Younger children become clingy and develop a fear of being left alone. Confusion, shame and guilt regarding the dead person are all a normal part of their grieving. Anger and denial may follow after a week or so after the death. Whatever feelings they experience, it's important for them to know and to be reassured that it's okay. It's very important to allow them their own personal safe space when they're comin' through the grieving stage."

"How would ya even go about explainin' to a child that somewan died by way of suicide?" asked Jim now feeling the guilt of his actions but somehow relieved that Peg had not found herself trying to explain a fatal instant to their son Johnny.

Looking at Jim over his half masked specs while nibbling at the nail of right index finger, Doc once again lets out another long deep sigh before replying.

"Jim, my dear man, it may seem impossible at the time to even try to explain suicide to children but that's exactly what one must do. The child's age will be a factor in how much they'll understand and how you'd go about explaining the situation. Some young children are content with a very simple explanation. Others will need more detailed information to allow them to come to terms with the death. It's best to keep your explanation short and simple. Make it known to them that it wasn't their fault and the person that died loved them dearly. Help them to overcome any fears or guilty feelings they may have regarding the death. Listen to what they want to say. Often, just being there for them in silence and givin' them a cuddle or a hug is more beneficial than speaking meaningless words. Allow them to cry out their tears. It's my belief that suppressed tears only germinate the seed of depression..."

"Emm, emm," nodded Peg.

"When children are ready, they'll want to talk to you about their inner feelings. If they feel comfortable and safe with you, they'll trust you. When a young child hears that the death was by way of suicide, one of the first questions a person can expect is, what's suicide? A simple explanation might be that people die from many different causes. Some people die from road accidents, strokes, heart attacks or cancer but others get sick in their minds, they find that the pain they suffer is so great that their minds tell them that it's time to die. They then decide with the strength of their minds to die and they end their lives. Children will need to know that the suicide wasn't their fault. They'll need to know that the feelings they're experiencing will pass. They'll always miss and love the parent that has passed on. Always allow them the right to keep the spirit of their loved one alive in their hearts."

"We're all so ready to moralise about suicide and have glorified critical thoughts about it 'til it visits our own doorstep, would ya agree, Doc?" asked Peg holding his attention with her intense stare.

"Indeed you're right, Peg," nodded Doc. "Often we tend to moralise about suicide. The social stigma and prejudice about suicide are our greatest enemies in preventing us from understanding the reasons why the victim was taken by the hand of death by way of suicide. The shame that the Catholic Church has instilled into its followers regarding suicide has laid the foundation stones for people's cruel attitudes towards the victims of suicide and in the long run is the cause of the guilt that many families and friends of the victim suffocate themselves with..."

"Shur, from a very young age many of us are taught that suicidal people are shameful, sinful, weak, selfish or manipulative," butted in Peg.

"I can tell you now, my dear Peg, they're certainly not. Suicide is neither right nor wrong. It's simply something that happens to a person when mental torment and agonising emotional pain exceeds their inner strength to cope with coping. It's a horrific permanent solution to often a temporary situation. By allowing a person to die with dignity, we give them the right to allow their spirit to go free and rest in peace. If we allow their spirit to go free, we too will find solace in our bereavement," said Doc looking at Jim and he could see from his hunched posture that he was very troubled.

Peg just sat there in silence gripped by the wisdom of every spoken word.

"Emm," nodded Jim.

"You see Jim, suicide isn't something that just happens to someone else, it can also knock at our doors and who knows maybe one day it might, God forbid it though," sighed Doc reaching out and dipping his finger into the holy water-font on his desk. He blesses himself by making the sign of the cross on his forehead and after a few moments of mental recollection, he continues speaking in his deep Limerick accent. "We don't truly know what really empowers people to take their own lives and I guess we never will. We can make scientific assumptions but we'll never really know. To me suicide is a subconscious vision followed through by a conscious act."

Doc was a little restless in himself this morning as today was the anniversary of his wife's death and talking about death was making him feel a little sad. But knowing that Jim now depended on his care, he takes a deep sigh while swallowing his inner feelings.

"People who attempt to take their own lives by way of suicide often feel so emotionally alone. Too many of them simply just struggle through life in an emotional abyss. They often feel friendless not only amidst a crowd but also amongst family and loved ones. They spend most of their days abiding by other people's wishes and desires but never comin' to terms with their own feelings and emotions."

Doc paused for a moment and then continued speaking in a low tone of voice.

"In life, many of us look for friends to need and care for us. I'm aware that this is an essential human need but too often we ignore the one true friend we've got in life and that's, oneself. If we could get to know and like ourselves then we'd come to love ourselves. By loving and understanding ourselves, we'd get to understand others better. We'd be less likely to be disappointed and hurt by others. But above all, we'd come to understand that people are human and as human as they are, they'll let us down in life. You see Jim, by befriending ourselves we'll never feel alone. Too many of us go through life not even knowing who we really are, simply because we have lived our lives in someone's footprints. We've set our goals by someone else's wishes and desires, living our life trying to prove that we're normal and likeable. Often, it takes a crisis in life to awaken us to how fragile we really are. Life has it's own way of alerting us to our limits, strengths and weaknesses. Jim my dear lad, you're one of the lucky ones, for truth behold, life has handed you a second chance. You'll need to start believing in yourself, Jim. And believe in yourself, you must, if you're to recognise, understand and accept the challenges that life has in store for you…"

"I guess ya're right. Are there many others like me?" asked Jim and there was a quiver in his voice as he tried to hold back the tears.

"Indeed they're, Jim. Do you hear those people out in that waiting room chatting away amongst themselves?"

"Emm Emm," nodded Jim.

"Truth behold, most of them can't be cured with pills alone. The reality of the situation is, they only need to chat about life's little troubles that'll probably cause the odd ache and pain or maybe a lowering of the spirit or a sleepless night," replied Doc pointing to the waiting room door. "Sometimes, it might only be that they've lost their reason to smile or laugh and as a result of that, their immune system has broken down. You see, our feelings and emotions have a lot to answer for when it comes to physical illnesses…"

"Doc, why is there such a stigma around suicide?" butted in Peg as she eases her chair closer to Jim.

"Ignorance will always bring stigma. Often stigma originates out of fear of the unknown. Years ago, people were of the belief that it was the fairies who took the person's spirit when the person died by way of suicide. And the troubled spirit was to remain in the fairy world until they decided it was time to let it go free. I guess though, the real stigma propagated from the Catholic Church. You must remember there was a time when the Catholic Church had a monopoly over souls. People believed that donating money to the Church was a sure way of buying their way into Heaven. The very thought of being denied the right to bury your loved one in holy ground was enough to give rise to the creation of the stigma around suicide and you must remember it was the Catholic Church that denied that right to the families of the victims of suicide. They drummed it into us that it was a crime again the Church and God to take your own life. So hence, the saying, he, or she 'committed' suicide. But, what I do know is, where people have interfered with fairy routes or disturbed the folklore resting places of the fairies such as fairy forts or rings, there's not only a higher rate of suicides or attempted suicides but also a higher instance of emotional torment. Some might say, that's all just hear'say, but I think there's more to it then we care to believe."

"Where does wan start when it comes to sortin' out Jim's situation?" asks Peg.

"Well, there're four major steps that one needs to abide by. The first one is, to have a realistic expectation. What Jim is suffering from is years of suppressed feelings and emotions that have got the better of him. It'll take time to unravel them and understand why they're causing him such inner torment. The second step, Jim, is to be willing to accept your limits. You can't climb mountains when you only have the strength and energy to climb hills. As I've said earlier, you need to listen to yourself. Don't let anyone push you or pull you beyond your limits. This is where you come in Peg. Be there for Jim when he's feeling low in spirit. Allow him his down days and by doing that, you'll allow him to appreciate his good moments. And as regard to the third step, think before accepting other people's reactions to you. Always remember that people are human and often they'll tell you not what you need to hear but what they want you to hear. The most important step of all is, try to mix with open-minded positive people. They're a tonic in themselves. Learning from their optimism will allow you to sort out your pessimism. Having a positive outlook in life is both rewarding and just. It'll allow you to be free of insecure feelings and thoughts. But above all, it'll allow you to accept your hurt and anger and help you to strive towards renewal health and life."

Doc paused for a moment to recollect his thoughts.

"Often emotional pain is good if we accept it to be the path of healing, it alerts us to the need to look inwards and take account of our lives. It gives us the strength to search out the right pathway in life that we need to follow to aspire to well-being and happiness. I'm a believer, that doing is often a quick boost to the ego and self-concept. Get involved in gardening and get in touch with your creativity and imagination. Revisit your dreams and set daily small goals that're in line with your well-being. I know all this may seem daunting now, but if we work through it as a team, we'll all be winners in our own right. I'd like you both to remember that the worthiness of your lives comes not in what you do, or even whom you know, but by who you are. You're special, don't ever forget that," said Doc raising his bushy eyebrows and giving them both a big hearty smile.

Peg smiled shyly back and nodded in acknowledgement, as she was very pleased with Doc's wisdom, for she herself needed to off load past negative baggage that has tainted the core of her being for years.

"Do… ya… think… I'llllll…. try it again?" Jim was referring to suicide.

"Jim, it's okay to mention it by name," timidly smiled Doc. "You may or you may not try to take your own life by way of suicide. I believe that's in the lap of the Gods. But there's one thing we can do to try and prevent it and that's to sort out what drew you to it in the first event. I don't think it was that blooming letter. That letter was only the siren that alerted you to your senses and allowed you the choice to accept a second chance. When we get to understand the reason for the present circumstances, we can advance forward. Don't be afraid to allow people that you trust and love to reach out to you, Jim. Love is a blessing that's germinated in one's spirituality…. and… the more you give…..the more…. there's to go around."

"Emm, how right ya're, Doc," replied Peg nodding in agreement and placing her hand on Jim's shoulder while looking at him in admiration. "I think that Jim needs to believe in himself more and give himself credit for all he has achieved…"

"Yeahhhh Jim, Peg's right, do give yourself credit for your achievements in life and I need to stress also that to believe in oneself, is one of the necessary steps of overcoming any crisis in life."

Jim is fully aware that Doc is no psychologist but he has a natural understanding of the workings of the human mind. In life, some of us spend years trying to study psychotherapy but the few that are born with it as a gift will shine through with easiness in their profession and Doc is certainly one of those chosen few.

"Will.... I need.... to come.... and see ya very often.... for the treatment?" muttered Jim while biting into his lower lip.

"The treatment and care will be an ongoing process. And it ain't really how often it is, but rather how you're responding to the treatment. You see, I'll be treating you both as individuals yet as a couple. This will also be an opportunity for you, Peg, to take recollection of your own life as a woman, as a mother and as a wife. We'll see how you're progressing in each section of your life. While on the other hand, you Jim, will be looking at your progress as a man, as a father and as a husband. Often over the years, an imbalance occurs in one of these areas and that alone can cause a problem in another area. When we've harmony in all three areas, we get fulfilment out of life. I feel if you work together and come through this phase in your lives, your love for each other will strengthen and grow..."

Jim and Peg both nodded in agreement.

"Often, life's problems left unsolved can choke the life out of love and marriage. What I intend to do today, is to take some blood samples and get them assessed as I need to rule out any physical element that may be causing you both to feel under the weather. Then maybe, in the next week or two, you'd come back to see me and I'll carry out other physical tests that need to be attended to. In the meanwhile, I'll draw up a mental renewal exercise that'll suit you both. Over the next few days, I'd like you to take a little time on your own and write down issues in your lives that're a challenge to you. I'd like you to make a list of all the things you've done with your lives from as far back as you can remember. It doesn't matter how small they seem, it's the joy and satisfaction they brought, that's important. On another list, I'd like you to write down all the things you like about yourself, this is no time to be modest, be honest and proud of yourselves. Then, I'd like you to take another piece of paper and make a list of what you like about each other. And the final list, is about Johnny. Tell me how he has changed your lives. Bring those lists back with you when you come to see me and we'll take it from there..."

"Grand so," replied Jim glancing across at Peg. "Ach shur, that won't be too much bother."

"But in the meantime, take care of each other and stay safe. There're too many people walking around, weight down with others people's problems. Remember, the first lesson of recovery is, don't let your mind become so distracted by other people's issues that you allow yourselves to lose all insight to who you really are. When we allow ourselves to feel comfortable with ourselves, we once again become aware, of lessons we learned, once known but somehow forgotten. We start to give ourselves permission to acknowledge, reason and understand our feelings and emotions while laying negativity to rest," sighed Doc sitting back into his chair, stretching out his legs and as he glances down at the dry dusty clay on his leather boots he clears it away by the flick of his heels. This might be a cause of concern to his medical colleagues in a city practice but not so to Doc, for his cares were country folk.

"Often I find that my mind is so clouded that I can't see the way forward. I suppose that's what brought me to Doulus Head," mumbled Jim in a broken tone of voice as he takes a handkerchief out of his jacket pocket and wipes the perspiration from his brow. "I suppose that's one of the reasons why I tried to search out death instead of allowing death to search out me?"

A momentary silence fills the room and with all eyes focused on the oak stained floorboards, the three of them take a moment to reflect.

"That... ain't.... surprising," replied Doc as his mind wanders off for a brief moment to the isolation of the countryside around Doulus Head, and the very thought of Jim intending to end his life there sends a cold shiver up his spine. "Your mind is like a mirror. If the mirror becomes too dusty or clouded, you won't see yourself clearly and the only thing to do is to wipe it clear. The same can be said when you find yourself engulfed in troubling moments in your life. The only way forward is to find time to clear your mind so that you've a clearer vision of yourself and the world around you. All through life, we feel so important, attending meetings to organise the workings of the world around us but few of us attend the most important meeting of all. Or should I say, even have knowledge of its existence…"

"What meetin' is that?" butted in Jim.

"A… meeting ….with ourselves," smiled Doc.

"A… meetin' ….with ourselves?" exclaimed Jim.

"Yep. That's right, a meeting with ourselves," insisted Doc tapping on the desk with his specs. "The agenda for the meeting is, your mind. The issues to be discussed are, your feelings and emotions and how you're coping with them. To me, that's the most important meeting in life. We're so busy running, racing, galloping and gambling with our lives that we neglect to spare a few moments each day having a meeting with our minds. And everyday we fail to meet with our minds, we're allowing more and more chaos to build up in our lives. We certainly wouldn't let our business run like that, for we know if we did, it'd fall apart. So, as from today Jim, I'd like you to take time out at the end of each day to have an appointment with yourself. Meet with yourself and focus on the reconstruction of a healthy mind, body and soul. That's one of the greatest gifts you can give to yourself. It's called personal time. If you do that on a daily basis, you'll not only come to know yourself better but you'll also become your own best friend. Peg, it's something you could do as well. I do it myself and I find it very rewarding…."

"Would ya say that men are their own worst enemies and carry a legacy of emotional constipation from their past?" asked Peg.

Doc paused and reflected for a moment while once again tapping the desk with his specs.

"From my medical and personal experience in helping men to come to terms with mental health issues, I feel that many men in the past have been raised on not how to be a man but rather on how not to be a woman. And for that reason alone Peg, is there any wonder why many of us men have difficulty in expressing our feelings and understanding our emotions? This social belief of the past has left many men suffering from emotional constipation as you yourself have rightfully described it and believe it or not, it's this inability to manage their feelings and emotions that has sown the seed and laid the foundation stone to many an abusive relationship."

"I suppose there's no quick fix to sortin' out emotional pain and grievances?" muttered Jim.

"Well, I could give you a pill and hope it'll go away but in my opinion that's only like brushing the dirt under the mat. The day will come when there's no more room under that mat and it'll need to be cleaned out. The same can be said about our suppressed feelings and emotions," coughed Doc trying to clear his tobacco tainted lungs. "I do however have a guide chart for helping people to overcome their emotional challenges in life. I've it somewhere here in the drawer. I myself call it my safe cross code. Or maybe it should be referred to as the first aid treatment for emotional difficulties. It's certainly of great value to me when I'm confronted with personal issues. Ach shur, why not take a copy with you, sit down, and work it through for yourselves…"

"Be happy to do so." replied Peg.

"Often, if you write down you feelings, you become more aware and alert to how you need to confront them. Life is like an undulation and it's only when you're on the downward slope you come to the realisation of the understanding of the sense of appreciation when the good times come again on the upward slope. But it's important to realise though, no matter what guidelines you choose to follow, unless you're prepared and willing to make your peace with yourself and life, you'll never achieve happiness," said Doc handing them a copy of the safe cross code regarding feelings and emotions. "You see, one in six people suffer some form of mental illness. Now with that in mind, we need to take a realistic view and attitude to the treatment of mental illness. Treatment of mental illness shouldn't be carried out to suit or fit in with an administrational system. It should be directed towards individual care, taking into account that each and everyone of us is a unique person. We need to have mental health units attached to general hospitals and not locked away in units behind high stonewalls. We need to start treating the mentally ill person as a whole person and not just look at the illness and treat it separate from the person. These people need to be treated with dignity, humanity and with supportive loving care. Until we'll accept that attitude, the reality of the situation will be that we'll always have a stigma around mental health...."

"I totally agree with ya, we certainly need to change our attitude in life regardin' mental illness. We need to start treatin' the person and not just the mental illness," insisted Peg gazing out the window. "But like many situations in this country of ours, it'll take another generation to come before we realise that mental illness is a part of livin' and that it's often the source of many of the physical illnesses that we suffer from."

Once again, there is a moment of silence and the ticking of the grandfather clock in the hallway seemed to harmonise the chirping of the small birds picking away at the crumbs on the windowsill.

"You see, too many of us live life carrying around burdens from the past entwined in hopes and desires for the future and because we continue to do so, we fail to live in the present moment," said Doc coughing once again to relieve his tobacco mucus lined lungs. "Too many of us have lost the ability and privilege to laugh like a child and that has become the source of many of our everyday illnesses. Our behaviour and attitude are a reflection of our mind. How we feel about the world around us depends on our state of mind. Life is simple, it's when we choose to make it complicated, we suffer. Our mind is our guide to our body but it's our will that controls our mind and because of this, our well-being is determined by our state of mind. When our minds struggle with negative concepts, we'll live in pain but when our minds learn to develop positive concepts, we'll live in joy. I'm a strong believer in the fact that our health services need to pay greater attention to the power of the mind when it comes to healing and curing."

As the time passes, they chat about the comings and goings in the community and of Jim's chances in securing more employment locally. Doc asks about Johnny's well being and tells them that he would like to check out his development to make sure that he is in good health. Johnny by nature is very hyperactive and has suffered from asthma and eczema since birth but is recovering well since he has gone on the goat's milk. Doc tells Peg to keep him on the cod liver oil, as it helps calm the hyperactive nature that many Down's syndrome children are born with. He explains to them that fish oils have the potential to improve the impressions and connections in the brain cells and this leads to better concentration and calmness in a person as a whole.

"If we can keep Johnny's lungs in order, he'd be well able to ward off chest colds or flu over the coming months. He was a lucky chap to recover from that flu of 1968, so many others weren't as fortunate. We had flu like that in 1945 and in 1957 as well. I remember it wiped out so many families. The flu strains seem to be getting stronger each year so Johnny will need to stay on the cider vinegar and honey as colds and flu don't take root in an acid flora body. The cider vinegar contains the essential trace minerals for a healthy body and the honey is a natural antibiotic in itself. In times gone by, honey was often referred to as nature's cure. The best thing to do at this time of the year is to make sure that he's wrapped up warm when he's out playing. I think there's some wisdom in the saying, button to chin, when October comes in, cast not a clout, 'till May be out," said Doc shaking hands with Peg and Jim and bidding them farewell.

"Ach....maybe Doc.... me problem... is that I've too much self-pity, I need to cop'on," smirked Jim.

"Well my dear man, in my opinion, self-pity is a privilege that we shouldn't indulge in too often," grinned Doc tapping Jim on the shoulder and winking at Peg as they make their way out through the waiting room.

On the way out, Jim's attention is drawn to a poster on the entrance door containing the slogan, *"Many people would cherish a smile so why not share one with a passer-by"*.

Chapter Five

Church Dues

It's the first Monday into New Year and Sean Og decides that it's time to pay his church dues. A big goose reared by Peg is just the very thing he thought to himself. And he being well known throughout the village for the kind resourceful chap he is, takes the goose in a plastic manure bag to the priest's home on the crossbar of his bike. The goose is alive and every-now and again it struggles with the wobbling of the bike as Sean Og tries to duck the potholes. He reassures her that the outcome will be favourable and all that is required is a little patience.

When he knocks at the priest's door, Betty, the housekeeper informs him that the Parish Priest is attending to the main altar for evening benediction. The Parish Priest with his inherited Christian attitude is content to take a goose anytime of the year but there are certain conditions attached to his acceptance and gratitude and that is, a goose should be seen and not heard. Today, just like any other day, the aul boy, as he is known to his parishioners is in his usual form, lets say, he certainly ain't backward in coming forward in what he has to say to his parishioners.

"Well Sean Og, there's a sayin' my dear mother used to use, always a day late and a pound short, but in your case it's more like 365 days late and many pounds short," he sniggered as he turns around to see what Sean Og has to offer.

"Well Father, I'm here now and that's all that matters and ya'll be happy to see I'm about to pay me dues," smirked Sean Og trying not to allow the attitude of the aul boy knock him off his tracks.

"Well, well, well, paying your dues, is that so," grunted the Parish Priest in his usual statistic self as he squints over his round rimmed specs.

"Now Father, here's wan of the finest Embden geese ya'll find throughout the whole of South Kerry. It was hand reared by meself and only fed the best of organic food. It's sure to make a hearty meal and shur, if ya're in need of feathers, these wans are good enough for any man's pillow, even yours Father. Herself inside, or should I say ya'r good housekeeper, would be glad to get her hands on wan of the wings, ach shur, wouldn't it make a grand duster for her. So, all-in-all, Father, I don't think ya can condemn or refuse the gift I bring ya today. With the scarcity of good geese around this year, it'd more than cover the value of me dues owed. I assure ya Father, none of us are losin' out here. Ya've a grand goose and I've now paid me dues. Shur, anyway the money owed in dues wouldn't cover the price of wan as grand as this wan. I don't' think ya can argue with that and ya a holy man of God," insisted Sean Og as he carefully hands over his overdue yearly dues.

"Itsssss….alive…HoooolyGoddddd…the blooming thing…. is alive," howled the priest in his familiar authoritarian tone of voice, as the bag is laid gently down in front of the main altar.

"Of course it is," smirked Sean Og. "Howlow do ya expect a man to go, kill his own, Father, shur if ya ain't intendin' to put it on the Sunday dinner plate and if ya treat it well, it might lay the odd egg or two. Now, how nice that'd be. A grand fresh egg for ya'r breakfast, that certainly would give any hungry honest holy man a healthy start in the mornin'. And shur, if ya're industrious enough ya might pick up an aul gander for it and with God's blessin' shur she might go broody and hatch out a goslin' or more. Now, how nice that'd be, wouldn't ya be rightly set up, Father…"

"Hmm," grunted the Parish Priest.

"Now think of it, ya've so many options Father, but I'll leave it up to ya'rself to decide which way ya want to go," grinned Sean Og leaving the Parish Priest puzzling out the equation with the bag containing the live goose in his clenched fist.

Approaching the door, Sean Og quickly genuflects and makes his way out through the tympanum. Dipping his fingers into the holy water fountain, he flicks the blessed water into the air and then makes the sign of the cross on his lips while mischievously giggling to himself. Replacing his bainin cap and tucking the collar of his donkey jacket up around his neck, he set on his way across the churchyard, and just as he had anticipated, it wasn't long before the goose passed him out. Now, Sean Og having worked as a farmhand for years and being a resourceful fellow in the making just happens to have a purse of ground-oats in his pocket. With a little encouragement and enticing he mutters, "honk, honk, girleen, here now, girleen," to the goose and soon he has her eating out of the palm of his hand. The goose stretches out her neck and with a squint in left her eye she looks up at Sean Og as if to say, "lets get the hell out of here." She has no resistance to being popped across the crossbar of the bike. And with that, they are both homeward bound leaving the roars of the Parish Priest echoing into the distance.

A safe trip home is granted to both of them. After all, Sean Og had paid his yearly dues and who was he to question the mysterious ways of the Man Above. Peg didn't know of Sean Og's commitment to paying his dues by taking one of her geese and why upset her now for she would be none the wiser, now that the goose had arrived safety back in the farmyard. The Parish Priest was certainly not going to question matters further, for after all, wasn't he the eejit who allowed the goose to escape, thought Sean Og to himself. But above all, the parish priest is a man of good statue in the village and has his honour to uphold. A man of such status is certainly not to be mocked or joked about, or become the topic of comedy especially over a pint of stout on a dark winter's night.

When the goose is returned to her rightful place in the farmyard, she runs off with a scattering of her wings and a loud gobble as if in her own way telling all present, "Ya'll never believe what that fella got up to now. I tell ya, there's ain't so queer as folk."

Peg believes that to avoid ill luck over the coming year that a household should make sure that all the Christmas decorations are packed away before the twelfth night of Christmas. So religiously without fail over the past years, she was sure to take down the Christmas decorations on the night of the eleventh of January. She would get Johnny to make a wish for all the people he loved just as the final decoration was placed in the box. This year is no different but she has her own wish to make. She wishes that everything would come right for the family and hopefully they would be able to cope with whatever challenges life has in store for them over the coming year.

"Do ya know Jim, Fr. Murphy told me when I was in service all those years ago that the twenty-fifth of December was not originally a Christian feast day. It was a pagan wan. It had to do with the feast of Saturn, the Roman God of Time. It was a Roman pagan custom to decorate their homes with flowers, trees and decorations. The Christian Church decided to take the idea from this pagan feast and make it their day for celebration. The mistletoe was only hung in houses and was never allowed to be hung in Christian Church because of its pagan association," said Peg as she helped Johnny unravel the balloons.

"I remember as a child, the aul folk held on to so many customs and beliefs and they'd religiously abide by them," said Jim to Sean Og who is sitting quietly by the fire flicking through the back pages of the daily newspaper in search of the racing results.

"I remember as a very young child, me mother would insist on windin' up the aul grandfather clock in the sitting room immediately just as the clock stuck the New Year in. By doin' this, she maintained that it'd brin' good luck and good fortune to all who lived and visited the house over the comin' year. She'd also insist, that on New Year's Eve, all the cleanin' together with the sweepin', and dustin' around the house, sheds and yards should be completed before midday, so as not to sweep away the good luck of the new year ahead," chuckled Peg to herself as her thoughts wandered back to the time when her mother was alive.

"I guess the folks long ago had their own reasons for believin' what they believed," replied Sean Og pencilling around the racing results and passing them over to Jim who is sitting at the small table at the back window completing the therapy exercise that Doc had laid out for him.

He is intending to return to see Doc in the morning and is determined to sort out issues that are holding him in the rut of life that he now finds himself trapped in.

"Goin' to be a change in the weather," frowned Peg looking out onto the evening sky. "I'd say there's frost on the way, I can feel it in me bones."

"I think ya might be right, I noticed a strong smell of soot comin' from the open fireplace in parlour this mornin'," replied Jim smiling to himself as he watched Peg potter around the house in her apron and slippers humming Silent Night while making sure that there's a place for everything and everything is in its place.

For a woman who's childhood was stolen from her, she certainly holds no bitterness in her heart, maybe sadness and doubt but there is certainly no bitterness and every living moment she mothers Johnny, it's as if it's her way of compensating her lost childhood.

Chapter Six

Jim And Peg Revisit Doc

Jim and Peg are up at daybreak the following morning and are eager to spend some quality time with Doc working through their worries and hopefully get an insight into why Jim was so ready to seek out death and throw in the towel in the arena of life. The clinic is quiet and this is a relief to Jim for he was nervous that some of the nosey locals might try to sniff out as to why he was calling upon Doc.

"How's the form?" asked Doc greeting them with a hearty smile.

"Yerra grand," replied Peg.

Doc had arranged the furniture in the clinic so that the three of them could sit comfortably during the session and on his desk he has a night-light burning in front of a little statue of Our Lady.

"As a couple, how're you coping?" asked Doc.

He is eager to get down to their relationship as a married couple. Especially now that they are spending more time in each other's company since Jim had lost his job. He is aware that a change of situation from the normal routine can put a strain on any relationship especially when Peg isn't used to having Jim under her feet, day in and day out. Jim too, must be missing the daily comings and goings that went on at the creamery where he used to work.

"Ach shur, truth behold, like any marriage we've our crazy lunatic moments of rantin' and ravin' at each other while doin' the leprechaun poka followed by the few hours of silence, just like the calm after the storm. And then life seems to come together for us as normality once again sets in," giggled Jim winking at Doc.

Peg blushed, as she was well aware that Jim was referring to her high-spirited temper that he is capable of stirring up every now and again with that stubborn streak of his. Noticing that Peg is uneasy, Doc winks at her and replies in his normal jolly gesture.

"I can see you've your work cut out, trying to keep this man of yours in toe…."

"I do me best," she butted in giving Jim the evil eye, which told him, ya just wait 'til I get ya to meself and then lets see who's havin' a crazy lunatic moment.

"I suppose every marriage has its ups and downs," shrugged Jim.

"Indeed they have and the reality of the matter is that happy marriages ain't all that thick on the ground these days," replied Doc sorting out his records on his desk and putting his pen in his breast pocket of his tweed jacket. "Unravelling, challenging marriages, yeah, indeed there're plenty of those around but happy ones are certainly scarce. Marriage is like an oil painting, the more you look into it the more the scene changes. The first stage of your marriage is like a romantic voyage and once the voyage is completed you've to work at the realities of life. Married couples have to work together through good times and bad times for a marriage to thrive. When a man and woman live as isolated beings when they're married, marriage just simply exists and eventually wears out like a tread worn vest…."

"Do ya think that the availability of divorce would break up marriage?" asked Peg, now feeling more at ease.

"Indeed it won't, it ain't the readiness of divorce that breaks up marriage. It's people. If marriages are goin' to cease to function, they do just that. People may put on a harmonious show in public but behind net curtains and closed doors, the untold truth exists," Doc responded looking over his specs as his own thoughts wafted back to his own marriage with Betty.

"We've brought back the exercises ya gave us on how we're feelin' and ya told us the last day we were in, that ya'd do out a therapy exercise for us to follow," said Peg.

"Indeed I did, I've it here in the drawer and I'll go through it with you shortly. But first I'd like to take another blood test from you Peg. To tell you the truth, I wasn't too happy with the last results," said Doc taking a needle and syringe out of his medical bag.

"Somethin' wrong, Doc?" Jim asked anxiously.

"Well I'd rather wait until the next test comes back and we'll have a better picture of what's goin' on. Have you felt a little under the weather lately?" Doc asked her as he takes the blood from her right arm.

"Ach shur Doc, I haven't been feelin' meself for a long time now, but I put that down to issues that I need to deal with from me past. I feel tired and I'm startin' to feel me age creepin' up on me, but other than that I think I'm grand."

"I'd like to make an appointment for you to see a consultant in Tralee hospital early next month. I just want a second opinion. Let's say, better be sure than sorry," replied Doc putting the blood samples in an envelope ready for the evening post.

"Yerra, Peg, ya'r body has waned away slowly over the past few months," said Jim knowing in his heart that Peg was never a woman to complain about her health. She might complain about other things but certainly not her health.

"How's the stomach, any tenderness, pain or diarrhoea?" asked Doc.

"Strange ya'd ask me that. I've a little tenderness every now and again and diarrhoea twice a day now. I don't know why that is, for I'm ain't eatin' anythin' out of the ordinary. I guess it's all down to a bit of worry and bother," said Peg a little puzzled as to why Doc is taking it all so serious.

"We'll see, the test results should tell us more but in the meanwhile, I want you to keep that appointment in Tralee."

Doc isn't too hasty in telling them what he thinks is wrong and knowing that his diagnosis wasn't his imagination, he somehow wanted to be certain before he prepares her for the outcome of his findings. Deep in his heart he is hoping that he is wrong, for he has grown very fond of Jim and Peg over the years. Giving bad news to any of his patients was sad at the best of times but having to deliver bad news to a friend is devastating both emotionally and mentally for any doctor.

After quietly reading over what they both had written regarding their personal lives, Doc takes off his specs and sits back into his chair as if to relax himself into his thoughts.

"Peg, you spend so much time and energy trying to make Johnny into a normal child. He is normal under the circumstances and perfectly normal with that. He is a normal, loving, Down's syndrome child, no more or no less. He'll never be anything else. What you should be doin' to get more fulfilment out of parenting is, enjoying his ability to live within the capacity of his disability. Down's syndrome children are wise and fun loving. They learn from example and action. They need rhythm and familiarity in their lives. They love to interact with people. They're open to creativity, love photography, nature, animals and music. Cultivate these talents and you'll come to discover what great joy there's to be found in parenting a child such a Johnny…."

"Emm." nodded Peg.

"Peg, from coming to know you over the past few years, I can see that you've placed all your energies into mothering Johnny and Sean Og and you've neglected Jim and yourself. While you Jim, have placed all your energy into trying to be a man, so much so, that you've neglected Peg and Johnny. Outside the home you've tried so hard to please others, that when it came to running a home and parenting, you left it all up to Peg. Johnny is growing up so quickly and I feel that you may be missing out in the little everyday joys that a child can bring. Both of you see security as important in life, but I see your vision of security has a different meaning for both of you. Jim, security for you is having money and a good job. While in Peg's view, it's about having a safe and caring home. While both of you are correct, you may have a tendency to take your views to an extreme. Even though you live as a family, each of you are living separate emotional lives and this is where you've drifted apart and done so totally unaware of it happening. Each of you have found your reassurance in other parts of your existence and that has cushioned you to stay ignorant of the emotional drift, you Jim, in your job and you Peg, in caring for Johnny and Sean Og. It seems to me that Sean Og has become a child in your eyes and maybe that has something to do with your past. You're tending to mother him rather than be a sister to him. I think it may have something to do with him goin' to the Industrial School at such a young age. But somehow, I fear that it has to do more so with something that's taunting you from your past. You're using Sean Og to compensate for something precious in your life that's missing. I think you're aware of what I'm talking about, Peg. That's something you and I might need to work through together."

Peg smiled shyly.

"Ya're probably right Doc, I want him so desperately to feel cared for and all I want is for him to be happy. And I know there's wan other issue that I hold dear to me heart and need to find answers to...."

"But Peg, while Sean Og may need friendship and care, happiness is something that he has to sort out for himself. As for that other issue, I think that's the key to unlocking the door to the underline reason for you mothering him so much. When you feel the time is right, I'd like to talk to you on your own about that."

Doc was referring to the baby that Peg gave birth to in the Magdalene Laundry and the nuns had told her that the child had died. He was aware that Jim did not know about this child and had promised Peg that he would not reveal her secret to him until she herself was comfortable with letting go of it.

"Emm, maybe so," nodded Peg.

"While mothering Sean Og as a child you've isolated Jim and he now feels alone and lonely in the periphery of your care. He has compensated this vacuum by needing to feel wanted in his job. That's why losing your job came as such a shock to you, Jim. It became your life and your identity. It allowed you a route to feel more of a man. Actually, I'd go as far as to say, it may have made you feel a complete man. You may have felt that all the extra hours were about money but realistically it was about self-approval and recognition. You see, where we lack in one area of our lives, we'll compensate in another. Jim, you'll need to accept that men are human and just like women and children we too are entitle to express our feelings and emotions. You've suppressed your feelings so much that it has started to raise your blood pressure. Even your digestive system is starting to clog up. As for the pains and aches you're suffering from, these have to do with your suppressed emotions. If you don't learn to express them, there'll be a volcano style eruption of anger, or maybe the opposite, your body may clamp down and you'll end up suffering from a very bad breakdown. You're like a pressurised machine at the moment, if we don't find the release valve, we're certain to have an explosion on our hands," said Doc squinting at Jim over his half masked specs.

All this time, Jim was doodling on his hand with a pen he had found in his pocket. He was accustomed to doing this when he was listening and concentrating on something that he found interesting. Although during his school going days he was often scolded for doing this and often found himself, nursing the after effects from the lashes of the Christian Brothers strap, but somehow they didn't manage to beat it out of him. After mentally recollecting and reflecting on Doc's words of counselling, he stops his doodling, looks up and responds in a low tone of voice.

"That makes a lot of sense Doc, I've felt so alone and often jealous of Peg's and Sean Og's relationship. They're so close and even in silence, they're able to communicate with each other. They seem to be able to get on without me. I know this may be terrible for a father to say but there're times I'm resentful of his relationship with me Johnny." Putting the pen back into his pocket and with his hands clasped tight under his chin, biting his lower lip while nervously looking at Peg he continues speaking. "I feel so guilty about this, but Peg, I can't help it. But, the truth of the matter is, that's simply how I feel…"

This somewhat startles Peg.

"I never realised that, I'm sooo, sooo sorry for makin' ya feel like that. It's just that Sean Og and I've so many hidden silent torments regardin' our past. And I guess that in some strange way it has brought us closer over the years. Always lookin' out and protectin' each other…"

"But Peg, why do ya feel ya need to shut me out?" butted in Jim, looking her straight in the eye with an open hand gesture and a tone of justification in his voice.

"I never meant to, but I guess I was afraid, if ya knew about me past, ya might think that I wasn't the woman ya thought I was and deep down I was afraid ya might stop lovin' me. Ya see Jim, I need and ache for ya'r love so desperately," replied Peg and the tone of her voice alone let him know that it was all innocent and no hurt or malice was ever intended.

"Peg, don't ya know after all these years, I couldn't ever stop lovin' ya. I fell in love with ya for the person ya are and not with what happened in ya'r past. But if knowin' what secrets cause ya torment from the past, then maybe I could understand ya better, but I don't think I could love ya any more. Yerra Christ Peg, ya're me life and I told ya that in the note. I idolise ya and I don't think I could love ya any more or any less," replied Jim placing his hand on Peg's arm, comforting her with a gentle squeeze.

"One thing we all have to accept in this life is that change is ongoing. Externally by what we see and internally by what we feel. How change changes us as human beings is determined by how we think, feel and act," sighed Doc standing up and placing his hand on Jim's shoulder.

He then quietly slips out of the room to make a pot of tea. From his professional experience, he realised that they both needed a quite moment or two together to recollect their thoughts.

On returning with a plate of biscuits and a pot of tea he could see that for once, they were now connecting on an emotional and spiritual link, something that had been neglected or left on the sideway of life as often happens in many cases when couples get burdened down in the worries and anxieties of everyday living.

Chapter Seven

An Eye Opener For Jim

Over the coming week, Jim finds it hard to believe Sean Og's and Peg's stories about the abuse they claimed to have experienced in the Industrial Schools in Tralee. Could such terrible things have happened? These religious people after all were the models of Christian morals within society. They were recognised to be the chief leaders, teachers and preachers of the Catholic Church. If these people did such terrible things, how could they preach the Gospel of God? These were just some of the thoughts that tormented Jim and gave rise to restless nights.

One afternoon while clearing out the out-sheds, he comes across a poem, "A Stolen Childhood" that falls out of a journal written in Sean Og's handwriting.

A Life's Stolen Treasure
The Month was November, the Year 1949
In a grey yard huddled many boys,
Heads held low from fear and inner misery.
Amongst them I hunched found guilty of a crime,
No Ma nor Da to love or care for me.
It was there I became a number and soon learned to run to the call,
Slowly my birth name was allowed to become
A fading memory on a courtroom wall!

Reading and writing I did quite well.
But why had each day to be a living hell?
I felt so undignified with my clothes held low,

As that Leather Strap gradually grounded me to the floor.
I cried out in silence, 'Please God, don't let the tears flow.'
But my encouraging Spirit responded
'Hang in there lad, you've the willpower to endure a lot more.'
That harsh voice still sends quivering shivers up alone my spine
As I recall him count the lashes right up to nine!

Each night I prayed,
Why God why me?
I've tried so hard to please Thee,
I've learned to learn well
Even endure the duties of a man.
Tonight please God, don't let it be Me!
As I prayed with hands clasped tight
Is it too much tonight to let me lie low?
When that Handle turns on that Great Door!
With sprat like muscles so weak
Can I really endure much more!

At the age of sixteen
They claimed I was free.
Saying, 'they've no further use of me.'
Free to roam and search the world
Looking for ways to become a man.
Struggling to recover my lost identity!
Dear God, I've one last request
Please be my Guide and stay close by my side,
For the only crime I was found guilty of,
Is that I had nobody to love me when I was a child!

How could it have happened? I hear people say,
Little kids marked by the crimes of heartless men!
Where were the Good Ones when those kids cried out!
But were there really any Good Ones I still try to puzzle out?
For each and everyone of them just stood by,

Hearing and listening to the echoes of our screams and
cries!

Years later I heard I was labelled one of the 'Specials'
A stamp that embodied me with their mystic satanic rituals!
Enforcing me to abide by my measure,
As they engulfed themselves in their bodily pleasures!
Haunting memories of bread and dripping
Still engraved in my gut!
As I live my life reclaiming A Life's Stolen Treasure…
My childhood dignity.

Sitting on the windowsill, Jim flicks through the pages of the private journal in dismay. He is bewildered by what he finds out about Sean Og's memories of his childhood in the Industrial School for boys in Tralee. Up to now, Jim was unaware that Sean Og is having treatment for his past from Doc. It shocks him to find out in the journal that he too had suicidal thoughts and yet Jim had always seen him as a happy go lucky fellow. Was he carrying around such dark emotional torment in his heart for years and yet the people that loved him were unaware of it. Throughout the journal, he refers to "the mark". Returning into the house, he shows the poem to Peg, who gets very upset. As the both read the journal, they now realise that, it turns out that Sean Og has kept a journal for years and this is his way of coping with his taunting feelings and emotions.

That evening they talk to Sean Og about their discovery and he is happy that they are now aware of his deep buried emotional torments. Pasted into the journal are little pictures drawn by Johnny. The crayoned coloured drawings tell little stories of how Johnny relates to life. Peg and Jim are over whelmed by the fact that Sean Og has taught Johnny so much about life and are very touched by his love and commitment to him. Jim now realises that he has missed out on so much of Johnny's life. Over the years he had spend so much time trying to please others that he forgot to spend time with his precious ones, Johnny and Peg. And even though Johnny was his son, he was beginning to look upon him more so as a child rather than a son. A reality that happens in many a family if the truth was told. But he made one promise to himself that this would change, for now he fully understood the reality of the saying, *"any man can be a father but it takes a special man to be a Dad."* And that was what he intended to become, a Dad in every sense of the word.

"Sean Og, ya've been spendin' all this time teachin' Johnny and Good God, I wasn't aware of it," said Jim holding the drawings in his hand and the more he looks at the simplicity of the drawings, the more he is overcome with the rebirth of the umbilical pride that a Dad feels for a son or daughter.

"Just fan linn, shur, ya've seen nothin' yet. Ya'll be very proud of ya'r little boy when I show ya what I've abroad in the shed," chuckled Sean Og making his way out to the out-shed and after a few minutes he returns with a small pine box that contains a small willow basket and six little framed water coloured paintings that Johnny had painted.

"Johnny helped to make the frames. Ya see, ya've a very clever wee fella and ya didn't know it. Here is wan of the baskets he made with me last winter. I think it's very good and with practise, who knows he might manage to make a few for the tourist season. He is very creative and is eager to learn. Look at the picture he drew last month of ye'r home. I asked him to draw it after I wrote this verse."

What makes a House a Home
It's not the fancy mirror on the wall
Nor the candelabra in the hall
But the loving arms that are always there
Whether you want to share a joy or shed a tear
That's what makes a house a home

It's not the glowing car in the garage
Or any other fancy carriage
But knowing someone is waiting for thee

Happy to transform your worries into glee
That's what makes a house a home

You may wish for riches and seek out wealth
That doesn't guarantee happiness or fair health
But knowing there's always a welcome and a bed
To lay down and rest your tired weary head
That's what makes a house a home!

"Ach, that's so nice, Sean Og I never knew that ya wrote poetry," exclaimed Peg in admiration.

"Well, ya learn somethin' new every day. Johnny made the frame with me. We used the wood from the aul oak tree that Jim cut down last year. Ya should've seen his wee face when we finished it. He was so chuffed with himself. It was meant to be a gift for both of ya and we thought of givin' it to ya on a special occasion maybe a birthday or an anniversary or so. And I suppose, this is a special occasion for all of us, for I've now released me past to ya both and that's such a great relief for me. Do ya know that Johnny has a great love for nature and he's able to recognise most of the wild flowers? What I notice is that he loves the aul camera and of late he has taken a few photos. They're a little blurred 'cause of the shake from the excitement in his wee hands when he took them but if I persevere, I think he'll manage to take some good wans. I think it's great to see him come on so well over the years. Ach shur.....he's a grant fella.... and ya....don't even know it Jim," chuckled Sean Og.

"Indeed he is, emm he certainly is," nodded Jim and he was proud to call himself, Johnny's Dad.

Chapter Eight

The Journey To The Industrial School

After the death of Peg's father, her mother returned to Ireland and lived in a small three-roomed cottage outside Tralee on the Castlemain Road. Times were tough and food was scarce. She took laundry and sowing into her home to provide for her family. In 1947, she came down with tuberculosis, when Peg was eight and Sean Og just five years old. While she was ill, Peg stayed home from school to care for her. The local Parish Priest found out the reason for Peg's absenteeism from school and reported it to Tralee Garda. Following a visit to their home from the Garda, a summons was issued and a week later Peg and Sean Og found themselves in front of a Judge in Tralee courtroom. Peg remembers the Judge to be a kind elderly man, who spoke with a deep husky voice. During the hearing, the Judge asked if there was any living relative willing to take care of the two children while the mother received treatment for her illness. The Garda present responded, "not to me knowledge ya'r Honour." Arrangements were then made for them to be transferred into the care of the Religious Orders who were responsible for the running of the Industrial Schools in Tralee.

On the morning when the Garda came to take them away, their mother tried to convince him that she would have a friend take care of the children, she pleaded for them to remain with her so that arrangements could be made. The Garda was very stern and showed no compassion for her in her state of illness, and simply said that the matter was out of his hands and it was up to the courts to do what they wanted with the kids.

"I remember her cuddlin' us and promisin' that she'd come to collect us within the next week or so. She asked us to be brave and to pray to God every night. We were to be good and have our manners at all times. She asked the Garda if she could put clean clothes on us," said Peg as she told her story to Jim. "But he responded, now missus, these kids won't be needin' too many clothes where they're goin' to…."

"Ya mean he just took ya both away. Was there not a doctor or nurse present?" asked Jim in disgust.

"Just as we were leavin' the house, a doctor arrived to see me mother," replied Peg with a deep sigh.

"In the honour of Jaysus, did ya understand what was happenin'? It must have been very frightenin' for ya both," Jim interrupted, now bewildered by what he was hearing as he stood by the stove with the poem in his hand.

"Sean Og wasn't aware of what was happenin', he was only interested in havin' a spin in the car. I knew things weren't right but didn't cause any fuss so as not to upset me mother. On the way out, the doctor patted me on the head and said, 'good lass, off ya go and look after ya'r brother now'. Mother waved from the small cottage window and shouted out, 'I'll come for ya in a few days, I promise, in a few days I'll come for ya darlings', that was the last time I saw or heard from her. It wasn't 'til years later when I told Fr. Murphy about her that I found out that she died a short time afterwards and she was buried in Tralee graveyard…."

"Fr Murphy?" exclaimed Jim.

"Yeah, He took me to see the grave and arranged for a little headstone to be erected in her memory. At the time, we had difficulty in findin' the grave 'cause it was unmarked. The caretaker helped us find it because he remembered the funeral. Seemly the priest, the undertaker and the gravediggers were the only people present at the burial. They never told me in the Industrial School that she died. I thought, I was prepared to protect meself as by nature I was a quick-tempered child and well able to handle meself in the schoolyard even when the other kids called me 'bastard spawn of an Englishman'. At the time I didn't really understand what they meant, but with a few blows of me fist, they'd be off on their trotters. But when it came to the bullyin' and abuse in the Industrial School in Tralee it was a different matter. It hit me like a bolt of lightnin' and I was totally unprepared for it. When we were in the National School in Tralee ya always had the teacher to run to for protection if ya found ya'rself in a wee bit of bother but in the Industrial School ya'd no wan. Ya were made feel dirty and insecure. Ya were told day in and day out that ya should be grateful for what was being done for ya. Even though there were moments of happiness there were much more moments of anxiety and terror and I often wondered what I really had to be grateful for. But I guess it wasn't the nuns that got me through, but the girls as we struggled to make playful moments out of scraps twigs and stones. The way of gettin' on a nun's good side was to shout out the prayers in parrot fashion. Whether they meant anythin' to any of us, I never really knew but day in and day out we'd recite them at the top of our voices, all standin' in rows with eyes closed, heads bowed and hand jammed together," said Peg glancing across at Sean Og who stood silently by the stove with his head hunched into his shoulder pits.

"When did they separate ya and Sean Og?" Jim asked with his hand on his chin and shaking his head from side to side in horror. Wanting to believe what he was hearing but found it so difficult to understand and come to terms with it all.

"They separated us outside the courtroom. Do ya remember that Sean Og?" asked Peg putting on her apron to make a pot of tea.

"Ahhhh Christttt, I don't really, all I've is an impression in me mind of meself cryin'. That's all, I can remember now," replied Sean Og taking off his cap and sitting on the sugan stool by the corner of the table.

"Well, wan of the Garda gave ya a sweet and tried to console ya as he tried to pull us apart. We hung onto each other and didn't want to let go. I remember him whisperin' to me that I'd see ya later and I was to go with the other Garda. I was then driven by car to the Industrial School for girls. At the entrance of the school we were met by a tall stern lookin' nun who said, 'Well Garda, I see ya've another wan for us'. She held me by the chin and asked me to put me tongue out. 'She's a nicely mannered kid', the Garda remarked. Then she looked into me eyes and responded, 'hardy enough', and with that, she slammed the big wooden door shut and took me by the hand to a room with so many small beds in it. I learned to call it a dormitory. The beds were clean and tidy and the dark wooden floor contrasted with the cream and green coloured walls...."

Sean Og didn't say a word he just hunched his head into his shoulders.

"I remember askin' for ya Sean Og and the nun responded in a scornful voice while firmly holdin' me by the chin, 'here madam, you'll do what you're asked and told. And I don't' know anythin' about any Sean Og, so ciunas now'. I didn't know what ciunas meant but from the way she said it, I knew that I was to be quiet. Later I was to learn that ciunas was the Irish for quiet or silence. No matter how many times I'd ask about ya Sean Og, I'd still got the same answer, 'ciunas'. I asked about mother, but nobody would tell me anythin' or help me contact her. The girl in the bed next to me told me, 'ya'll never see ya'r Mammy or Sean Og again for that's what happened to me'. I remember tellin' her that me Mammy was comin' to get me when she was well. But this girl was adamant that me Mammy wouldn't come and how right she was. I never gave up hopin' and prayin' day in and day out..."

"Holy....Jaysus," exclaimed Jim.

"When we'd say the prayers before our lessons and we were requested to pray for the poor black babies in Africa, the Pope and bishop's intentions. I never did pray for any of them, for in me heart I said those prayers for mother and ya, Sean Og. As the days, weeks, months and years passed by, I learned to accept that ya nor mother were ever comin' hither. In some strange way, I guess I become a part of the bewildered pack and learned the ways of survival. Ya learned to buy and sell favours by partin' with ya'r food and as ya got older, ya demanded the respect of the younger wans. I guess for ya Sean Og, it was much the same."

At this stage, Sean Og was just sitting quietly with his head buried in the palms of his hands.

"Yeah Peg, it took a while for me to realise that ya were never comin' back either. I guess in the first week or so the Christian Brothers walloped the tears out of me, for all I can remember is that if ya were seen cryin', ya got ya'r ear togged and told to be a man. When I got over the tearful stage, the first year at the school was fine, as far as I can remember, it wasn't 'til I was seven years of age or so, well it was a few weeks after me first holy communion when the bad times started. It was then they started to abuse me. It was then that life become hell, always watchin' out in the yard to see if the Christian Brothers would give ya a clatter from behind. Ya got that lash from their leather strap to the back of ya'r legs whether ya were in the wrong or not. I think they used to get some satanic joy out of how ya'd react. If ya cried at all, they'd continue to do it. But if ya showed no reaction and walked away, they'd give up after a while and move on to some other poor misfortunate fella…"

"Fuck'in…..hell," exclaimed Jim in dismay.

"Yeah no word of a lie, that was so. Night after night, I'd drift off to me imaginary land of livin' in a happy family with a lovely mother huggin' me. But strangely, I could never see this imaginary mother's face. Well, that's how it was. Many of the days in the school were certainly not days that a young boy would have cherished memories about. Filth that happened to me and the other boys in that blasted place, I'd rather forget, for it upsets me when I talk or think about it. When, I was let go from the school at the age of sixteen, yerra Jaysus, I must have been, almost nearin' me seventeenth birthday or so, I was given a half a crown and set on me way. Wan of the Brothers at the time advised me to take the boat to England for he said that there'd be plenty of work for the likes of me."

"Take the boat to England?" muttered Jim.

"Yep across the Irish sea. I remember makin' me way to the train station and wanderin' around the platform ain't knowin' how to go about gettin' a ticket. At the station, the ticket-master must have seen that I looked lost and approached me. He queried, if there was anythin', he could do for me. When I explained me story, he told me to wait in the station until he had finished his shift. He then took me home to his wife and they gave me a bed and a meal for the night. By Christ, I remember it to this day, for it was a grand feed of spuds, crubeens and cabbage with a big bowl of custard and stewed apple, I was allowed to ate as much as I could fit into me hungry belly and darn hungry I was. His wife told me as she filled up me plate, 'Don't be shy laddie, for shyness never fed a hunger or quenched a thirst'. The following mornin', a man who was goin' to England to work on the buildin' sites called to their front door. I could hear him ask, 'Where's the young misfortunate?'

'In here Paddy,' replied the ticket master's wife, 'he seems to be a nice twig of a gearsun, but very shy. Shur, they're all shy comin' from that place. Those schools never offered any young laddie or lassie neither print nor plan for life and ain't that the reason why so many of them run away from life itself. It's sad, but ach shur, that's the way it was, that's the way it is and no doubt that's the way it'll always be'. I could hear her say. 'Don't worry, we'll look after him and see him right,' the man replied…"

"Almighty……Jaysus," muttered Jim.

" Anyway, with that, I was asked to get me things together and we set out on our way to catch the boat to England. I didn't say too much to the man who was to take responsibility for me but I do remember followin' him around like a little lost puppy that just had its tail docked. 'Got to speak up for ya'rself laddie, ya got to speak up for ya'rself laddie, that ya must do, ya'll certainly have to do so when ya get to London. There are some tough hobos and langers out there. Don't ever tell them how much money ya've and ya'll be just grant. We'll try and get ya a job as a navvy on the lump, now that'd get ya a nice few bob. If fate smiles nicely on ya lad, a few bob in ya'r breeches should see ya through the bad times and give ya a good start to ya'r independence. Wan thin', ya'll need to do is to hold ya'r head up and be proud of ya'rself. Ya'll need to stop thinkin' that ya're inferior. Remember no wan can make ya feel inferior without ya'r permission. And there's no two ways about it, me dear laddie. I know I'm no father to ya and dear say ya've none at hand but that's the advice a father would give to an immigratin' son,' he said to me...."

"Almighty.... Christ," muttered Jim.

"He sorted out a place for me to live alongside other Irish chaps and after a week or so, he had me workin' on wan of the buildin' sites. After that, I never laid eyes on him again. To this day, I often think of him and wonder what became of him. In the evenin' on me way home from work, I'd pop into the Church to say a prayer and it was there I met with a priest from Donegal. Yerra Jaysus, grand chap he was. I felt I could talk to him. Wan evenin' I mentioned to him about the abuse that was goin' on in the Industrial School in Ireland. He advised me that the best thin' to do was to close the door to that chamber of horrors and get on with the rest of me life. He said, that he understood what I was talkin' about but if I was to've any life out of that school I was to put what happened to me in that dreadful place to the back of me mind. But somehow, as much as I'd like that door to remain locked every now and again it'd unlock itself if I came up on a smell, a vision, an expression or even a word. Aspect in life would shock me subconscious mind into action and I'd start to remember the horrors again. I now know that it'll never go away. I can try to walk away from it, suppress the memories, even pretend it didn't happen, but now I realise and have come to understand that these bad memories are a part of me identity and me life. I've to live with them but I've the choice not to allow them to take over me life..."

"Jaysus," exclaimed Jim.

"Doc has helped me. It wasn't tablets that helped me at the time, it was confrontin' me emotions and acceptin' that abuse was somethin' that happened to me. Doc helped me to realise that I didn't cause it, I didn't want it, but it happened. I was a victim of abuse but I can allow meself to be a survivor and get the best out of life. All I ever wanted as a child was to experience a normal life. When I left that blasted school, life was alien to me. I was afraid of me independence. Me mind had become so institutionalised that I was totally depended upon people and instructions. I needed noise and people around me. I feared me own company. I developed a third eye, always watchin' out in case somethin' was goin' to happen. I even feared silence. I didn't trust people. If somewan got close in friendship to me, I'd misread the signs and think they were intendin' to abuse me. The fear of the darkness would send shivers up me spine. I went everywhere with a candle and a box of matches in me pocket. I guess I feared me own existence. It took years to come to terms with meself as a person. There were times I felt a misfit in me own body, strugglin' with emotions that I simply couldn't understand, tryin' to seek out answers to unanswerable questions. Fears that I needed to confront and manage as many of them were of me own makin'. I now, with the help of Doc have come to like meself as a person and hopefully, wan day, I'll be able to love meself for the person I've become," sighed Sean Og sipping the drags of tea at the end of his mug as he watched Peg and Jim once again read through his poem, A Life's Stolen Treasure.

"Peg, what happened to the family home, why did ya'r mother not leave it to wan of ya?" asked Jim

"Fr. Murphy looked into that for me when I was in service with him and all he could find out is that she sold it two days after we went into the Industrial Schools. Mysteriously, the money was never accounted for. Seemly, the locals claimed it was sold for ten quinines and that a businessman from Tralee bought it. He was a brother of wan of the Gardai that attended the court the day we were sent to the Industrial Schools. There was no will made, all we know is that the deeds of the home were transferred to this man's name," replied Peg shaking her head with arms folded as she gazed out the kitchen window wondering what really happened to their home and whether her mother was treated unjustly by the greed of the moment.

"I see," hemmed Jim doubting the honesty of the transaction and he too was wondering if there was a bit of skulduggery carried out. But deep in the core of his marrow he knew that was one injustice and dark secret that went to the grave with their mother.

"Do ya remember Daddy's photo on the kitchen wall, Sean Og?" asked Peg as she poured out another cup of tea all round.

"Emm, I can barely remember. He was in uniform. There was another man sittin' beside him in the photo and a woman with curly hair stood in the background."

"That's right, that was Daddy, Mammy and Daddy's brother, William. Seemly, Daddy and William joined the British Army and become Radio Officers in the Second World War. They were both killed in action near Caen in 1944 on D-Day and after that mother left Cornwall and returned to Tralee with the two of us to look after her sister Joan who was dyin' of tuberculosis. After Aunty Joan died, mother became the rightful owner of the family home and she made an income from makin' alterations for drapery shops and takin' in people's laundry. She had a little garden out the back and kept a cow, a pig and a few hens on the acre of land adjacent to the cottage. Do ya remember we called the cow Daisy?"

"Now, 'tis all comin' back to me," sighed Sean Og picking up his cap from the floor and hanging it on the chair. "Was there a brown aul dog as well?"

"That's right, he was called Borach. Mother gave him that name 'cause he was bow-legged and Borach is the Irish for bow-legged. Mother used to go crazy when ya sat on his back 'cause he was always full of fleas. And no matter how many times he was treated he'd get infested again. I loved that dog and he was a loyal friend to all of us. God, mother was so particular about cleanliness and each day she'd have us scrubbed from head to toe. I was never without a new dress. She'd make them out of left over material from the alterations. She did everythin' for us. She made us her whole world. Even though times were tough, we pulled through and there was always a warm meal on the table. I remember, the neighbours would say that she could make a tasty stew out of a turnip and a few wild herbs. Mother was a very placid woman and kept to herself. She was fond of the quiet life and didn't harbour too much on gossip. I guess in many ways, ya're like her Sean Og, I must have got me wary temperament from Daddy and his brother. May the Lord God have mercy on their souls," said Peg getting up to open the front door to let Sally the dog out for a run.

"That war left many a home without a loved wan," said Jim.

"Indeed it did. Seemly, up to forty million lives were lost to that war. I remember the neighbours used to try and console mother about Daddy by sayin' that he died with honour. Mother could never accept that. She'd always say, truth behold, when it comes to war there's no glory or honour, for war is crude and cruel, vile and inhumane, it deprives the innocent of life by plunderin' the lives of decent people, leavin' gallons of blood and guts and thousands of unacceptable corpse lyin' around together with many broken homes and hearts. So if that's the end result of war, how in the name of Jaysus can somewan say that there's honour and glory attached to it?" replied Peg.

"And how right she was, it certainly messed up our lives, for if Daddy didn't die in the Second World War, maybe we wouldn't be robbed of a childhood in those dreadful Industrial Schools," sighed Sean Og picking up his cap from the floor and placing it on his knee.

Darkness was now setting in and looking out the back window Sean Og could tell that it was going to be a cold night as the moon was high and the stars were bright. Having bid good night to Jim and Peg he rambled off to the back shed and settled down for the night. Once again, the candles were lit on the windowsills. Over the years, these two candles would flicker into the darkness of the night. One was lit by Peg in memory of a secret that she had carried in her heart and haunted her with doubt, day in and night out. Its light flickered in memory of her little baby that she gave birth to in the Magdalen Laundry. The other is lit by Sean Og to protect himself from his fear of the darkness. A phobia he has had to live with ever since he left the Industrial School.

Two weeks later, on the way home from Peg's appointment in Tralee hospital they stop off at Rath Cemetery. Over the years, Peg and Sean Og frequently visited this graveyard where their mother was laid to rest but they also visit two other graves, the grave of Peg's abuser and the grave of a young boy who died after a beating while in care of the Christian Brothers in St Joseph's Industrial School for Boys in Tralee. At the grave of her abuser, Peg would stand still for a moment or two and mutter time and time again, "Why… did… ya.. do it? I'll never… never… forgive ya…"

In the car on the journey home, they get engrossed in conversation regarding the abuse. Jim feels so sad for Peg but feels so guilty for being so blinded to her silent grief all these years. Jim promises Peg that he'll get the abusers to answer for their crimes and he intends to ask questions in the locality to see if any of the locals are aware of the horrific secrets that the Religious Orders are harbouring regarding the abuse.

Sean Og tells Jim about the death of his school pal Joseph, who died because of a beating he received from a Christian Brother. Sean Og was one of the young boys at the time that helped to make Joseph's coffin. A Christian Brother who was a notorious bully and feared by many was responsible for Joseph's death, but truth behold like many other antisocial happenings in that school the people in charge had once again managed to cover it up and no proper investigation was carried out into the cause of death.

The older boys at the school who witnessed the beating were ordered by the Christian Brothers to keep silent regarding the matter.

As Jim listens quietly to their conversation, he now understands what the mark meant, a saying that they often referred to when they spoke quietly together. They would talk about how lucky Johnny was, not to have been affected by the mark. The mark was responsible for the shame and the emotional trauma that they lived with day-after-day due to the abuse they suffered while in care.

"Sean Og, I don't know if I can ever forgive the man that abused me and the nuns for allowin' it to happen," said Peg and at this stage there were tears in her eyes but she was doing her utmost to hold them back for Johnny's sake, who was sitting quietly in the back seat with Sean Og.

"So many priests and nuns have said that I should forgive them and move on with me life. But I seem to be stuck in a rut and it taunts me day in and day out. It must be very difficult for ya, Sean Og, for ya've ain't the memories but the marks to remind ya of what ya've suffered. Yet at times I look at ya and I resent ya'r placid attitude to life and people...."

"Peg, for years it ate me up like a cancer. But Doc helped me through and the wan bit of sound advise he gave me was that me real disability was me inability to let go of the hope that the past could have been different and this disability that I had inflicted upon meself was certainly gonna make an emotional cripple out of me in the future. It took me a while to understand what he meant, for I too was punishin' meself for feelin' guilty with the thought that I was unable to forgive me abusers. I don't need to worry about that any more, for as the years passed I've recovered the ability to try and be satisfied without the memories of me past controllin' me. It was the loathsome attitude of the Christian Brothers that allowed me to loathe meself and the more I held on to this horrible feelin' about meself, the more I was still allowin' the abusers to abuse me. I now know that I wasn't at fault. I was the innocent vulnerable victim. It was the Christian Brothers who set out to power and rape me innocence and they alone will have to answer for their horrific crimes, maybe not on this earth but in the Spiritual wan and that alone gives me some peace of mind…"

"Ohhhh…. Sean…. Og," wept Peg.

"I must admit, I still get a turn in the pit of me gut when I come upon a Christian Brother. I feel tightness in me chest followed by a shortness of breath. But, day-by-day I'm learnin' to manage and overcome me phobia and insecurities in me own way. I'm very proud of meself. Doc has told me that each day I should give meself credit for livin' the present and survivin' the past. He also said, that forgiveness is about empowerin' ya'rself, it ain't about condonin' what the abuser did, it's lettin' go of anger. As long as I'm infested with anger the abusers still control me," said Sean Og letting out a long deep sigh.

"Mother of Jaysus." exclaimed Jim.

"I remember the mornin' he said that to me, I was sittin' in the waitin' room of his clinic for hours and I allowed each and every person that came in to go ahead of me. I sat there on me own tryin' to build up the courage to go into his surgery. I had struggled with the thoughts of goin' to visit him for some weeks. When Doc shouted, 'Next', I did a u-turn and absconded out of the waitin' room. Doc must have spotted me leavin' the yard as he came out and called out, 'Howya Sean Og, what can I do for ya?'
Yerra, I'm grand Doc, I'm just collectin' the aul bike, I shouted back. But he was quickly on me footprints and somehow he could see that I was troubled and invited me into his house for a cup of tea. After a short chitchat about the Tralee races, he somehow had me spillin' out all me troubles. Ya see, me body had over taken me. I was unable to manage it. I was overcome with bouts of anger and resentment followed by periods of sadness and frustration. I'd get raged at small setbacks and ended up blamin' others. I was so angry at me past and at everywan and anywan for allowin' me childhood to be robbed from me. I felt very insecure and to be honest, I started to fear me own existence…"

"Jaysus," exclaimed Jim in dismay.

"Me head was tellin' me wan thing and me heart another, there wasn't harmony within me thinkin', feelin' or doin'. I couldn't concentrate. I couldn't sleep. I felt so alone and lonely yet I didn't want people around me. I just wanted to be left alone. I became imprisoned in me own mind. I stared turnin' to drink to numb and hide me disturbed emotions, but they'd come back to taunt me the next mornin'. Life was tumblin' in on me and I was on the verge of throwin' in the towel. Everyday seemed lifeless and I lost the will and ability to smile and laugh. I'd look at people and see them laughin' and smilin' and wonder what they had to be happy about..."

"Ohhhhhh.... Sean Og.... I do..... so understand," sobbed Peg.

"In the end, I went to see Doc and he gave me hope and an understandin' that what I was feelin' was normal under the circumstances. For in reality, he summed it up in a few words, 'ya're simply pissin' into the wind me dear fella, simply pissin' into the wind. What I mean Sean Og is that ya've become ya'r own worst enemy. Ya've put all ya'r energy and willpower into hopin' that the past could've been different. And now, ya're too tired to live ya'r normal daily life. Ya've come to an emotional crossroads in ya'r life and destiny is takin' ya out on a limb to tell ya, to sort ya'rself out before ya become an emotional cripple. And as long as ya go on pissin' into the wind, ya'll continue to struggle with the natural flow of life and in return it'll continue to torment ya.' Ohhhh Peg, how right he was. Ya see, Doc always knows best..." yawned Sean Og placing his right hand on her shoulder, reassuring her, all would be okay.

That night before they went to bed, Jim was anxious to find out how Peg got on with the consultant in Tralee hospital but she isn't very forthcoming with answers. All she is willing to say is that Doc would tell her the results of the test in a fortnight or so. But she does let Jim know that the consultant has recommended that she goes on a course of medication and she is to remain on it until further notice.

Chapter Nine

Jim's Love Affair With The Local Barmaid

Over the years, Jim's and Peg's sexual relationship in their marriage has been almost non-existent and this has lead to many in-house arguments but whenever Jim would confide in Sean Og about his inability to relate and find fulfilment in his marriage, he would find no outlet. Time and time again, he would say in his frustration.

"Ya'r darlin' sister, has become a fulltime mother and only a part-time lover and I simply ain't understandin' why….."

But each time, Sean Og would plead with him to be kind and go easy on her.

Jim's sexual frustration within his marriage has resulted in him having a relationship with another woman named Mary O' Sullivan, the local barmaid. She provided well for Jim's starved appetite for sex. Jim could never understand whether it was the excitement of the unknown expectations or the secrecy of deception that gave the climax to the orgasm he experienced during his sexual encounters with her. But one thing for sure, Mary's sensual moans and groans during her own sexual climax were a welcome tonic to any man who was suffering from sexual malnutrition.

Mary was the envy of many a woman in the local village and the surrounding town-lands for she was well blessed with upper curves. In her male circle of friends, her curves were known as the two weapons of mass distraction that could become weapons of mass destruction if a man was fortunate enough to embrace them in his arms or simply rest his weary head on them. Mary's beauty was enhanced by her dress code as it embraced the curvature of her tall slender body. She was well aware of the power and magic she held over the opposite sex and used this to her advantage. Many a poor aching soul in the male kingdom became hypnotised as she handed a pint of stout over the bar. Could any poor fellow be blamed for adoring the wonders of the artistic creation designed by the Man Above? One thing for sure, Mary possessed amazing powers of magnetic influence over the local lads, something not even the Catholic Church possessed. The lads that stood at the back of the church huddled in prayer due to lack of courage, stool up front, night-after-night at the bar huddled in deep meditation as they ogled at her with their telescopic eyeballs. No doubt, it would be correct to suppose that God works in mysterious ways.

It was the week before the June bank holiday weekend 1969 and the weather was a blessing not only to the farmers for the early cut of hay but also to the roadside lovers. With weather like this, you were sure to have a warm glow to any night. Jim was on his way back from work when the thirst caught up with him and nobody would begrudge a hardworking man a hearty pint of stout. As the Shebeen was on route home he thought to himself, "yerra, a quick wan ain't gonna do any harm, shur it ain't?" He was in no doubt that he would make it back home before Peg returned from her ICA outing with the Cahirciveen ladies.

As he entered the pub, he was hailed by Mary O' Sullivan and the scent of rose perfume that graced her was enough to send any man on a trip down fantasy lane. That evening, for some unknown reason, the back snug in the pub was very quiet. Jim found solace in its peacefulness. Jim by nature was a deep thinking man and loved his aloneness but this very evening his thoughts were distracted by Mary's beauty. The more she glanced at her, the more he felt, there was a strange uniqueness about her that he had never found in another woman. But one thing for sure, he had come to realise is that Mary didn't make wife material but she was certainly a decorative arm trinket for any member of the male species. When their glances connected there seemed to be a link that he could not explain. Mary smiles and nods of recognition were the signals that sent his sexual appetising juices in motion. Jim was trapped in Lunacy Lane, enrolled in a sexual fantasy that only appeared to him in his daftest dreams. But now, it was there to be served up to him in reality. Could he be guilty of wanting something that he was starved of, for so many years? Not so, according to Jim's inner lunatic voice. What harm could a little fun do, surely it was only a way of exploring knowledge. After all, he wasn't intending to have a full blown relationship outside his marriage, he was only learning about the boarder aspects of the sexual world. Shur, what harm was that and if anyone was to reason it out, after all, he was only trying to spice up his marriage by bring new unfounded sexual knowledge to it, he thought to himself. Well that was Jim's way of justifying his sexual encounters with Mary O' Sullivan and putting his questioning mind at ease.

The phone in the back room rang and Mary slipped out to answer it. When she returned, she delivered news that could only be wished for in a dream.

"The aul wans on the ICA outin' will be stayin' in Knock overnight as Johnny Burn's aul bus broke down again. They won't be back 'til tomorrow evenin'," she yelled over the heads of the thirsty punters.

"Grand girleen," grunted the punter over their pints.

"I guess that means ya've to fend for ya'rself," whispered Mary to Jim.

"Ach shur, I'll manage, I'll grab some fish and chips on the way home," replied Jim sheepishly.

Well Mary wasn't having any of it. She wasn't going to see Jim go hungry.

"Jim, I'll finish early tonight, shur, I'll stir somethin' up for ya. We'll go back yonder and have a bite of grub. Ya just hang on there for me laddie and everythin' will be grand. Just grand…." she whispered into Jim's ear as she handed him another pint of stout.

Jim was in clover; his dreams were now coming true. Peg and Johnny away for the night. The poultry sorted out, the cattle fed and Sean Og staying overnight at the big house where he worked. Shur, everything is grand he thought to himself. After all, Mary was only going to fix him up with a bite to eat and what harm was in that? Her home was on route and if he played his cards close to his chest, nobody would suspect anything. But he thought to himself, "I'll need to make sure nobody suspects anythin'." So, the bright and intelligent chap he was, he went out and took the air out of the back tyres on his car. With a smug grim and upper teeth biting into lower lip he thought, "now, who in their sane mind, would suspect anythin', after all, it only looks like Mary is doin' a good turn, seein' me home safely. Tomorrow mornin', I'll get a pump from yonder and put everythin' right again and Pcg will surely be none the wiser."

Mary didn't waste much time making small talk with the local punters that evening after her shift. Jim had arranged to meet her at the crossroads just outside the town on route home. When, he saw Mary's car pull up, a nervous guilty feeling hit the pit of his gut but his impish inner lunatic voice nudged him on and soon his heart convinced him it was all going to be okay. Opening the car door, he quickly hopped in and soon they were engrossed in chitchat and laugher.

Mary's home was warm and cosy and soon the kitchen was filled with a sizzle of a good hearty fry up. Mary's glances were enticing and Jim was engulfed with sexual urges. It seemed so right to hold her in his arms and as their tongues entwined, her rose scented perfume electrified their kisses and cuddles. Placing her hand between his legs and massaging his genitals, "nice luggage," she muttered as her tongue graced his aching craving trembling lips.

As she unbuttoned his shirt, the sensation of her hands gliding over his bare chest empowered him to release the belt on his trousers and unzipping it allowed comfort and ease to his aching erection. Mary shed her clothes with the ease of a snake shedding its skin. Their actions seemed so right. Jim was lost in his presence of reality and overcome with the magic of the moment. This sexual sensation was one he had never experienced before. Mary seemed to be guiding him around her sensual body with ease. The closeness of their bodies and the unity of spirits seemed to empower each movement. Her moans and groans of satisfaction in his ear added energy to the climax of his orgasm. His heart was now pounding and his respirations rapid for his sexual juices were well in motion. As Mary reached her climax, he felt his body overwhelmed with the urge to let go. His world moved, as years of sexual frustration were uncapped. It seemed so good and yet so wrong, so fitting yet so deceitful and unjust. He felt cheated that this moment should be with Mary O' Sullivan and not with the true love of his life, Peg.

"Mary, ya're a grand fit lass and a gamey wan too," hummed Jim to himself patting the pit of his belly in satisfaction while adoring the grandeur of his macho body and giving her one of his macho winks.

"Jim, me honeybun, I don't intend bein' a chromosome short of becomin' a cross between a hibernating peasant and a demented nun. I intend to live life to its fullness and that was a sure promise I made to meself the day I left that blasted convent. They're too many self-imprisonin' women out there and I ain't intendin' to become wan of them. I call them, the sex maidens trapped in granny knickers," delighted Mary as she slipped her slender long legs into her black-laced pantyhose.

The sensual licking of her lips, like the cat that got the cream was her signal to Jim that he had rated well in her standards. You see, beneath the rose scented perfume and the fancy underwear, Jim knew that Mary exhibited the spirit and nature of a whippet hound and that was the link to her mischievous ways. But, what had just happened was an exciting experience for Jim also, not unlike a discovery trip of Ireland, something new to be encountered around every bent and curve of the Irish roads. And with knowledge like this, it was reasonable to hope that his marriage could only flourish once Peg allowed herself to accept her sexuality, well that was what Jim thought to himself anyway.

As he looked around the yard the following morning, he came across an old sheela-na-gig statue at the backdoor of the Mary's house.

"Where in the honour of Jaysus did ya get this?" chuckled Jim stooping down to take a closer look.

"Ach, that's a family heirloom. It's an aul sheela-na-gig, it's a medieval fertility statue. I think it belonged to me grandmother or great gran-aunt, God rest their souls. Don't ya dare touch it or ya'll end up fatherin' a child," sniggered Mary as she handed him a cup of tea and a slice of jammed toast.

It's amazing how denial has a way of making people secure in a distorted sense of reality and this was so in Jim's case as he soon fitted into the comfort of his misplaced guilt. As the morning progressed, Jim noticed that there was a strain to his step. "Ahhhh Christ, that's to be expected," he thought, after all he had put muscles to the test that had laid dormant for years and Mary introduced him to others that he thought he never had. But his manhood was none the worst for wear and routine exercise was a good health guide for a long life was what he had read in one of Peg's magazines a few weeks back. A little drop of Winter Green would sort out the muscle strain and have him tipping over for another night with Mary he hoped. He reassured himself as he strolled to the village that morning. Ach shur, he could tell Peg that it was a bag of grain that got the better of him, if she was to put a sympathetic word towards his direction. What happened last night could only be good for it had lifted his spirits and put his singing voice back in tune.

As the weeks turned into months, Jim and Mary met up on a regular basis after work. As time went on, the sexual encounters he experienced with Mary didn't live up to his fantasy world. He was to discover that sex wasn't a way of discovering what he himself missed out on so much, which was the attention he craved from Peg. Soon the excitement of his adventures with Mary were unfulfilling and inwardly he scolded himself for his stupidity and devious lunatic nature. But, to keep Mary sweet he continued to deceive himself and Peg.

How could he have put his family at risk? If Peg were to find out, she would surely run out on him. What would happen to Johnny if she took him away? He could not bear to think of the outcome. Now he was to live with the deceit and the burden of a secret that would haunt him day in and day out. If he was to come clean and tell Peg, he had so much to lose. If he was to stay silent and swallow his guilt, he had to live with a twisted gut every-time he laid eyes on Mary. But his greatest fear was, would Mary let the secret out of the bag. Could he trust her? With her fun loving nature and whippet hound spirit, he could never count on her. The villagers were always thirst hungry creatures by nature for gossip and somebody else's misfortune was the food that fed their curiosity. But, he thought to himself if he could keep Mary sweet and Peg in the dark, this skeleton in his cupboard would hopefully dissolve with time, or would it?

Chapter Ten

Peg's Past

It's a lovely Sunday afternoon in March and Jim and Peg take a stroll along Rosbeig strand while Johnny and Sean Og happily pick shellfish from the rocks. The strand is very quiet and other than the odd stroller, the noise from the sea gulls together with the whistling of wind through the rocks complimented the sound of the incoming tide lashing up against the far distant cliffs. The sky is clearing up after the morning's showers and the clouds seem to be settling down. Dingle peninsula is just about visible in the distance. There is a strong smell of seaweed coming from the rocks as they stroll along the water's edge. Peg happily picks a bunch of dulse to make a mixture for Johnny's chesty cough. Every now and again Jim edges a stone off the incoming tide and takes great joy when it bounces as it skims the water. As Peg looks out yonder into the distance of the ocean, her mind wanders back in time and flashbacks from the past of a framed picture of Galway Bay that hung long side a picture of the Holy Family in the hallway of the Magdalen Laundry in Cork bring tears to her eyes.

"What's the matter, Peg?" asked Jim looking at her mysteriously.

At this stage the tears had now turned into choking sobs coming from deep within her throat.

"Jim dear, ya've no idea of the secret that I've carried in me heart for years. Day after day and year after year, I feel it gulpin' me up inside but I don't know how I'll ever get to the bottom of it," sobbed Peg sitting on a nearby rock and totally uninhibited by the waves gushing up against her boots.

"Ahhh Jaysus I don't like to see ya upset. Whatever it is, it can't be that bad. Just tell me. In the honour of Jaysus what's upsettin' ya, shur we'll sort it out whatever 'tis," he said for he knew that it couldn't be a love affair, for Peg had a problem with attraction and attention from men due to her hang ups with her own sexuality. He thought that maybe it had something to do with Johnny and maybe she was blaming herself for he being Down syndrome. Doc had often said in the past that many mothers often secretly blame themselves for mental or physical handicaps in their children.

This stroll along the water edge turns out to be a trip down horror's lane and Jim was certainly not prepared for what he is about to hear. Looking at him with a vague expression Peg mutters out in a broken tearful voice.

"When I was in the Magdalen Laundry in Cork, I gave birth to a baby girl and the nuns said that she died 'cause I didn't look after her. They said that I was a stupid evil girl and that God would punish me. But Jim, I wouldn't let me baby die. I know I wouldn't. Somethin' ain't right, I've always felt it in me heart that I didn't let her die and me gut feelin' eats away at me everyday tellin' me that the baby's alive and well."

There is a brief silence and Jim just stands there staring at her, trying to make sense of what she was telling him.

"Ahhhh Christ, if me baby died, I would've seen the little body laid out in the mortuary and shur the Magdalen Laundry girls would've gone to the funeral. Surely, the priest and nuns would've said a prayer for her at Mass on Sunday. That was the custom if other girls' babies died. Ohhhhh Jim, I swear to Christ, I didn't kill me baby," wept Peg making the sign of the cross on her forehead while stunting Jim with her concealed skeletons of her past.

Standing there, knee deep in the tidal wave he could feel a sensation of numbness coming over him from the knees down. Sitting down beside Peg and cupping her sobbing face into the armpit of his coat, he just allowed her to cry and cry. There seemed to be no end to her sobs. He could feel a tightness overcome his throat just at the back of his Adam's apple. Words would not come from him so he just soothing her by patting her head.

The wind had now entwined both of them and in the distance is a blurred vision of Sean Og and Johnny. Time seemed non-existent and the only thing that really mattered now to Jim was the grief and sadness that Peg had carried around with her in silence for so many years.

"Ahhh Peg, let me get me head around this, the Laundry was a place where ya worked. What had the nuns to do with it?" he asked as he tries to fit the pieces of his wife's past together. "In the name of Christ, who was the father of the child and what happened after the death of the baby? Did the father live with ya when ya carried the child? What did the nuns have to do with all of this anyway? When ya left hospital where did ya go…."

Peg raised her head as if to relieve her throat and allow the sea air to revive her lungs and with a sobbing sigh mutters out.

"Do ya remember when I told ya all about Sean Og and meself when we were put into care? Well, I was sent from the Industrial School in Tralee to the Magdalen Laundry. The nuns were in charge and I lived there under their care and supervision. There was no hospital, the Magdalen Laundry was a place for awful sinful girls who got themselves pregnant, or so the nuns told us. The nuns were meant to look after us and make sure we repented for our sins. I stayed there for almost three years and then they transferred me into service to Fr. Murphy in Cahirciveen. The father of the baby didn't care about me. He had his evil way with me every time the nuns sent me out to him. Mr. Keating was his name. He was a local businessman. He'd give the nuns a few bob when he'd return me after havin' his evil way. He made me commit grievous sins. He forced me to touch his privates and he used me in an awful sinful manner. I was just fifteen at the time…."

"Fuck'in…. hell," gasped Jim.

"When I told the nuns, they sent me to the laundry after the school doctor checked me out. But before that, they gave me a beatin' when I told them about the horrible thin' that this man was doin' to me. They didn't believe me, I was ordered to go to confession and beg God for forgiveness for my horrific lies. I didn't know I was pregnant. Shur, God bless me ignorance, I knew nothin' about babies or pregnancy. It was wan of the older girls in the laundry that told me I was goin' to have a baby and that was why I was transferred there. The girls all laughed at me and it was a joke they shared amongst themselves in the earlier weeks after me arrival. Three days after the baby was born I went out to get a bottle of warm milk, 'cause the baby was cryin', when I came back me baby was gone."

There was a pause and Peg just stood up and gazed out yonder to sea with a vague look in her face. Removing her blue cotton scarf from her head and using it to wipe her face, she walks out into the tidal waves. Her red hair now blowing into the wind and as she cups her bewildered face into the palms of her hands, she continues gagging the words out. Jim was in her footsteps and placing his hand on her shoulder stood by and just listened.

"When I asked for me baby, the nun in charge of the maternity section of the Laundry told me that me baby suffocated while I was out. God, I wept bitterly. I totally lost me head and turned the cot and bed upside down. I bawled at the nun, where's me baby please, give me back me baby. I hate ya and this blasted place. She hit out at me and told me to behave meself and she ordered me down to the lockup room, which was better known as the haunted closet. I can still hear the nun yellin' at me, 'Ya better pray that God is all merciful and that He doesn't sent ya into eternal damnation for ya'r horrific sins. Ya're a no good evil rip. Murderin' ya'r own baby, how can God ever forgive ya?' I pleaded with her, please Sister, let me out. I swear I didn't kill me baby. Please give her back to me. Please Sister, I'll behave and do whatever ya ask of me. Just....please...please.....give me back me baby. But nobody would help me. They just left me in that dark cold damp smelly closet...."

"Closet?" exclaimed Jim try to come to term with what Peg was saying.

"That haunted closet was under the main stairs where girls were sent if they misbehaved. The nuns would lock us in there for a number of days with only water and bread to eat. The place was full of mice and cockroaches. It was a scary place and the girls used to say that a dead nun haunted it. I hated it and it's 'cause of that blasted place I now fear the dark...."

Turning around and looking Jim straight into the eyes as if to convince him of her innocence, yet doubting herself, Peg continues in a feeble sobbing voice.

"I remember when they left me out I hit out harshly in anger and frustration at the nun but the nun got out her strap and gave me a trashin'. I started to bleed from the womb. The blood poured out of me body like water from a tap. I destroyed the hallway with me blood. Then the doctor came and gave me an injection and I don't remember anythin' else 'til I came to me senses a few days later. And when I did, I discovered the nuns had shaved off me lovely head of curly red hair. This was me punishment for actin' out of order and causin' such a commotion. I didn't rebel for I had no energy left in me weak marrow to do so. I just accepted me punishment gracefully and prayed to God that He'd take me. Do ya see....I don't know? Maybe....me baby....did die...... maybe they did say prayers..... when I was doped for those few days......I really.... just don't know, Jim."

"Mother of sweet Jaysus," sighed Jim.

"There was wan kind nun in the Magdalen Laundry, Sr. Dominic was her name and I remember she was very good to me. Actually, she was good to each and everywan of the girls that found themselves in trouble. I could talk to her, she said, she'd get me out of the Laundry and somehow when I did go into service, I felt that she'd somethin' to do with it. I missed her when I left..."

"Uk, Ma and Da," called out a familiar voice for the distance.

"Jim, please go to him, don't' let Johnny see me like this," sobbed Peg as she wipes the tears from her eyes and brings herself to the attention of the moment.

"Ma whawha wha's wong?" asked Johnny as he came closer with his little bucket of muscles and periwinkles.

"Ach son, ya'r Ma got some sand in her eyes from the sea breeze," quickly replied Jim. "And I was just sortin' it out for her. Shur she'll be grand after a while. Peg dear, maybe we should make tracks and see ourselves home?"

"Grand," muttered Peg.

There was no objection from Johnny's side for he had enough of the sea breeze and was getting weary and hungry. Jim gently embraces Peg and hand-in-hand they set out on their way to the car that is parked at the far end of the strand.

"We'll talk later darlin', when Johnny goes to bed and everythin' will be grand, I'm sure of that. Take it ayezee now and we'll sort everythin' out," whispered Jim to Peg as he opens the front passenger's door for her.

There are very few words spoken between Peg and Jim on the way home. Sean Og entertained Johnny with stories in the back seat. Sean Og was always a bit of a storyteller and had a wonderful collection of stories when it came to children. Johnny could sit for hours listening to these stories finding great joy acting out the characters. There was always a little boy named Johnny in the stories and each story started with, "Once up on a time..." and ended with, "Have a good night sleep, stars are shinin' bright and the moon is out tonight, so sleep well little Johnny, sleep well little Johnny tonight..."

At this stage, Johnny is able to recite the beginning and end of each story and never minded the repetition of words. Funny enough, he seems to be happier with the familiarity of the words and gets great mileage out of the same story. Every now and again on the journey home

Johnny would sneeze and he would prompt Sean Og into reciting the nursery rhyme,

"Monday sneeze; watch out for danger
Tuesday sneeze; kiss a stranger
Wednesday sneeze; expect a letter
Thursday sneeze; await something better
Friday sneeze; is for woe
Saturday sneeze; a long, long journey you must go
Sunday sneeze; tomorrow expect a lover."

Then Johnny would ask what day it was and insist that Sean Og tell him what he should expect from his sneeze.

Even though people thought that Johnny didn't understand much, he would prove them wrong, time and time again and have many a person wondering, how a little Down syndrome boy's head could carry all he knew. Johnny was like a sponge, he soaked up everything he heard and saw. But the one thing that would amuse Johnny for hours was when Peg would make hand shadows of different animals and birds on the bedroom wall. She could move her hands and fingers around in various positions and create numerous objects. The one that gave Johnny the greatest joy and fun was Toby the terrier wagging his tail. Johnny was able to manage Grumpy the bulldog and the piglet. He would sit patiently for long periods of time trying to create Peter, the munching rabbit and would giggle to himself when he had just about got the knack of it.

As they pull into Glenbeigh, Johnny shouts out while tapping Jim on the shoulder. " Ite keam….pese Da.. ….yuk….. thop."

Little Johnny is as glic as a fox. Even though he is unable to tell one day from another, somehow every Sunday he would ask for sweets when he would pass the small shop and filling station at the end of the village. Jim pulls in at the main entrance of the shop and Sean Og takes Johnny in to get his usual Sunday treat.

Shortly after getting home, Peg attends to the supper while Jim feeds the cattle and fowl for the evening.

Johnny is eager to go to bed as he is very tired and Peg fears that he might be coming down with a chest cold, as he is a little hot and wheezy. After having some garlic and thyme ointment rubbed onto his back and a small slice of lemon bandaged to his left radial vein to keep a fever at bay followed by a bedtime story from Hans Andersen's Best Fairy Tales read by Sean Og, he is well on his way to dream world.

The sitting room is nice and cosy, but Jim feels a bit of extra firing might be needed as he is in no doubt that Peg has a lot on her mind. And if they are to continue what they spoke about on the strand, it could be well into the early hours of the morning before they get to bed. He feels a little uncomfortable and uneasy in himself with Peg anxiety for she has always been the strong one in their relationship and was the person to make everything okay when things went wrong. He isn't used to seeing her down in spirits and certainly not in the state that she was in today. He goes out to the back shed to get a gabhail of turf and bids goodnight to Sean Og.

"Ahhhhh shur, she ain't herself Jim, she's a little off form and low in spirit tonight. The past can do that to ya if it fetches up with ya at all. Just take her ayezee. Jim, please be patience with her. Time will sort it out, for time is a great healer. Although, poor aul Peg had it tough with those awful nuns in that Laundry. Terrible stuff happened to young lassies in there," muttered Sean Og to himself as he boils up the kettle for his water bottle and a mug of cocoa.

"Peg is a strong lass and will pull through, we'll both see to that," replied Jim.

When Jim returns to the front room, Peg is already huddled up in her rocking chair by the fire in silence, she didn't even notice him coming in.

"I've the kettle on and I'll make ya a nice sup of cocoa. Would ya like a buttered scone with it Peg?" asked Jim kneeling down to put a few sods of turf on the fire and building up a good hearty flame with the bellows.

"Naaaa Jim, I'm fine. Ya've been very good to me today. I shouldn't have got into such a state on the strand. I should be able to put me past to rest by now and be grateful for the good life ya've given the three of us. If it wasn't for ya, where would me and Sean Og be now? Ya're a good kind man…"

"Peg, don't be so hard on ya'rself. Ya're a great wan to have come through what ya came through. I don't think I'd been as strong and as courageous as ya. By Christ, they were tough times. Why didn't ya tell me about it before? Ya must know by now that I'd have understood," replied Jim looking in admiration at Peg but with sorrow in his heart as it was really only sympathy he could share with her as he felt he could never fully empathise with her past suffering as he himself was fortunate to have a happy childhood.

"There's stuff that's difficult to put words on. I guess in some way I was ashamed for years that I was reared in that Industrial School and wanted everywan to think that I was normal and had a normal upbringin'. Ya see Jim, been reared in an Industrial School does strange stuff to ya'r mind. For instant, ya never feel as good as other people. Ya feel that there's somethin' wrong with ya. Ya see, after I went into service, I used to think that people were gawkin' at me on the street and sayin' that wan came from an Industrial School. It was only about a year of workin' in service with Fr. Murphy when I realised that people took no notice of me and it made no difference to them when they found out anyway…."

"Peg, I don't want to upset ya any further but what really happened in that special home or so called Magdalen Laundry?" meekly asked Jim settling himself into his armchair and sipping his cocoa.

"When I was in the Industrial School, the nuns farmed me out to a businessman in Tralee, well that's what we, the girls used to call it. His name was Mr. Keating. He was a tall, middle-aged man and I remember now, there was always a fierce aul smell of tobacco and whisky from his breath. He was a buildin' contractor, married with six kids livin' on the outskirts of Tralee. Yerra Christ, he was looked upon as wan of the respectable citizens and was always givin' a few bob to the nuns for the black babies in the missions. He'd come and collect me on a Saturday afternoon 'cause his wife and kids went to Limerick to visit their grandmother. I remember wan afternoon he told the nun in charge that he preferred it that way 'cause I'd get more done and anyway he didn't want me mixin' with his kids. I never met his wife. I only saw a photo of her. She was a heavyset woman with black hair. He'd refer to her as the missus. He was a good bit older than her, maybe twenty years her senior...

Jim sighed in disgust.

"When I was first handed over to him I was told to be good, have me manner and do what was requested of me. Me job was to clean the house and attend to the sheds where the buildin' materials were stored. It was in wan of those back sheds he'd get his evil sinful way with me. It all started on me fourteenth birthday, he claimed he was goin' to make a woman out of me. He touched me all over me body with his hand inside me vest and knickers. And then insist on placin' me hand on his privates and get me to arouse him, then he'd enter me body. I felt so uncomfortable and resisted at the start but he warned me that he'd tell the nuns that I ain't doin' me job and that I'd get into trouble. That man got his sinful way with me for a whole year. On me return to the school after spendin' the Saturday afternoons in his care, the nun in charge would meet us at the main door. Smiles were exchanged between both of them. He'd then hand her an envelope sayin' 'a little somethin' for the poor starvin' black baby's collection box' and her reply would be, 'I'm ever so grateful, ever so grateful.' ..."

"Fuck'in.....hell," gasped Jim shaking his head in dismay.

"Wan day, I told her what really happened while in this man's care, I was severely punished, me body lashed black and blue followed by an ice cold shower in full view of some of the girls. I felt so ashamed, horrified and humiliated. The followin' week, after the beatin' from the nuns in the Industrial School, I was farmed out again but this time I was beaten and violently raped by Mr. Keating. He told me by the time he'd finish with me I'd never again forget to keep me big gob shut. His vicious attack took place in wan of the back sheds. Grabbin' me by the back of me neck, he walloped me on the face, forced me belly downwards over the bags of cement, ripped open me knickers with his pen knife, forced me legs apart and with his hands over me mouth, he got his evil sinful way. It was so painful and me belly and thighs ached. I can still hear his groans and deep respirations and smell his whiskey tobacco-tainted breath as I struggled. The more he forced himself into me, the more me body became saturated in his sweat and me head became buried in clouds of cement dust. I struggled and bawled out, 'please stop, please stop', but he yelled back, 'take it….. ya ugly little whore…… take it like a woman…. ya filthy good for nothin'….. little skinny whore'…."

"Sweet Jaysus….. say not more…. ohhhhh Peg say no more," quivered Jim.

"No Jim I need to tell somewan and get it all off me chest. Please hear me out, ya need to know," bitterly sobbed Peg. "I started to bleed and I could feel the blood pour down me legs onto the saw-dusted floor. At this stage the pain was horrific, he was forcin' himself into me back passage. I bawled and bawled, he put his fingers into me mouth to shut me up which were tainted by me soilin' and as he did so, he groaned out, 'Shut up…. ya feck'in… whore…. shut up ya feck'in whore…. I'll give ya some thing to bawl about.' In some strange way, me strugglin' seemed to edge him on and arouse him. Ohhhh Christ, it seemed to go on forever. The more he forced his weight on me, the more I gasped for air and the more I gasped and cried out, the more he seemed to get agitated. He pushed me to the floor and forced his dirty organ into me mouth. I gagged and vomited but that didn't stop him. Then he got up and kicked me into the belly, draggin' me onto me feet by me hair and pointed to a rope hangin' from the rafters.

'Ya see that rope.... now... take a hard.....long....gawp at it... ya dirty little skinny whore.....mark me words ya'll hang from it the next time ya bad gob me,' he roared out. Then he flung me back onto the saw dusted floor, zipped up his pants, straightened his collar and tie and left me there covered in me own vomit and blood mixed with the soilin' from his secretions. Ohhhh Jim, it was awful. Nooooo.... Jim.... it was both vile and disgustin'."

At this stage, Jim was sobbing into his cupped palms.

"Ya see, I didn't have a monthly bleed for a few months and didn't tell the nuns. It was a sin to talk about that unclean time of the month. Anyway, shur, I didn't know that I was meant to have a bleed every month. I didn't even know that I was pregnant. Ahhh shur Christ, I knew nothin' about babies and how they were born, not to mind how they were conceived. All I remember is, in the mornin' I'd get violently sick after breakfast and durin' the day I was faintish and weak but said nothin' I thought that somethin' terrible was happenin', I guess I thought I was goin' to die. And in some strange way, I was happy about that, 'cause for me, it seemed the only way of escapin' out of that damn place that I hated so much. Ya see Jim, everyday was the same, I didn't even know what age I was. I didn't even know when me birthday came. I only knew that it was Christmas 'cause the nuns allowed us to play all day and gave us chicken and roast potatoes. We got parcels but they contained soap and face clothes and bits of torn books. No sweets or toys."

Jim sat with gagging gasps and watched on in shock and horror. What Peg was telling him was beyond his wildest thoughts. He had never spoke of a rape before, not to mind hear the details of it. Could a person have come through so much hardship and cruelty and still be normal he thought to himself. Peg went on, but now it seemed that it was only her body that remained in the chair, one might say that her spirit had left it or was hovering around but to look at her, she was motionless and her eyes just focused on the flame of the turf fire.

"Mr Keating asked for another girl that day and said that I was trouble. He said that I stole money and that he wanted a girl he could trust. The nun in charge apologised to him for me sinful actions and told him that she had a girl who had just come of age. Young Kathleen Malone was sent out to him. Kathleen was a slow learner and they both probably knew that she wouldn't make much fuss, ya see, she didn't really know right from wrong. I can still hear the nun whisper to Mr. Keating, 'This wan's a bit of a pleidhce but she'll be able to manage a mop and a bucket and whatever else ya need of her. She'll certainly won't be any bother like the other madam'…"

"A pleidhce?" frowned Jim.

"A pleidhce is the Irish word for a simpleton, I guess to the nuns we were all simpletons in their eyes…"

"Jaysus Christ….. say no more," butted in Jim shocked by Peg past and suffering.

"Nooooo… Jim… I need to tell ya… I need to get it off me chest and clear me head…. That evenin', I fainted in the dormitory. The doctor was called to the school and he informed the nuns that I was with child. He was a kind man who spoke with a soft voice. I don't think he was a native of Kerry. I tried to tell him about me experiences and the terrible stuff that were happenin' in the school. He reckoned that I was about three to four months into me pregnancy. I remember Mother Superior comin' into the room while the he was examinin' me. He questioned her about the marks on me body and asked if there was anythin' happenin' in the school that'd be a cause of concern to her. I'm in no doubt that Mother Superior knew what he was referrin' to but she said that I was a difficult girl to handle and was well known for me lies. She went on to say that I got into a fight with another inmate and that they'd see that I'd behaved meself in future. The doctor requested that I get dressed and asked the nun to brin' me a warm drink. He told Mother Superior that he wanted a word with her in private and on leavin' the room he turned to me and said, 'Take care, I'll see ya're looked after. Don't fret now, everythin' will be taken care of,' I guess he too was in no doubt what had really happened to me..."

"Fuck'in hell," muttered Jim shaking his head in horror, "I don't want to hear anymore, I've heard enough."

"Please.... Jim I need to get it.... off me chest. Ya need to hear me story," insisted Peg grabbing a hold of Jim's arm. "That evenin', I was called to the Mother Superior's office and told to pack me stuff and was hoisted off to another Institution which turned out to be a Magdalen Laundry in Cork and there I was suppose to stay 'til the nuns decided what was to become of me future. I worked hard in that laundry day in and day out doin' me best to survive amongst the pack of young girls, starved and raped of their innocence."

"Was it.... such a terrible place?" Jim sighed.

"Believe it or not we had good days but it's the bad memories that have lived on with me. Life were never the same after the birth. I was very down in spirits and cried meself to sleep each night. Wan'night, I tried to leap out the top window, hopin' to do away with meself. Ya see, Jim, I'd nothin' to live for, or so I thought. The nuns told the doctor and priest that I had become a bit of a lunatic. If I tried it again, they said they'd have to send me to a Mental Institution or the madhouse as many of us used to call it at the time. From then on, they kept a close eye on me. Sr. Dominic was to supervise me. She was the nice nun that I told ya about earlier at the strand. She was very kind and used to brin' me special treats and helped me with me work when nobody else was watchin'. God, I remember now, she gave me a little picture of the Mother of Perpetual Succour when I was leavin' that place and I gave her a rose that I had plucked from the rose garden. She told me that the Mother of Perpetual Succour would keep me safe if I prayed to her every night just before I dosed off to sleep. And I guess she did for I did pray to her every night. I often think of that nun when I'm alone and wonder what became of her. She got me to pray to God after the birth of me baby so that I'd be happy again..."

"Yeah," muttered Jim with eyes focused on the fire.

"And shur, I suppose God did answer me meek prayers. I met ya and now I've a lovely son, a good aul life and Sean Og is safe as well. That's all thanks to ya, Jim. Ya see now why I was so angry when ya tried to take ya'r own life," sniffled Peg as her eyes fill up with tears but they didn't flow, it was like she was trying to be strong in front of Jim. Her face looked drawn and the blueness of her eyes had lost their sparkle. Her carrot red wavy hair framed her pale skin and even thought she was overcome with sadness and grief, there was an unusual beauty surging from her.

"Dear….dear…..Peg," said Jim now on bended knee in front of her holding her hands.

"Ohhhhh…….darlin', ya've given more to me than ya'll ever realise. Ya're me whole world and without ya, there'd be no life for me. I love ya so much," he whispered as he embraced her.

This was the first time in their marriage that their embrace seemed to fit and both felt at ease in each other's arms. It was like when an air lock is released in a pipe, it eases the flow of water. Peg's suppressed emotions and bad memories had left a mark of uneasiness to physical touch.

"Good God, I hated that blasted place. The mornin' I arrived at the Magdalen Laundry, I was asked me name, and when I replied, Peg, the nun in the main office said, 'Ya'll not be called Peg here, we've enough Pegs on our books. From now on, ya'll respond to the name Maire Beag'. But me name is Peg, I've always been called Peg. Ya see Sister that was me mother's second name, I responded shyly. 'That's of no importance to me. If ya'r mother cared enough about ya in the first place ya'd not be here in this state. Here, girls like ya do what they're told, God knows ya've sinned enough and makin' immense for ya'r sins is what ya should be doin', not worryin' about ya'r name. How far gone are ya?' she asked. Excuse me, Sister, I replied 'cause I didn't know what she was referrin' to. She looked at me in disgust and replied, 'Good God, they sent us an other stupid wan. Don't ya know ya should never sit on a boy's lap unless there's a newspaper between ya and him? Get her out of here and get her into this dress and apron. From now on, Maire Beag ya'll wear these. The devil makes work for idle hands so get her to work, there's plenty of it to keep her goin' in the washroom,' she requested of the young nun standin' beside me. In the boiler washroom, there were so many young girls. Some of them were sent to the Laundry for just simply being disobedient or for mixin' with boys in the streets. The older girls all had babies but they didn't speak about them. 'What's ya'r name? ' Wan of the younger girls asked me. The nun in the office said I was to be called Maire Beag but me real name is Peg," I whispered shyly. 'That's okay,' her friend replied, 'we'll call ya Peg amongst ourselves but be sure to stick to Maire Beag when wan of those aul wicket hags are around. Keep ya'r nose clean, work hard and ya'll get on okay. Volunteer to say the rosary every now and again and don't smile in front of the nuns and ya'll get on just fine. They don't like to see us happy, they say this is our penance for our sins. They'll pay ya two bob a week but ya don't get it. Ya'll get the hang of it if ya stick with us. They're just aul wicket bats from hell, that's what those nuns are,' she smirked flickin' some of the dirty suds at me…"

Jim just knelt in silence holding Pegs hand.

"Are ya pregnant or just simply pure devilish?" another girl asked me as she rushed by with a basin of dirty water in her gabhail.

"I don't know," I remember replying.

"Well don't let that worry ya for ya'll soon find out which wan ya are, 'cause the pregnant' wans are sent upstairs a few weeks before they get a baby," she assured me.

"The nuns didn't tell me they were goin' to give me a baby," I answered. Ahhh shur, God Bless us from all harm, lookin' back now, we were so innocent and ignorant. To think, at the time I didn't even know enough to know that I was pregnant and truth behold, I didn't even know what the word pregnant meant. When I heard the word for the first time I thought I was diseased with some strange illness," muttered Peg with a nervous giggle.

The colour started to come back into her cheeks and she seemed more at ease as she continues to relate her experiences to Jim.

"The sleepin' areas in the Magdalen Laundry were like little cells, we had a pisspot in the room that was to be kept under the bed and we'd to slop out each mornin'. The workdays seemed endless. I found out in later years, that it was a commercial laundry run by nuns. They said that we used to get paid but I never saw any money. The wages used to be accounted for in a book and money would be deducted as a form of punishment. God knows, thinkin' back now, I must have been very disobedient for all I got when I left was the price of me ticket to Cahirciveen. Ohhhh yeah, they gave me a flowery dress that was too big for me. I'd to tie a blue ribbon around me waist to stop the wind from gettin' under it and not've it lookin' like a tent."

Peg went silent and sat gazing into the smoke that found its way up the chimney from the burned out embers in the grate. It wasn't long before the silence was disturbed by the sound of the night wind and rain but the ticking of the grandfather clock seemed to harmonise the moment.

"Let's go to bed, Jim. I'm very tired. Thanks for bein' so understanding and lovin'. I didn't know how I was ever goin' to get around to tellin' ya about the baby. Now that I've told ya, I feel much better in meself. Ya see the moment I held me baby, I dreamt of her takin' her first step and her gurglin' out her first word. In me mind, I could picture her first day at school even her first Holy Communion. I called her Blathin, it's the Irish for me little flower. Ya see Jim, I was goin' to be a wonderful mother. I promised her that from the moment I laid eyes on her. I made a promise that I'd look after her and never let her go. When I cuddled her and fed her I felt somethin' in me heart that had been missin' for years, I guess, 'twas love. The love that was quenched the day me and Sean Og were taken from our mother's bedroom. But, somethin' ain't right I feel it in me soul and heart that she didn't die but I can't for the life of me understand why I've that feelin'. I simply can't, it just taunts me everyday of me life. When I first met with Fr. Murphy niece Geraldine, his sister Kate's little child, I felt a special bond with her, ain't that strange? When she looked at me, I could see Sean Og in her. I can't explain that either. Maybe I wanted to believe that me baby girl didn't die," said Peg shaking her head and biting her lower lip as a sudden tightness clinched her throat.

"I don't know why ya'd feel like that, I really can't say," said Jim looking puzzled and shaking his head in dismay.

"Ahhhh Jim, don't take any notice, I'm just ramblin' on. Maybe I simply can't accept the truth. I just don't know," said Peg as if to ease Jim's confused mind.

"Peg dear, I'm only sorry that ya've carried all this in ya'r heart for so many years. It makes no difference to me what ya did in the past. I love ya and nothin' will ever change that," he muttered holding out his arms to embrace her once again.

After locking up for the night and looking in on Johnny, Peg lights the little candle on the landing window and as she looks out onto the night sky, she asks God to put her agonising and frustrating thoughts to rest. Then slipping off her slippers, she joins Jim in bed and they both settle down for the night snuggled up in each other's arms.

Chapter Eleven

Given Into Service

One week into her nineteenth birthday Peg returned to her native county when she was given into service by the nuns to work as a housekeeper for a parish priest called Fr. Murphy who resided in Cahirciveen, Peg found him to be kind and committed to his parishioners. The work arrangement and transfer was organised by Sr. Dominic who befriended Peg in the Laundry but Peg was unaware of this. During her time there, she trusted Fr. Murphy and looked upon him as her new family.

When Peg arrived at Cahirciveen, Fr. Murphy knew little about her previous life other than that she was one of the girls from the Magdalen Laundry in Cork that gave birth to a baby while in care. Sr. Dominic who was a life long friend of Fr. Murphy from their childhood days had informed him that Peg would be a good replacement for the previous housekeeper who died from a stroke. She did notify him though, that Peg had developed a strong constitution for getting her own way and this was one of the reasons why she didn't settle too well into the life at the Magdalen Laundry. But when it came to trustworthiness and hard work, she was one of the best. Fr. Murphy, who in himself was a rebel by nature at the best of times felt that Peg would be the woman to keep the old fashioned priests that resided with him on their toes. And anyway, a good feisty woman around the place was sure to bring a bit of spirit to the atmosphere or so he thought. They both agreed that giving Peg a chance would do no harm and after all, it was the Christian thing to do.

Peg settled in well to her new surrounds and soon befriended Betty the housekeeper from the Convent. They both had Sunday afternoons off and would spend their time going for long walks, having picnics up in the Fair Green, hanging around the streets watching the local talent and judging the corner boys that stood shoulder-to-shoulder day after day helping to hold up the town's Court House wall!

As time went by, Peg was soon to become bewildered by the kindness of the nuns in the local Convent. All her life she had learned to fear nuns but these nuns welcomed her with open arms and she felt very much at ease in their presence. In the evening time, when things were quiet and her work in the Priest's house was done she would slip off down the small boreen that lead to the back entrance of the convent. And from there, she would wander up to the sewing room at the top of the stairway where she had full use of the old foot sewing machines. There she would happily spend hours designing and sewing, turning out beautiful dresses, blouses and skirts for herself and Betty. Every now and again, the nuns would give her material and wool that she could use. They also allowed her full access to their library, which was wall to wall graced with books of knowledge just waiting to be read and digested. It was there in that very room that Peg learned to read and write. In the Industrial School she never grasped the skill of reading and writing as she spend more of her time in the corner of the classroom facing the wall with a Dunce Cap on her head and with her left hand tied behind her back. Pinned to her back for all to see was a card that said, 'amadan ciotach', which meant, left handed fool. No matter how hard she tried to write with her right hand, she could never achieve the recommended standard that would please the nun in question. To this day, Peg often wonders if it was the fear that inhibited her from learning. Yet in the Convent in Cahirciveen, her left handed literally skills didn't seem to matter. The nuns were just proud of her for her ability to learn.

She was also granted the pleasure of learning to read music and play the piano. Something she prided herself on over the years. All in all, life was wonderful, plenty to eat, warm bed to rest her head and for once she even had kind friends that cared and accepted her. For the first time in years, she had started to enjoy life and not fear it. The nuns and priests from Cahirciveen had now become her family. She became accustomed to their way of living, joining them in evening prayer, sharing their joys and listening to their woes. She had come to realise that beneath that starched habit the nuns were really women and not bats from hell, as she had come to know of them in the Industrial School in Tralee and in the Magdalen Laundry in Cork. When she was sentenced into service in that Magdalen Laundry she could never understand how women who claimed to be Brides of Christ could be so cruel to their earthly sisters.

One autumn evening, just as twilight was settling in, Peg found herself sitting in the Convent conservatory amongst the geraniums wondering about life. Her thoughts wandered back to that dark November's evening in the Magdalen Laundry in Cork and of what Sr. Dominic had said to her as she tried to comfort her in her grief and muddled moments, 'Goodness has nothing to do with being a nun, goodness comes from deep within a person. Nuns are also human. Some of them are just not as kind as others. You see Peg dear, everyone is born with goodness but badness infests the soul of a person when they refuse to listen to their conscience. Also, it's important to remember that none of us are born evil. It's just that we learn to be evil on whatever pathway we choose to follow in life.'

It took Peg to come to Cahirciveen to really understand the wisdom of Sr. Dominic. And how right she was, Peg thought as her mind drifted off into reciting the Lord's Prayer.

Amongst any congregation and community, you are going to have characters that stand apart and the Church in Cahirciveen had certainly inherited its own over the years. Some priests were to be feared, others were to be love while more were there to be honoured or pitied. As time went by, Peg learned to understand the different personalities of each of these characters. She got on well with the old retired priest or 'the aul boy' as he was better known amongst his parishioners. They had a fondness toward him and one thing for sure, when it came to the practices of the Church, he worked miracles day and night. Midday mass on Sunday was over in fifteen minutes and evening devotions also completed in ten. Not too many complained about his ways of administration, for if they did, he would assure them, they could have his permission not to attend the sacraments at all.

Soap and water didn't visit him too often but as long as he had his sup of whiskey and his old clay pipe he didn't worry for much. During the day he was to be found digging over the Convent back garden and cleaning out the cow and poultry sheds.

The locals would have you believe that he was a true man of God but deep down he had a gra or in other words a deep fondness for one of the old nuns. It was a well-known fact that this nun would stand just inside the convent window overlooking the garden watching him while doing the rounds of her rosary beads. Every now and again, he would glance up at her and smile while resting his weary arm on the handle of his spade. Even thought fate didn't allowed them to be with each other in body, they were certainly kindled folk in spirit. And here in the convent garden in his twilight years he had found his Heaven on earth knowing that love wasn't always about the pleasures of the flesh but that true love germinated in the soul and glowed through the human heart. Sadly though, that's one thing, many of us fail to realise as we travel through the pathway of life.

Then there was Fr. Thomas, who on the other hand was as cranky out of the confession box as he was within it! He was nicknamed the Misery Miser. Always counting his money from the Sunday collection and making everyone aware of what the other person owed in monthly dues. Needless to say, he wasn't liked much by the locals but Peg had come to understand his ways. A good plate of spuds for supper, mixed with plenty of fried onions and milk was sure to get her in his good books and as long as she didn't touch his collection boxes and never answered back other than offering him the odd nod and smile then he was grand to deal with. Some would have you believe, he was doomed to be cranky from birth 'till death. But it was the corner-boys that had the tailoring of him. On his approach, they would tilt their caps and say in one harmony, "Father." But once he had passed by, they would wink and joke amongst themselves and if you happened to be near, you would hear them say, "there's a right laticho in that hobo…."

One cold March evening at the back of the church, Fr. Murphy found Peg sobbing. Approaching her, he soon ferreted out the reason for her unhappiness and gloom. She confided in him about the abuse in that Industrial School in Tralee and how the girls were suffering while in the care of the nuns. He was totally bewildered by the facts she confided in him regarding what was going on behind locked doors in the institutions. In his heart, he so dearly wanted not to believe it but something in his gut feeling urged him to look into it. He requested a meeting with the Bishop regarding the matter. Peg also confided in him about her past and how she ached to find out the whereabouts of Sean Og. He promised to keep an ear to the ground and make enquiries through Sr. Dominic and the Industrial School for boys in Tralee. After making a few phone calls, he found out that Sean Og had left Ireland for England after been left go or one might say released from the school at the age of almost seventeen. And from getting in contact with some of his Irish counterparts in one of the Catholic Churches in London he was able to trace Sean Og down. It turned out that he was working on a building site just outside London. Fr. Murphy dropped a letter to him regarding the good news. From then on both Peg and Sean Og keep in contact by letter and by phone.

While he was dabbling and doing his own investigation into Peg's past, what Fr. Murphy stumbled upon, really came as a great surprise to him. On visiting the educational department in Dublin and having searched through the files regarding Peg's family background, he found out that Peg's mother died one month after the children were sent to the Industrial Schools. Peg was horrified about the news of her mother's death but more so, for the fact that she blamed her mother for all the hardship she suffered in that Industrial School because she didn't come to collect her or even make contact with her.

Other confidential information that he stumbled over in the files urged him to arrange a visit to the Department of Registration of Birth and Deaths. A Bishop, who was a close friend of his family arranged for him to have access to the Irish adoption files held by the Catholic Church. He was horrified with the results of his research. All this time, Peg had led him to believe that her baby had died or so the nuns had convinced her. He discovered that to the contrary, the child was still alive and was adopted by an Irish couple now living in America. The adoption application forms in the confidential file revealed that a doctor and his wife adopted Peg's child. The names of the adopting parents on the adoption papers shocked Fr. Murphy, as they happened to be Kate, his eldest sister and his brother-in-law Peter. Fr. Murphy was well aware that Peg suffered a deep sense of grief for the loss of her baby and she felt so guilty. Now knowing that Peg is the mother of his sister's child, he felt a special bond and responsibility towards her. This information was something he intended to keep to himself but one summer's evening he revealed the news to his sister Kate, who was excited and requested to be introduced to Peg.

Fr. Murphy now knew there had to be some truth to Peg's story regarding the terrible abuse that was going on in the Industrials Schools and in the Magdalen Laundries and felt it only fair that it deserved some form of proper investigation. Equipped with his rebel nature he was determined to get to the bottom of it. Over the coming weeks he decided to hop his ball of investigation and see whose yard it would bounce in or in other words he would set the bait and wait to see who would get upset by it. He set out to make enquiries about what he called the MARK, which stood for the 'Massive Abuse Regarding Kids'. But the end result wasn't what he was anticipating. The Brother Superior of the Industrial School in Tralee got a whiff that a priest was stirring up a storm and having got in contact with his other counter-parts in the Industrial Schools around Ireland requested that the Bishop put things right and silence this priest. After all, they felt they had schools to run and how they ran them was their business.

A week after the complaint had been lodged with His Lordship by the Christian Brothers, Fr. Murphy received a letter which stated that he presence would be better served in the missions and arrangements were put in progress for him to leave straight way. He was also informed that the issue wasn't up for negotiation. By Friday, Fr. Murphy found himself in a small missionary community in the Congo. From there, all his correspondence and contacts outside this small community were to be closely monitored. Peg was dismissed from her position and given a one-way ticket to England with the compliments of His Lordship and the nuns were gracefully informed to cease all contact with her.

Peg made off Sean Og in London and once again went into service with an English family but this time it was by choice. It was here, she was to meet with Jim who was fifteen years her senior and who worked as a handyman at the same estate. After a few months into their courtship, they married and continued in service until they returned to Ireland. They settled down in the small holding a few miles outside Glenbeigh in County Kerry that Jim inherited from his Uncle Jack.

Chapter Twelve

Jim Takes Matters Into His Own Hands

Jim takes matters into his own hands and is on a mission to fish out the truth regarding the horrific abuse that went on in the Industrial Schools of Ireland. One evening, while having a quiet pint in the local pub, chatting about gone by days with a retired guard, better known to the locals as Dick Senior, the conversation lead onto Sean Og and the abuse he suffered as a young lad while in the care.

"Can ya believe that this was goin' on durin' ya'r time in the force, Dick?" asked Jim.

"Indeed... I've.... no doubt... no doubt...Jim, 'cause I can give ya a name of a Garda who has had to live with his own experience regardin' this matter. And I've no doubt what he'd have to tell ya, is true, for there's wan thin' I can assure ya, he was a honourable Garda in his day. Mick McCarthy is his name. He was stationed in Galway when I knew him. But it was durin' his placement in Cliften when the issue arose regardin' the abuse in the Industrial Schools that opened his eyes to the roguery and conspiracies that went on within the system and amongst the Religious Orders who were responsible for young kids placed into their care by the Irish State. Shur maybe, I can get in touch with him and he might have a word with ya. It might mean a trip to Galway if ya intend to follow it up," said Dick supping back the tail end of his pint of stout and repositioning his peaked cap while wiping his moustache with the sleeve of his green Aran sweater.

"By Christ Dick, I'd go to fuck'in hell and back to find answers," replied Jim holding up his empty pint glass to the barman signalling for another refill.

During the evening the thirsty punters get involved in the conversation and even though many of them had a story to tell about what went on in those Industrial Schools in Ireland few held out any hope of exposing the issue, as they felt that the Religious Orders were a law onto themselves with the backing of Church and State. And anyway, they felt they were in no position to question or accuse the Nuns or the Christian Brothers of their actions or deeds as they themselves were just simple humble God-fearing people, many with no education at all. The reality of the situation was that Ireland was a patriotic state run by the Catholic Church and humble people had neither hear or say!

Over the next few days, Jim keeps himself busy carrying out small repairs around the home. Johnny enjoys helping him. Peg is busy with preparations for the evening craft classes that are to take place in the Village Hall and plans to knit another sweater for Sean Og while attending them. The last sweater she knitted for him got mislaid or so he told her. But truth behold, he lost it on purpose for he looked like a stuffed lamb in it, as it exaggerated his pot belly or so he thought. Meantime, Dick arranges for Jim to meet up with Mick McCarthy in Galway. They plan to meet up in a quiet pub in Clifden on the following Saturday afternoon.

It's a wet Saturday afternoon when they arrive in Clifden and the local punters are engrossed in the horse racing on the goggle box. There is a better sound than picture but that doesn't seem to trouble the punters as they huddle together in anticipation and concentration. A strong smell of smothering turf mingles with the scent of ale and the whiff of smoke from the tobacco pipes clouds the back snug. But it's the familiar odour of dried pig dung entwined with the hum of wet donkey jackets and the appetising smell of bacon and cabbage from the backroom that gives a unique homely feeling to the pub itself. The clouded snug is to their advantage as what they have to say needs to be said in private. Dick calls out to the bean-an-ti for two pints of the black stuff as they make their way to the snug where Mick is awaiting their arrival. With a nod of recognition between the two retired Gardai, the three are soon united in their mission.

"Pleased to meet you, Jim. Dick told me all about you, but I fear you're on a wild goose flight, but anyhow, it can only do good if we can come up with something that'll stick and take those awful fuck'in bastards down," said Mick standing up from his seat and shaking hands with Jim.

He was referring to the Christian Brothers for Mick's memories of them weren't pleasant, neither from his school going days or from his dealing with them in the Industrial School in Letterfrack.

"Yerra Christ Mick, how did they get away with it, seemly the Christian Brothers were a fuck'in law unto themselves," said Jim removing a fly from his ale and flicking it onto the flagstone floor that was covered in sawdust to absorb the spillages.

"Jim, of course they fuck'in got away with it for they were indeed a fuck'in law unto themselves. You must remember that most of the families who had a son in the Christian Brothers also had a member of the same family in the nuns or priesthood and many of them had members of that very same family in law or medicine. They all protected each other. Anyone that rocked the boat or blew the whistle were deported to the missions or transferred, and that's simply what happened. Anyway, lay people weren't in any position to question their actions, after all, they were the people we raised our caps to as a mark of respect. Ahhhhh shur Jim my dear chap, they got away with murder and literally murder in many cases," muttered Mick as he sips the end of his pint. "They certainly left their mark on many a young lassie and lad. It's a wonder how any of them are half sane at all. I suppose only time will tell what the outcome will be."

There is a lull in the conversation and the three men sit quietly with heads bent low looking into their ale stained glasses.

"They were terrible times," grunted Dick. "Looking back now, it's a wonder how any of those young lads faced the outside world, ahhhhh Jaysus it was tough and tough it certainly was."

Jim orders another round of drinks and asks for a few ham and mustard sandwiches to be served up while he relieves his ale filled bladder.

When he returns to the snug, the two lads have already tucked into the sandwiches and he thought to himself, I ain't the only wan in need of grub. After straying off the conversation and focusing on the races on the goggle box, the local punters have a few words with them about the Rose of Tralee and Puck Fair in Killorgin. Many of them had fond memories of their time there and jokes and laughter fill the pub as they tell each other about their experiences.

The "bean-an-ti" makes a welcome appearance when she carries in a great big plate of boxty and crubeens together with a big skittle pot of colcannon and offers it around to the thirsty punters. For about five minutes or so, all that could be heard throughout the pub was the smacking of lips from satisfied tongues as each and everyone delighted in the pleasure of licking their fingers saturated in the salty tasty juices from the crubeens. But, Jim was a man on a mission and he soon brings Mick's attention back to the abuse in the Industrial Schools. After all, he had come a long journey in search of answers that would put his mind to rest and hopefully get a better understanding of what Sean Og and Peg went through while in care.

"Good God and no word of a lie, Jim," said Mick, "I wasn't long in the force myself and was stationed in Clifden when a call came into the station that two young lads had absconded from the Industrial School in

Letterfrack. My comrade and myself were sent out in search of them. Well, it wasn't too hard to find the misfortunate garsuns, for all we had to do was to go over yonder to Maam Cross and wait. As we waited late into the night, sure enough, just as we had anticipated, didn't the two lads come up over the fence and in their innocence they asked for directions to Galway? They were harmless creatures. Both of the lads were in the school 'cause they hadn't any kin to care for them. The little lad had a thick head of red hair and his freckled face somehow clashed with his bright blue eyes. He was tired, cold, hungry and dirty. His little body, thin as a rake with his bellybutton almost touch his backbone. His hands were covered in a rash, looked like scabies. Ahhh Christ, he was a pitiful sight. 'Sirs, do yees know the way to Galway town,' he politely but shyly asked. I don't think he really knew who we were..."

"Mother of Jaysus," muttered Jim.

"The older chap who was a bit wiser gave the wee lad a right nudge with his left elbow and mumbled, 'We're grand sirs, we'll find ours own way, thanks very much sirs.' My heart went out to them. Looking to my comrade I said, shur, what harm could a bite of grub do and maybe a sup of tea to warm them up. I knew what their fate was, a ride back to the school, back to a school with a bleak future ahead of them both. 'Com'on sons, ach shur ye'll be grand, just grand,' I said to them as we encouraged them along and took them to Clifden with us, into the station and gave them a mug of hot tea and a few slices of stale brown bread that I had in the drawer of my work desk. Holy Jaysus, I watched their faces as they tucked into the grub. It took me back to the Dickens novel that I had read in my school goin' days and how he described the lads on the streets. The two young lads' clothes were worn and tatty, their shoes were well soled down and sniffling back snotty runny noses with their protruding cheekbones, said it all...."

"Fuck'in hell," muttered Jim shaking his head in dismay.

"They told us that if we brought them back, they'd get their heads shaved and a severe lashing followed by a cold shower. They told us of horrific things that were happening to the lads. They said that lads were severely beaten and sexually interfered with. They told us that lads were taken from their beds at night to satisfy the sexual desires of some of the Christian Brothers. We asked, why didn't they complain to the Priest in confession or Brother Superior. They told us, if they told anywan about it within the school, they'd get a severe beating with a leather strap and then sent for a cold ice shower. Sick lads were put out to the hay fields to work if there was a shortage of farmhands. They told us about the meals of bread and dripping and seemly that was the stable diet for supper. They spoke about the boiler house and the henhouse, seemly that's where most of the sexual abuse occurred. They went on to tell us that lads would eat the pig slop to fill the hunger they felt in the pit of their bellies. They talked about when the Educational Inspector from the Department visited the school and how everything was put in good order for him but as soon as he left, things went back to the way they were..."

"Mother... of... Jaysus," exclaimed Jim.

"They told us about a little boy buried in the woods next to the school. They described it in great detail, how five of the older lads had to dig a grave in the woods leading to the main graveyard. According to them, the body wasn't in a coffin but in sacking, like a sheet wrapped around the corpse. No member of the dead boy's family was present. They went on to say that there was no Priest present either. Seemly the Christian Brother who attended the burial was more interested in a bird on the branch of the nearby tree than sayin' a few prayers. He told the lads to hurry up and cover in the body. Both of the lads were sobbin' at this stage. To this day, the memory of them is a clear as daylight, the sobbin' and the gaggin' from them still penetrates my brain. I can still see them in my mind, wiping their cold snotty noses and the tears with their dirty coat sleeves as they both told us of their experiences. They asked us to help them. They pleaded with us not to take them back. They offered to work for us or do anything that would find them a life outside the school. They both had no living relatives known to them when we questioned them if they had. Seemly, they were totally depended on the guardianship of the Christian Brothers. I made a promise that if I took them back I'd speak to the Brother Superior and everything would be okay. After all, not even the Christian Brothers were above the law or so I thought at that time. In time I found out differently…..."

At this stage, Jim and Dick were focused on every word with eyes pinned on Mick. The gruff voices from the punters hummed into the distance and they are totally oblivious of the comings and goings surrounding them. With folded arms and head held low Mick continued telling his story.

"We rang the school and told them that we had the lads and were on our way back. It was a wet windy miserable night and the journey back was slow. The lads said little as we came nearer the school. As they got out of the car the only remark that was made by them was, 'Thanks sirs, please tell the Christian Brothers that we're good.' They whimpered and hunched up like young hurt pups as we came closer to the front door…."

Mick let out a long deep sigh and loosened his tie. Dick shook his head in dismay and lit up his pipe. Jim just sat there in silence with eyes focused on Mick.

"A tall thin middle-aged Christian Brother with chiselled features and raven black hair met us at the porch of the school. Before I had a chance to say goodnight, he had one of the young lads on the ground with a blow of his fist and the other lad up against the wall, kneeing him in the groin and walloping him around the head. At this stage the lad was bleeding from his nose and mouth. Put a stop to that, right now, I yelled as I dragged the Brother off the young lad. I'll have you charged for assault, I shouted catching him by the collar…"

"Almighty….. Christ," exclaimed Jim.

"'Assault,' he jeered, 'who do you think you're, you and your side kick better get out of here and keep your gobs shut if you know what's good for you.' And with that, he slammed the door on our faces. You've not heard the last of this, I roared back in my anger and frustration as I walked towards the car. I fisted the dashboard in my frustration…."

"Fuck'in hell," gasped Jim.

"As sure as God, that did happen Jim, and that's no word of a lie. There were very few words spoken on the way back, I guess we were both in shock. To me, this was cruelty of the highest order and something needed to be done. What the lads had told us went around and around in my head. Could they be telling the truth or was it an exaggerated version of what they thought was the truth? But my gut feelin' kept telling me from what I witnessed in the porch of Letterfrack Industrial School that the lads were telling the fuck'in truth. I wrote up a report of what we witnessed in the Report Record Book that night and the following morning, I followed it through with my sergeant. When the sergeant confronted and cautioned the Christian Brother in question regarding his conduct and that of the school, the Christian Brothers reported the sergeant by lodging a complaint with the Minister of Defence regarding the matter. The sergeant in question got a caution and a month later, he was transferred to another station. I was also cautioned and told in a polite manner to keep my gob shut and mind my own business and that the comings and goings of Letterfrack Industrial School were of no concern of mine…"

"By Christ," muttered Jim shaking his head and clenching his fist in disgust. "The system was crooked, 'twas bad, really bad. So, the Christian Brothers were a rule onto themselves. But, what became of the two young lads?"

"I didn't follow it up Jim, and today I live with the guilt of not following through on the promise I made to those two young garsuns. I'm now in no doubt what those two young garsuns told us that night was true. Is it any wonder why lads don't trust the Gardai when they've experiences like that? Shur, I was worse than that fuck'in

Christian Brother, I should've gone back and bet the living daylights out of the fucker, but instead I was lookin' after number one, my job and myself. But now I tell you both, if I ever meet up with any of those evil fuckers now, I'll not hesitate to take them down with my bare fists. A few years behind bars would be a small price to pay for takin' those abusers down...."

"Ahhhhh, well Mick, ya did ya'r best under the circumstances and if ya did go after that fuck'in Brother in a violent manner ya'd ya'r family to think about. I feel it in me bones that those evil abusers are goin' to get their com'upins sooner than later. Enough public exposure will take them down. And only then, will the boys and girls that were abused while in the care of the Religious Orders find some solace in their lives," replied Dick scratching his bald head and turning his cap from front to back.

"Where's this famous school or should I say chamber of horror, is it far from here?" asked Jim.

"Ahhh, just a few miles or so back yonder," grunted Mick. "Do you want to take a quick gander over yonder?"

"Shur, Jim, it'd do no harm if we took a quick gander yonder. It might put ya'r mind to rest and give ya a better picture of what went on," said Dick.

"What's the time like? The evenin' will be soon closin' in," replied Jim gawping out the pub door and up the main street of Clifden.

He could hear the shouts of glee from children running up the footpaths chasing an old rusty bike wheel and just across the street an elderly man sat patiently on an old donkey cart happily smoking his pipe while awaiting someone.

"I'll give the O'Connor's a buzz and they'll let Peg know that I'll be late home and tell her not to wait up for me. She worries if I'm away from home so late especially if she knows that I've gone by car. I'll rin' from the phone box up yonder and put her mind to rest," said Jim putting on his brown tweed overcoat.

After bidding cheerio to the local punters, it wasn't long before the three men were on their way to Letterfrack.

"Very isolated....it certainly is......only madra rua territory, " remarked Jim looking around and taking in the countryside as Dick drove with ease. His car wasn't running too well on the long journey up from Kerry, the radiator was overheating but he had brought a gallon of water in the booth, should it cause any problems.

"Truth behold...ya're certainly right," muttered Dick wiping his nose on the back of his hand. "Ach shur....it's only...fox territory...indeed...that's all it is."

Sheep and cattle graze the long acre to Letterfrack. They just wander hither and thither around the road totally oblivious of the passers by. The wind is rising and there is a fair gale sweeping across the bleak countryside. As they approach Letterfrack they ask one of the locals where they might find the graveyard. The local just shakes his head and walks away.

"Not very friendly," remarked Dick as he looks around to see if there's anyone else around that might help them.

"Ahhh shur, I guess they don't want to get involve in matters they'd rather leave rested. I do know that it's up yonder by the local Church, shur, it can't be that difficult to find," sighed Mick.

Eventually they find their way to the chapel and sure enough just up from it is the entrance to the small woodland.

"That's the dreaded woodland where the young lad was buried," remarked Mick puffing his pipe and tucking his scarf into his overcoat.

The rain is now making its presence known and a cutting breeze is sweeping up the hill from the village below.

"Is there any chance you might have a flash lamp in the back?" Dick asked Mick as he looks up into the evening sky.

After spending a few minutes searching out their whereabouts, they make their way through the overgrown tree-patch and stumble upon a small patch that is for a better word, just a swamp. As they walk around it, they can feel their feet spring into the swampy ground. There, at the end of the swamp stands a memorial cross to the memory of the boys that died while in care of the Christian Brothers in Letterfrack Industrial School. Names are inscribed on the two sides and at the back of the cross. In the front there is an inscription of recognition to the Religious Orders for erecting it. The names and dates of death of the young lads are inscribed but Jim is surprised that no ages appear. There is a bleakness and a haunting feeling about the place As they make their way down the overgrown bramble pathway to the car Mick remarks about the airy and uneasy sensation he is experiencing as he stumbles through the overgrowth.

"Mother of Jaysus, they fuck'in buried the young lads in a swamp. Truth behold, it's simply just an aul bit of slough for the want of a better word. Up to sixty boys lyin' there. After all, they're somewan's relations. This can't be right and it seems to me, no wan gives a fuck'in damn," mumbled Jim to himself and at this stage he is very bothered and has worked himself up to tears. "Wan of our names could've been on that cross, only fate willed a different life for us three."

Turning to Mick, Dick remarks.

"Gosh, he's very cut up about all of this. He has taken it badly….."

"Well that ain't the worst of it, rumours say that lads were buried in a boggy terrain at the back of the school farm. And another lad is suppose to be buried over yonder by the small grotto as you come up the lane," whispered Mick to Dick as if not to upset Jim any further.

Jim wanders off into the Church and on bended knee, he asks God to give him the strength to seek out justice and to bring peace and contentment to Peg and Sean Og. He thanks God for giving him a second chance at living and vows that he will respect life and do his best to make the world a better place. On his way out, he wondered why didn't the Christian Brothers bury the boys in the patch of ground adjacent to the Church. If they had, the locals could have given them a thought as they passed by and prayed for them during Mass. But then, the

Christian Brothers were not in the business of remembering or showing any respect for these youngsters lying in that slough up yonder. They're only hoping that time would forget the past and shur what other reason would anyone have, for disposing of innocent children's bodies in such a manner he thought to himself as he makes his way back to the car. Darkness has now settled over the village of Letterfrack and the night is well in.

"Would ya like to see the school, Jim?" asked Dick. "We've just come from there…."

"Ahhhh Christ no, I've seen enough for wan day," replied Jim shaking his head and biting his upper lip while rubbing the palms of his cold hands. "We'll make our way back. Mick has been good enough to share his time with us and I'm sure he'd be glad to get out of this fuck'in hell hole of a place anyway…."

"Ahhh well," replied Mick wiping the muck off his boots. "I certainly have my own haunting skeletons and ghosts in my cupboard regarding this fuck'in place…"

"I suppose ya wouldn't be able to put ya'r hands on the record book from the Garda Station where ya wrote in that complaint?" asked Dick.

"Indeed I can and better than that, I've the aul note-book I used that night. The young lads' names are in it. It's in an aul shed back yonder at home. Follow me back from Clifden and I'll get it for you. Shur, it's on your way home to Kerry anyway," replied Mick.

Mick lives in a little cottage about six miles outside Clifden on the Galway road. It's a quaint little white washed cottage, hedges nicely trimmed and flower borders well kept. The inside had the mark of a bachelor, not dirty, but certainly in need of a woman's touch. His wife, Annie, had passed away a few years back and all of his family are now living in England and America.

Mick pulls his car into the narrow driveway next to his cottage and wanders off to one of back sheds while the two men sit silently in their car. It's not long before he returns with an old dusty weather beaten notebook covered in mice droppings. He wipes off the dust and the droppings with the back of his hand and then tears out the page where he and the sergeant had taken details about the event. It contained the date and time of the incident, the names of the two boys in question, where they were collected from and the name of Christian Brother that made the complained to the Minister was written in black ink that had blobbed from the dampness of the years.

"Hopefully this will be of some help to you Jim, and the best of luck with your quest. I'll keep an ear to the ground, should I hear of anything that might be of interest. I'll let you know. God Bless you. We need a few more people like you. But something tells me, you'll have a struggle on your hands. You'll certainly be ploughing a long lonely furrow in your search for the truth regarding the abuse that went on in those Industrial Schools of Ireland and elsewhere. These evil abusers aren't ready to put up their hands and admit to their wrongdoings. I guess they never will for they saw no wrong in what they did. It was like a pre-Christian ritual they practised. But for any justice to be delivered, the truth needs to be fished out. There're no two ways about it, the truth and only the truth needs to be fished out. It'll take good people like you to tow in the rod of the truth and expose it so that evil can be wiped out...."

"Ahhhh shur, I'll do all I can to fish the truth out, Mick," nodded Jim. "I'll let ya know how I get on, ya've certainly been a great help to me."

As a sign of gratitude to Mick, Dick beeps the horn as he reverses out the gateway pointing his car in the direction of Galway.

"A nice chap. Very honest I'd say," Jim remarked about Mick.

"That's wan honest man. He never got over what happened with the two lads that night. Ya see Jim, meself and many others in the force had no real say. We were sent out to catch the innocent fool of a lad without a flash lamp on his bike makin' his way home on a dark winter's night but we weren't allowed to go after the real law-breakers. There were times when I'd expose a wrongdoin' and was ordered by my seniors that I was to overlook it. Puttin' it mildly, there were times, when I was told that stuff I saw and reported I wasn't to say I saw it and would be threatened with a caution if I took it any further. Ya see, there were different laws for the rich and the poor," said Dick loosening his upper dentures with his tongue to clear a piece of trapped ham.

"Jaysus," sighed Jim.

"Yeahhhhh Jim. And that was simply the way the system was back then. Often, we were only made feel like feck'in eejits in uniforms. And with the squarin' that was goin' on in the force, there were times you'd wonder what was the reason in havin' a police force at all. Yerra Jim, truth behold, it was a time when laws were made to keep fools like ya and me in order while the rich made a fool of the Irish State that made the laws…"

"Squarin'?" butted in Jim with a puzzled frown.

"Squarin' is when somewan asks a Garda to drop a charge and to make sure that it doesn't appear in front of the Judge. In return, the Garda is offered a favour or a backhander. Very often, political influences are behind the squarin'," replied Mick repositioning his dentures. "Ach truth behold, there were very few straight people in the police force, many of them were only dressed up thugs in uniform."

"Do ya honestly think any of these abusers will be brought up the steps into a courtroom to answer for their wrongdoin'?"

"Well Jim, I'd like to see the day come when that'd happen, but even if ya did get them into a courtroom that wouldn't mean they'd be found guilty. Ya see, in a courtroom justice is a game of wits. Ya've two legal teams battlin' it out, tryin' to convince a jury that their client is the honest wan. The legal teams ain't interested if the clients are honest or not. The courtroom has nothin' to do with honesty or the truth. Yerra, in many cases, the Bible is only made a mockery of. The Bible should be removed from the courtroom. Ya see Jim, the work of the legal teams have nothin' to do with searchin' out the truth. They've a job to do and that's to get the best outcome for their clients. And on the day, the team that presents the best case will convince the jury to waver in their favour and the rest is up to the His Lordship, the Judge. In many cases, the guilty walk free and the innocent never get justice. Especially in the case of abuse, ya need hard facts to take an abuser down. It's often harder to prove ya'r innocent when ya ain't guilty. But there's wan thin' I can assure ya, the abusers can run and hide under the umbrella of denial and silence but they can't hide from their conscience. That'll haunt them until the day they die. So, no matter what happens they can never go to bed and rest in peace with themselves and hopefully that might be some consolation to the victims of abuse," replied Dick winding down the window and throwing out the butt of his cigarette. And as he does so, a night moth finds its way into the car and settles on the dashboard.

"Out with ya, we're pickin' up no hitch hikers tonight," chuckled Jim picking up the moth and letting it fly free out his window.

"Ya certainly wouldn't want too many of those little feck'ers in your wardrobe," joked Dick.

The journey back was quick as the roads were quiet. The headlights of the car seemed to attract the night moths and every now and again, an odd rat or fox would dart across the road causing Dick to brake sharply. The night sky was beginning to brighten as the rain was easing off and in the far distance if you looked close enough you could see the plough and the odd falling star.

It was into the early hours of the morning when they arrived back to Glenbeigh. The village was at rest, but Tabby the Travellers Inn's tomcat sat proudly on the windowsill of the pub, quite content with himself. The contentment a cat would exhibit ready to sit down to a meal with mouse on the menu. All the way home, the two man were engrossed in recollection of what was spoken about and no matter how they tried to reason it out, neither of them could understand how so called Christian men could be so cruel. They spoke about the Holocaust and how thousands of men, women and children were robbed of life.

They both felt that was an era of strange and savage times. But for many young Irish girls and boys they too experienced their own emotional holocaust while in care in the Industrial School in Ireland.

Once children have the bare necessities in life, warmth, food, affection, support and love, they develop a high resilience to overcome and accept hardships. But, the children in care under the Religious Orders that ran the Industrial Schools in Ireland were starved of these basic necessities and for this reason alone how could they ever be expected to overcome their horrific experiences. And as the saying goes, *'The only thing necessary for the triumph of evil is for good people to stand by and do nothing'.* This certainly happened when it came to the abuse in the Industrial Schools, evil flourished because good people did stand by and do nothing. And that's how it was. Hopefully this is one lesson that history won't allow us forget.

Chapter Thirteen

Sharing Words Of Wisdom In The Local Pub

"Is that little retarded chap yours?" a well-dressed elderly man sitting at the bar whispered to Jim as he orders a pint of stout for himself and a small glass of orange juice for Johnny. From the sound of his accent, Jim could tell that he was English.

"Ha?" replied Jim in a defensive manner. "Who?"

He was well aware that the man was referring to Johnny. And over the years, he had always taken offence at someone calling Johnny retarded. In his eyes, his son is very normal in the body and mind he had chosen to be born into.

"That little red haired chap with the freckles sitting over yonder in the snug," replied the English man lighting up his pipe and taking another sip from his half filled glass of ale.

"Yepppp," grunted Jim looking across at Johnny. "That's me little Johnny and I'll have ya know, there's nothing retarded about him. He's a perfectly normal Down's syndrome boy. And a very clever and astute one at that, I'll have ya know, Sir. Come over here Johnny and say hallo to this man."

He then beckons to Johnny to come forward. With that, Johnny jumps up from the snug and skips across the pub floor with a beaming smile on his face.

"Say hallo to this gentleman here," Jim requested of Johnny.

"Heeeee," giggled Johnny putting his hand out to the man.

"Please to meet you, my dear chap," greeted the English man

"Wats ud ame?" Johnny asked in his strong Kerry accent.

"What's my name?" replied the English man surprised at the hearty response of the little lad standing in front of him, "I'm George and I'm here on holidays from London."

"Dat hice," replied Johnny shaking the man's hand and then embracing his Dad in his usual childish manner.

"I see what you mean," said George to Jim while looking in admiration at Johnny. "He's certainly a very clever little chap. I do apologise if what I said caused you some offence. You see, I was a headmaster in London many moons ago and I knew of a family that had three little Mongolian children in the family, well that's what we called those children back then. I remember just like you, their mother looked upon them as normal. And how right she was. She'd often say to me, these three lads see us as retarded in their eyes. She'd tell me that they were better able to cope with their disability that we were able to cope with their acceptance of it. I guess in many ways, we're the ones that add to their inability to cope with certain situation in life because we don't even think of accommodating for them in our everyday routine. And that's not naivety on our part but plain ignorance and no excuses should be accepted or tolerated for our actions…."

"Ya never spoke a truer word," replied Jim patting Johnny on the head and requesting that he pull his stool up to the bar counter to drink his orange juice.

Locals in the pub are chatting amongst themselves at how life is so unfairly divided up. George over hears what they have to say and is eager to join in the conversation.

"Success in life is a moment in time and that moment is when you retire to your bed for the night with the contentment in your heart. And, you can turn over and have a peaceful night sleep knowin' that you've done your best during the day," said George holding his hands in the air. "Success ain't about the car you drive, the status you hold or the big house you live in. These are often only commodities that we hide behind to protect us from facing our true selves. The way to value how much we've made in wealth in life is to see how much we can take with us to the next world. And that's nothing. So, the question that should be asked, why are we all strivin' to make more wealth and riches? Too often, wealth far, far beyond our needs."

All this time Johnny is sitting quietly at the bar stool gurgling away at his orange juice and nibbling on Tayto crisps. On hearing what George has to say about life, he is determined to add his own words and tells all present in his gleeful childish manner that he has no problems and life is easy when you just love people and Holy God. And he goes on to tell them that the next thing in life is to be nice and that's easy, just be nice. On hearing this, George stands up from his bar stool to stretch his legs and wanders over to the front door to chat with one of the locals standing nearby in a pair of work-overalls. He had come in for a quick pint. There is a slight hum from his muscular body, not a dirty one but one that arises from an underarm sweat that comes from doing a hard day's work in a confined space.

"I think the only retarded people walking around are the so-called normal ones and I myself could be included in that category with the way I've dealt with my life's issues," muttered George to himself.

"Yerra Christ, I guess, if we were all to be honest with ourselves we'd say the same. Ahhh shur, we spend so much time tryin' to find fault with the disabled that we often overlook their normality in their disability. It takes a child like Johnny to show us, the very people who ironically claim to be normal, how retarded we really are, in our inability to recognise our abilities in life. God bless him, he's a credit to his parents, they much be so proud of him. It takes a lot of parentin' and time to turn out a lad as capable and as nice as that young lad." replied the local man blowing his nose on his oil stained handkerchief as he gawps out the pub door drinking his pint of stout.

Jim is certainly very proud of his son and prides in telling George and the other punters about the joy and sensibility that Johnny brings to the family. The locals are amazed at how much Johnny is in tune with life and are taken back by his words of wisdom. But mostly at how clever, curious and obedient he is.

George asks for another glass of ale and taking it in his hand holds it high and offers a toast.

"To the future and all who choose to travel on the train of life."

"To life," hailed the thirsty punters.

With that, George stands erect and recites a verse on, **Days of Yore,**

"They matched us; we married and then came love.
We strive to live life as best as we could.
Turf fires smothered, as loaves were turned out.
Food on the table, no State Aid and no need to shout.
Candles flickered light, no locks on the doors.
No carpets, but a squeezebox to put a shine on the floors.
No television just an aul wireless bought for a dime
And at Christmas a noggin of poitin was no great crime!
We abided by the Church, no condoms no pill.
When it came to the kids each house had its fill!
A flowery spud topped with hot dripping
Was sure to keep a young farmhand tipping!
While a decade of Rosary was thought to determine our fate
But one thing for sure it kept Aul Nick away from the gate.
Most bills were paid with a sack of spuds or a half cock of hay.
People helped people and a cuppa sent worries on their way.
A morning thrush was out sung by a whistling tune
And the postman was as welcome as a hot day in June.
Castor oil was certain to send many ailments away.
Just as a few bob was classified a big loan of the day.
Shur, an aul bottle of porter was grand
After an evening searching for muscles on the strand.
Dancing at the crossroads were moments to treasure.

And hay fields were the evening places of our leisure.
The crowing of a cock was sure to wake us from our pillow
Just as summer was timed by the return of the swallow!
Strives and punches were just upheavals of another day
Just as we accepted the song of the blackbird to be pleasant
and gay
Engulfed in a donkey jacket as snug as a bug
We revisited our dreams on a flea-hoppin' rug.
As I take the time to look back over the years
There were good times, sad times and certainly some tears.
I remember the blessings I remember the smiles
But most of all, I now laugh at those crazy hairstyles.
I've lived life and welcomed each pleasure,
My days may be numbered and the years I can't measure.
But I thank the good God above for sharin' with me his
special treasure... LIFE."

With that, whistles, cheers and a well appreciative hearty clap could be heard throughout the pub and a complimentary glass of porter was ordered for George by one of the thirsty punters.

As they sat in the snug late into the evening reflecting on life and the wonders of living, one thing they all agreed on was that we only borrow a few years on this earthly existence before we move to the next stage of the development of the Being that dwells within each and everyone of us. Sadly though, too many of us become hangers on in our own lives and by doing so we fail to reach or have the ability to recognise our full potential. They also agreed that the right to die was the only right in life that we can't be deprived of.

"After living my three score years and ten I now know that too many of us are of the opinion that education finishes the day we leave school or college, when it actual fact it only starts," insisted George.

"I guess ya're right," replied Jim.

"Well, put it like this, because we make the mistake of thinking that education ends the day we leave school or college," gurgled George as he downs his final sup of ale.

"Too many of us go through life taking orders from people with their brains up their arses and their heads full of shit."

"Ya might have somethin' there," chuckled Jim putting on his jacket and getting Johnny ready for the road home.

"My good man, apologies if I offended you when I said that Johnny was retarded when I met you earlier on during the day. You're right, he's certainly a perfectly normal intelligent little happy Down's syndrome boy and any man would be proud to have him as a son. I certainly would," smiled George shaking hands with Jim and Johnny.

"He certainly makes me proud," replied Jim as he nudges up against Johnny and gives him a mischievous punch on the chin.

"See you again next year, God willing," hailed George holding up his pint glass as Jim and Johnny head off out the front door.

Jim glancing back over his left shoulder and bids farewell to the punters.
"May the road rise to meet ye,
May the breeze be always at ye'r backs,
May the sun shine warmth upon ye'r faces,
Ans may the rain fall soft upon ye'r meadows,
So 'til we meet again,
May God comfort and hold ye
In the palms of his hands."

"And yar's," shouted out the punters. "Bail ó Dhia ort."

"Agus rath Dé orthu," smiled Jim.

Chapter Fourteen

The Parish Priest... Not A Happy Bunny

One evening on returning from the village Sean Og informs Jim of the news that the Parish Priest in Glenbeigh has got a whiff that Jim is asking questions about the abuse that went on in the Industrial Schools.

"Nora whispered in the Post Office today that the aul Parish Priest has got the whiff that ya're sniffin' out information about the MARK and she said that he's in a right tri-na-cheile about it. Seemly, his housekeeper was in the shop this mornin' and left it be known that the aul boy was bullyin' and puckin', roarin' and gaddin' after a phone call he received last night and no word of a lie, he was like a bull with a camp of ants up its arse. He thinks that a Fr. Murphy who has returned from the missions on a sabbatical has somethin' to do with it. So, Nora says that ya'll need to keep a low profile for a few days 'til the aul boy cools down," giggled Sean Og tapping Jim on the shoulder, who is reading the racing results from the daily paper.

"Emm, he'll be effin' and blindin' a lot more when I'll tell him what I know," smirked Jim. "I'll certainly give that aul bucko somethin' to go berserk about."

But, little did Jim realise the power of the spoken and unspoken word of the Parish Priest in a small village. Over the coming days, the priest requests that his parishioners shunt and boycott Jim's family. Jim is upset with the locals' response and how easy it is for the priest to persuade and influence them. After all, over the years these were the people Jim helped through good times and bad times, standing by them through thick and thin while working at the nearby Creamery. But Sean Og tells him that eaten bread is soon forgotten.

One Sunday morning after Mass, the old Parish Priest makes it his business to dart a few stabbing words in Jim's direction.

"If you intend to set out blaspheming decent Christian leaders of the Catholic Religion, you ain't welcome at my church," roared the old Parish Priest at Jim.

"Ya can't stop me attendin' the sacraments," replied Jim who is somewhat taken aback by the Priest's attitude.

"I'll request from the altar that you and your missus be removed from the church if I see you attending Mass from here on out. Those so-called abused children of the past that you're so intent on helping, should've been glad and grateful for the food, shelter and education they received while in the care of the Religious Orders. In actual fact, it was the Religious Orders who rescued many filthy, hungry, bad smelling kids from the width and breath of Eire and gave them a new life and a clean bed to sleep on, " huffed the Priest sternly.

"I think not," replied Jim and before he could say another word the Priest butts in.

"The community was a better place without the likes of your lot in it. Why don't you go back over the water to England and that's where you and your missus belong. The people here don't want your type. If you want my advice you'll leave the past rest in the past and get on with your own business."

"Now ya listen to me Father, truth behold," shouted Jim and at this stage there was anger building up in his nerves. "If ya knew what I know now, I dare say ya'd be more backward in comin' forward with that fuck'in righteous attitude of ya'rs…"

"My dear man, leave the past in the past and if you don't, I'll have the villagers boycott you and your family," grunted the priest angrily and with that he struts off back into the church.

Over the coming days, the cold isolated glances and shrugged shoulders that Jim and Peg receive from the locals sent the message home to them that they aren't welcome. But Sean Og's understanding of the matter was, the locals weren't to blame for they were only following the unquestionable instructions of their Parish Priest. And many of them after all, had put their trust in this man to fulfil the fate of their spiritual destiny.

"We'll reject that Catholic Church and all its teachin'," scorned Peg in her frustration on hearing what the Parish Priest had to say. "I'll set up me own altar and say me own prayers here in me own kitchen. We'll all be better off without those Holy Joes and Genuflectin' Biddies that're only in the church on a Sunday mornin' to equip themselves with next week's bloomin' gossip...."

"No Peg, they've no right to take away what's rightfully ours. We go to Church to honour God and not that fuck'in priest. We'll go to another church, Foilmore Church is just a few more minutes drive over the mountain and what's more we won't have to mix with a bunch of fuck'in hypocrites on bended knee," scoffed Jim determined that nobody is going to bully him around.

"Maybe so," huffed Peg with a shrug of her shoulders. "Yeah Jim, we'll go there and shur Sean Og can gander along as well. Anyway the villagers' reaction ain't surprisin' for we never partake in their gossip and their ALS and for that reason alone, they were never too fond of us. Ach shur, they're only a shower of spreasans as we'd say in Irish."

"ALS and spreasan," replied Jim with a puzzled expression across his brow.

"ALS stands for Arse Lickin' Sessions and spreasan is the Irish for good–for–nothin'," giggled Peg giving him a mischievous clatter across the ear.

"Hmm, hmm," grimed Jim shaking his head in amusement for Peg always seemed to amaze him with her terminology and sayings.

From then onwards, the family set out to attend Mass in the Foilmore Parish every Sunday morning and were made feel at ease there. Foilmore Church is a small community Church four miles out of Cahirciveen on the Killorgin road. There, the parishioners are decent, kindly, hardworking friendly people, who come from farming backgrounds and who are more interested in earning enough money to feed their families and pay the bills than grabbing a quick buck and wallowing in wealth. Johnny fits in well and is amused by Champ the old flea ridden sheepdog that sits quietly at the back of the Church and waits for its owner to receive Holy Communion. Following communion its owner would genuflect at the end of Church, bless himself, replace his cap, tie a piece of baler twine around his donkey jacket and then both of them would leave the praying congregation and wander off towards the direction of Kells.

During the Mass the priest would often be out sung by the shouts of children, the crying of babies, the cooing of nearby pigeons and the cawing of the crows that nested in the tall trees at the front entrance. But nobody seemed to mind. They would continue to pray in one verse and voice. Every now and again, a local dog would wander throughout the parishioners in search of its master. A quiet whistle from its master would alert it to whatever pew it needed to sniff out. The whiff of perfume that would hit your nose on route to receiving Holy Communion in Glenbeigh Parish Church is replaced in this church by the homely smell of animals, milk and silage. Sean Og is happy to attend Mass in the Foilmore parish but remains loyal to his claimed position, standing at the back door. The only times he is accustomed to making a full entrance is on Good Fridays for confession and to receive Holy Communion on Easter Sunday and Christmas Day.

Chapter Fifteen

Things Aren't Going Too Well For The Family

Over the coming weeks, things don't go too well for the family and the local children set out to bully Johnny. Many of them have over heard their parents gossiping about Johnny's family being rejected by the local church and in their childish naivety and ignorance they set out to bully Johnny and take matters into their own hands. One day following a local football match, they gang up on him and start calling him names and begin pushing and shoving him around.

"Satan's son, Satan's son," they jeered.

"Wha tat?" asked Johnny running up to them trying to befriend them.

"Away wit' ya Brit Prod, go back to England ya Brit Prod," yelled out one of the younger lads.

"Dav twet," said Johnny offering them his packet of sweets.

When the young lads become aware that name-calling meant nothing to Johnny they start pushing him around and one of the older lads in the gang calls out, "Mongolian pig face who cries, dribbles and talks like a wee bobeeee," and with that he gives Johnny a blow in the eye with his right fist. By the time Sean Og arrives on the scene Johnny is in tears, his little specs trampled into the grass and he has a great big shiner over his right eye.

"Away with the lot of ya, ye shower of little feck'in thugs," yelled Sean Og.

Doc happens to be passing and stops to check out the situation. He reassures Sean Og that Johnny will live to fight another day but insists that he intends to have a word with the parents of the local children involved.

That evening, Doc calls around to have a quiet word with Peg and Jim to put their minds at ease as he feels that it might only be an isolated case but advises them to be vigilant just in case things may stir up again.

"Ach shur, kids will be kids and when they hear adults bad mouthing other adults they often feel they've the right to take matters into their own hands and even the good ones turn into little villains," he tells Peg and Jim who're worried for Johnny's well-being.

Just before he was about to leave for home he insists on going to Johnny's bedroom to have a little word to console him. On the bed tucked into his teddy bear Johnny is quietly sobbing and nursing his bruised eye with crushed ice wrapped in one of his Dad's hankies.

"Shush shush, here my brave wee warrior, things will be grand," he hushed to Johnny picking him up to give him a hug and a cuddle.

"Uuk nie, uuk meee nie," sobbed Johnny squinting up at Doc as the little tears poured down his cheeks.

Doc takes another look at the bruised eye and reassures Johnny that tomorrow he will be feeling much better but the bullyboys that did this to him would be scolded and punished for their actions.

"Do you remember what happened to Ipsey Wipsey Spider?" hushed Doc, patting Johnny on the head, "He too was upset when he tried to go up the water spout, 'cause down came the rain and washed him out. Then….to his surprise…..what happened? Out came the sun and dried up all the rain and once again he was happy because he could go up the spout again. So you see Johnny dear, there's always a bright side to life even though it might seem dim and dull now."

On hearing this, Johnny somehow feels better, after a few moments forgets about his bruised eye, and is deep in discussion with Doc. He tells Doc he doesn't want to be different any more, he wants to be like the other children, be special and grow up to be a hero. Doc tells him that to be a hero, one doesn't have to do wonderful things in life.

"My dear dear Johnny, heroes are people who do ordinary everyday things but respect and appreciate the simple things in life. You're.....a very....special boy. You're the special child of your Ma and Pa and without you, life for so many people in the village would be so dim and that includes me," smiled Doc.

"Yu luv meeee?"

"I… love… you… like a son…. I look upon you Johnny, as the son that I wasn't fortunate to have," grinned Doc winking at Johnny and giving him a playful clatter across the ear.

"Yahhhhhh, yahhhhhh," cheered Johnny leaping up and down on the bed and playfully punching out at Doc.

"Come now lad, your Ma has supper on the table and a young warrior like you can't go without his grub," chuckled Doc as he encourages Johnny down the stairs into the kitchen.

"Meee," replied Johnny as he skips ahead.

"Yep," chuckled Doc tapping Johnny on the shoulder. "You be good now for your Ma and Pa, I'll call tomorrow to see my little brave warrior…"

"Yaaaaa….yaaaaaa." Johnny screamed out with excitement.

"I'm off now and hope all goes well, It's sad when kids get caught up in the grievances of adults," Doc called out to Peg who is in the backyard putting the hens in for the night.

"Cherrrrio and thanks Doc for cheerin' him up, that young lad looks up to ya, the same way he looks up to Jim and Sean Og," said Peg handing Doc a dozen of fresh hen eggs from the nest.

Doc smiles to himself and feels a sense of satisfaction with the thought Peg had just left him with. You see in life, it's the simple things that bring the greatest joy. Simple things, like knowing that people care.

As the weeks pass by, Jim finds it hard to get work to bring some money to cover the bills. The local farmer who employs Sean Og helps them out. Jim barters his work for food and turf. One early afternoon while sitting by the open turf fire in Sean Og's living quarters, the two men are having a hearty man to man chat over a sup of Poitin that Sean Og had made in the back shed three years ago. As they look back over the years they come to realise that Jim is only a feck'in eejit and Sean Og the village idiot. They both have spent the greater part of their lives living in somebody else's shadow, trying to please every Tom, Dick and Harry. They decide that they are no longer going to be every man's fool.

"Jim me dear aul chap, a person's life is like a cesspit, there's only so much crap a cesspit can take and if it ain't shovelled out, it'll fail to function. The same can be applied to a person, for there's only so much crap a person can take and then there comes a stage in a person's life when they've to confront the crap and clear it out so that they can start livin' their life to their full potential. Well, that's what Doc says and I've no reason to doubt him," said Sean Og laying out some willows on the floor to make a basket for the caorans.

"By Jaysus, ya ain't far wrong there," chuckled Jim as he watches Sean Og carefully select the willows as he clips the ends and measures them up one-by-one. All this time, Johnny is hunched up with his teddy bear on the windowsill digesting every spoken word.

"Wha ditanc bitwan iodit and eckin' ddit?" he stuttered out chewing away at his teddy bear's ear with a puzzled frown across his brow.

"Whoooooo," replied Sean Og pausing for a moment as he was taken off his trend of thought by Johnny's question. "To tell ya the truth, Johnny lad, I can't really say. Though I guess wan's a foolish intelligent man and the other is just simply an aul foolish fool and which is which I can't really say."

"Emm emm," responded Johnny wiping his nose on the sleeve of his sweater and gawping over his round rimmed specs at his Dad and Uncle as if to wonder which one was which. He is just about to ask another question when his Dad stops him on his tracks.

"Johnny my dear laddie, what did the wise aul owl do?"

"Uld ulllll?" smirked Johnny and he knew his Dad was asking him to stop interrupting the conversation.

"Yeahhhhh," grinned Jim reciting the verse for Johnny,

"A wise aul owl sat on an oak
The more he heard the less he spoke
The less he spoke the more he heard
Why ain't we all like
That wise aul Owl?"

"Yaaaa, yaaaaa," chuckled Johnny hugging his Dad and after giving Sean Og a quick kiss on the cheek he sets off across the farmyard to seek out Peg who is in the kitchen happily preparing Irish stew for the evening meal while listening to a recorded tape of her favourite radio programme, The Kennedy's of Castle Ross.

As Jim and Sean Og happily sit there chatting of gone by days while making the willow basket, their trail of thoughts bring them back to memories of their childhood. One of Jim's memories of his childhood days is of the big old farmhouse he grew up in. It was so cold that the big fluffy black cat would creep into the oven to get warm. He remembers the fly spotted lamp hanging in the hallway that led into the back bedroom that he shared with his four brothers. The smell of sour cream coming from the butter churns in the pantry. The welcoming smells of crusty bread with the bacon and cabbage that filled the kitchen. The clatter of plates accompanied by the laughter and chatter that echoed throughout the house during meals times. He remembers Fred the farm dog and how he would stretch out night-after-night in front of the big open fire in the parlour only to jump up when a spark would escape from a blazing log.

His school days were clouded with memories of the smell of sweaty bodies of boys and girls with farm muck under their nails. The scabby knees and the holed leather soled open laced boots that were always two sizes too big. But most of all, the one memory that stands out in his mind was the comforting smell of his mother's apron when she cuddled him when he had hurt himself from a fall or when his spirits were just feeling low. He had the wonderful memories of the evenings when family would go 'bothantaiocht'. This was when families would visit each other to play cards or simply sing and dance the night away to the sound of an old squeezebox. People shared joys and sorrows and of course, there was mileage to be made from the gossip involving someone else's misfortune. Even though times were tough and food was scarce, somehow, there would always be plenty to go around. It was like the miracle of the loaves and fishes. People shared not only their time but also their food and clothes. Struggling through struggles made them strong in character, body and Spirit.

"When it came to me aul fella, yerra shur he was a grand aul chap. He never laid a hand on me. Maybe the odd time he let an almighty roar out of him if I was misbehaving," chuckled Jim. "He'd yell at me 'Ya'r better stop that, rrrrrrr.' Well truth behold, I'd stop me mischief and never waited round to get to know what rrrrrrr meant. But I certainly didn't want to find out either for I knew from the roar of me aul fella's voice that rrrrrrr was not somethin' ya wanted to wait around for...."

"Ahhhh Jim, it's good to hear what happy memories of childhood should be like," sighed Sean Og as he pours out another sup of the good aul mountain dew as he himself calls the poitin. "Ya see for months after leavin' the blasted fuck'in Industrial School, I'd make up an imaginary childhood I never had. I'd tell the lads on the buildin' site in London that I was reared on a big farm outside Tralee. Had a mother who was a teacher and three sisters who were all livin' in Ireland. I'd pretend that we had full and plenty. I even went as far as tellin' them that me uncle had left me two grand farms outside Limerick. And when anywan asked what I was doin' in England, I'd joke that I was the wild son that needed to stretch me wings a little. It wasn't until Peg made contact with me with the help of Fr. Murphy that I decided to wake up to me past and eventually return to Ireland and accept me background. But I guess, deep down inside the imaginary life I developed about me childhood allowed me to temporarily bury the past and not think about it. I had me own way of dealin' with the awful stuff that went on in that blasted Industrial School...."

"Ahhhhhhh Christ, I suppose so," replied Jim letting out a long deep sigh.

"Ya see Jim, I wasn't a child in me childhood 'cause from the moment I went into that school in Tralee I became a number. The Christian Brothers stole me birth right from me and that was me name. That number is embedded deep into me brain and me aul soul. Thinkin' back now it was like a German concentration camp. We responded to the call of a number just like the Jews did, so many years ago imprisoned in those horrific camps."

"Emm," responded Jim shaking his head and thinking to himself if he was granted one wish now at this present moment in time, he would wish to turn back time and give Peg and Sean Og a second chance at living a proper child's childhood.

Sean Og's memories were far from nice smells and memories of comforting moments. The Industrial Schools seemed to attract abusers just as a light in the darkness attracts moths. Memories of meals of mouldy bread and dripping were deeply embedded in his gut while thoughts of eating some of the pig slop to fill an empty belly were enough to turn a man's stomach. He remembers the town's folk watching them walk to the strand every Sunday come hail, rain or snow and there they would be expected to strip off and take a swim in the cold sea whether it was summer, spring, winter or autumn and then walk the long journey back in marching drill formation feeling cold, wet and miserable. Each lad, conscious of the glances of the town's people, glances of pity rather than glances of admiration. He told Jim about the human-rack that the inmates formed in the meadows to gather up the hay that took place in some of the Industrial Schools. In the summer time a row of boys would stretch across the meadow on their hands and knees and would be expected to rack back the hay row-by-row with their hands. If the Christian Brother thought you were not putting your back into the work he would give you a lash of his cane or strap right down onto your shoulder pit.

"Almighty God, I can still hear the shriekin' cries of young boys comin' from the henhouse, everywan knew what was happenin', but nobody said. Every time I go to Tralee and pass the location of that school, flashbacks of the boys walkin' in drill formation come floodin' back. Not to mention, the depressive memory of sobbin' humiliated young boys stumblin' around the schoolyard, carryin' their urine stained mattresses on their shoulders," sighed Sean Og throwing another few sods of turf on the smothering fire and oiling up some of the willows to make them more flexible for entwining in the handle of the willow basket.

"Almighty…..Christ," muttered Jim counting out some more willows for the basket.

"I don't think our school was special and the abuse that went on was just an isolated situation. An Irish man on the buildin' sites told me while I was in England that he was sentenced by the court to Letterfrack Industrial School, for stealin' a loaf of bread and a half a sack of spuds. And while he was detained there, he witnessed at the age of twelve a boy bein' beaten by the big leather strap to an inch of his death at the foot of the long stairway that led up to the dormitories. He too, fell victim to the ice cold shower in the middle of the night after an inhuman Christian Brother got his evil way with him, just like meself. But the memory that stood out mostly in his mind was that he was wan of the boys who dug a grave in the woods leadin' to the main graveyard for a little boy who died, seemly this little lad was buried without a Priest present. Seemly the Christian Brother present was more interested in the bird on the branch of a nearby tree than sayin' a few aul prayers," said Sean Og standing up and stretching to relieve his aching back.

"By Christttt, that's interestin' now," replied Jim as his thoughts wandered back to the conversation he had in the pub in Clifden with the two retired Gardai " A retired Garda from Galway told me of that very same incident."

"The Christian Brother who sexually abuse me would get a group of inmates to work each other off in the showers. 'Wank boys, wank boys, com'on, wank like men, he'd jeer, I'll make men out of ye yet. Wank ye filthy swine,' is what he'd yell as he walked up and down in front of our naked bodies and as he did so, he'd his own hand inside his cassock workin' himself off. I remember wan winter's evenin', wan of the younger Christian Brothers must have heard the yellin' and shoutin' and he walked in and caught us at that crazy manhood ritual. He lost the plot. 'Stop that filth, stop that filth', he yelled and with that, the Christian Brother who was in charge of us grabbed a hold of him, pinned him up against the wall and kneed him into the groin. There was a right struggle between the two of them. 'I'll complain ya to the Brother Superior I'll complain ya to Brother Superior', was what the younger Brother kept yellin'. After that, I never laid eyes on that young Brother again, I guess he did make that complaint and like many others he was transferred," sighed Sean Og.

"So, ya're tellin' me, that all the Christian Brothers didn't involve themselves in the abuse?" questioned Jim.

"Good God, of course not, there were some who certainly tried to carry out their work in a Christian manner. They certainly were a few that I could name. The Brothers that did partake in the sexual abuse seemed to have a code and a recognised honour amongst themselves. Shur, the wans who didn't partake in those crazy rituals really had no say at all," muttered Sean Og putting a few more sods of turf on the fire.

"Pure....utter....fuck'in.....filth," muttered Jim.

"When I look back now, over me years in that fuck'in Industrial School, many of the Christian Brothers weren't trained to teach. Most of them it'd seem were just out in search of power. They used that power to express their anger and frustration, while relievin' it by abusin' young boys placed in their care. We all tried so hard to please them, just like a son tries to please his father. I guess in some strange way, they did replace our fathers," mumbled Sean Og as he looks out the small front window on hearing Sally bark.

"Well, I guess all kids will look for a mother or father figure if they haven't got their birth wan at hand, I dare say ya were no different," replied Jim and his heart was now full of sorrow for Sean Og.

"It's funny that ya'r mother is the wan person that stands out in ya'r mind of past memories, yet for me it's wan of the Christian Brothers. Almighty Jaysus, did I fear him and so did everywan else. The only way I'd describe him was that he was an unusual cross between a Saint Bernard and a Doberman but the roar of a constipated Jackass, he certainly had. He was a big hefty man with hands the size of shovels. He'd catch ya by the ears and hoist ya off the ground if ya happened to cross his path when he was havin' a bad day. He was wan of the Brothers that sexually abused the specials…"

"The specials?" butted in Jim.

"Emm, the specials, they were the lads that had no contact with the world outside the school. They had no relatives to care for them. I meself was in that group. The Christian Brothers could do what they liked to us 'cause we had nobody to run to and tell. The nights I was ordered from me bed and sexually abused, this Christian Brother would stand by the door and watch on with a smirk on his face. And when it was all over he'd give me a wallop across the back of the neck and tell me to go and clean meself off. If a young lad cried while been sexually abused he'd sneer in a sarcastic manner, 'Ach shur, our poor little gearsun is cryin' I'll give ya somethin' to cry about, out of here ya dirty little skunk and wash. We don't want the sheets to get dirty, now do we, so wash that dirty slop off lad…..."

Jim shook his head and sighed in dismay.

"Com' to think of it," gasped Sean Og. "That very same Brother had a desperate hang up about women."

"Hang up about women?"

"Yep," nodded Sean Og. "In the classroom he'd bawl out like a constipated Jackass, women are impure ......they're pure filth. What're they boys?.....They're pure filth Brother....we'd yell back. That's right boys, he bawl out and his face twisted like a corkscrew."

"Mother....of...Christ," muttered Jim.

"Ahhhhh, he was a horrible bastard and there was no other way of puttin' it. In the classroom, he'd take ya to the top of the class to his desk pretendin' to explain a sum or an Irish passage to ya, but while ya stood by his side, he'd place ya'r hand inside his cassock and get ya to touch his privates. The other boys at the back of the class would smirk and giggle quietly for they knew what the Brother was doin'. It was so humiliatin', but there wasn't a feckkkk'in thin' ya could do about it," said Sean Og and Jim could tell from the sound in his voice that he was living the memory as he was describing those horrific childhood memories.

There was a silence and after a few moments of thought Sean Og continues telling his story.

"The wan thin' that really stands out in me mind is the size of the feck'in rats. Mother.....of....Jaaaysus, they were big long, healthy, hairy, grey bastards. They terrified me. I remember, Tom, wan of the lads in the dormitory would take great joy waitin' for them to com'out at night and he'd feck pebbles at them. I guess after a while, it became a game for the lads, seein' who'd hit the rat. 'Got the fucker, hahaha, got the little fucker', is what ya'd hear when wan of them hit a rat. Thinkin' back now, I guess the rats were better fed than us and to make it worse they'd no fear of humans. There were nights I'd lie huddled up under the blankets, listenin' to them scratchin' and runnin' hither and thither under the floorboards.

"Fuck'in hell," sighed Jim.

"Lookin' back now Jim, in the Industrial School in Tralee boys were taught to abuse boys from the example and actions of the Christian Brothers. I guess it was a ripe breedin' ground for bullies and abusers. Some of the older wans would bully the younger wans. Ya always had, what I'd call the scouts. These were the lapdogs for the Christian Brothers. They were always runnin' and racin' with tales and getting' young boys into trouble. There were times when these so-called scouts would be handed the leather strap to whip other boys. The harder they'd lash, the more praise they got from the Christian Brother. There were wan or two who actually sexually abused younger lads. I guess they felt they had a God given right to do so, as they themselves were ordered to wank each other off in the showers by that nutcase of a Christian Brother who become knowin' amongst the older cheeky inmates as Willie Wanker. Nothin' could be done about it. If ya complained, ya not only got a trashin' from the Superior but also from the bullyboy. I guess ya'd say it was like livin' in an abyss. The longer ya survived the darker it got....."

"Wicket abuse....pure.... utter abuse," gasped Jim.

"Wan thin' I've come to realise from me robbed childhood is that our childhood years are only a dozen and no more and if ya've the misfortune to experience a bad dozen, ya'll never again get the chance to relive them to put them right. And for that reason alone, every kid should be allowed the opportunity to enjoy the formative years of life, for these years will become their happy memories that'll help them through adulthood. Children should never be taken for granted. They should've the same rights as adults and be treated with respect. But more importantly, they should never be punished for the sins and wrongdoin' of adults."

Sean Og stands up to get a handkerchief from his coat pocket that is hanging at the back of the old pine door and wipes his brow and clears away the unshed tears that are starting to fill up in the corner of his eyes.

"By Christ, they were horrific times, good God, they really were horrific times," was all Jim could say.

"Then....when it came.....to the Irish dancin'.... that was another......feck'in story," sighed Sean Og picking up another bunch of willow and continued making his willow basket for the caorans from last year's turf, which were used to start the fire in the mornings. "Good God, I never got the hang of it. I could never take on the stance as if I had a black thorn stick pocked up me arse right up to me tonsils. No matter, how hard I tried to command that stance, the more me head would jet forward when I lifted me legs. I'd end up spendin' most of the dancin' class in the corner wearin' a dunce cap, nursin' the calves of me legs from the lashes of that big leather strap. 'Still sufferin' from the here's me head and me arse is comin,' the older inmates would whisper as they passed by."

Jim didn't respond he just sat there and shook his head in dismay.

Over the coming days, the two men keep themselves busy, cleaning out and painting the farmyard sheds. The paint is made out of sour milk and lime, which is coloured with farmyard dung mixed with some water. This is something Jim had learned from his father. It took him a while to get the consistency right but when he did, it worked wonders, as there was a nice tint in the whitewash that blended well with the thatch and the farmyard surrounds. Repairs are made to the thatch roofs with the reeds that were gathered last year. This is Sean Og's speciality and he certainly takes pride in it. Although Peg would have you know that he did more gawping and gaping around to see who was coming and going, as there was a great view of the Ring of Kerry road from the rooftop.

Every year the weathercock that was put up on the east gable of the main house to teach Johnny the movements of the wind is painted and greased. Jim had made it in one of the night classes that were held in Cahirciveen Vocational School a few years back. He had learned much valued skills at those classes and these were to stand to him over the next few months, as he would have to attend to the farmstead and learn to value and respect nature. One thing he found out, it is not until a man has to totally depend on nature for his food and self-appreciation that he truly understands the need to respect it while fully recognising the wonders and miracles of each season.

One of the jobs that appeal to Jim is the laying of the hedge groves. Sean Og had done it five years ago and it was well overdue for another cut back. Laying the hedge groves not only tames them but it gives good coverage for the inhabitants such as the small chaffinches, sparrows, robins, blackbirds and much more. It's lovely to peep into a nest of young nestlings in the summer time and watch them mature while they learn the ways of the world around them. Taking time to tame and lay the hedges also gives a nice profile to the fields and meadows.

In the corner of each field, Jim and Sean Og have made seats out of old railway sleepers and stones. These are much-loved spots where time grants you the privilege to see the world around you, not only through your eyes but also through your heart. It's grand to sit there and spend a moment having a quiet smoke or simply watching a spider making its web or a snail cross your path carrying its shelly home on its back or every now and again delight in a sparrow patiently hammer a shell of a young snail against the stones in anticipation of a hearty meal. While sitting there, watching the world go by and wondering about the miracles of nature, your mind would somehow wander off to whatever dreamland it choose to visit. There were times when Sean Og would sit there with Johnny and recite the poem while explaining the wonders of nature to him.

Wonder Why.
Have you ever wished upon a rainbow?
While allowing you imagination to flow
For your imagination energizes your creativity
Which encourages your inner child to grow

Have you ever wished upon a falling star?
While the night sky curtains off the day
Have you ever smiled at the wonders of life?
As a child kneels down to pray

Have you ever touched a snowflake still afloat?

And wondered at the magic of it all
Or watched a butterfly sit so still
While we, life's passengers daily rush by

Have you ever wondered at the beauty of a web?
Catching the morning sun flickering through
Do you ever wonder why the swallows return?
Or why a crowing cock mystifies the noon

Did you ever wonder why Mother Nature cares
Winter Summer Autumn or Spring
Whether you stop or simply refuse to stare
She'll continue to cherish and look after her kin.

Chapter Sixteen

Jim Tracks Down Fr. Murphy

It is coming into late spring and there is a good stretch in the evenings when Jim decides to trace the whereabouts of Fr. Murphy in the hope of tracking him down. He is determined to find out what really happened and why he was transferred to the missions all those years ago.

Doc informs Jim that Fr. Murphy is residing in a Rest Home just outside Limerick city since his return to Ireland from the missions due to failing health. Doc makes contact with the matron of the Rest Home and arrangements are made for Jim to meet up with Fr. Murphy.

"Peg I'm takin' ya for a drive today and Johnny is stayin' with Sean Og for the afternoon," chuckled Jim placing his arms around her slender waist and giving her a mischievous hug and kiss on the cheek.

"Doka Da," mumbled Johnny happily slurping his way through a bowl of bread and broth.

"Where're ya takin' me?" exclaimed Peg, surprised by Jim's spontaneous invitation.

"Patience me dear missus, patience, that's what's needed," chuckled Jim in anticipation that everything would turn out the way he had planned as he embraces her once more. "Ya'll simply just have to wait and see…"

"I hope we'll be back before six, 'cause I need to bake a few scones for tomorrow, I'm off to see Joan's mother, she has been feelin' under the weather for a while now," replied Peg as she continues stirring the soup for the lunch.

"Ara, gra geal mo chroi, fear not, I'll have ya returned to ya'r kitchen before the clock strikes midnight and if I don't, yerra Christ shur, the worst that'll happen is ya'r carriage will turn into a pumpkin," giggled Jim giving her one of his macho winks.

They set out on their journey shortly after lunch. The road to Limerick was busy due to a football match that was on in Tralee but on the whole it was a relaxing journey and it wasn't long before they were pulling up outside the gates of the Rest Home.

"What on earth...are we...doin' here?" exclaimed Peg looking up at the building and admiring the spread of daffodils and wallflowers bordering the front lawn. "Is this an nursin' home of some type. Is someone we know ill or something?"

"No dear, there's somewan in here, I'd like ya to meet," replied Jim turning off the ignition and leaning across to open the car door for her.

But, before they could make their way down the hallway of the Rest Home, Fr. Murphy had made his way towards them. Peg is lost in the moment and for the first time in her life she is struck dumb.

"Peg my child..... ohhhhh... Peg my dear child," was all Fr. Murphy could say as he held out his arms to her.

As they both stood there in silence with outstretched arms, the tears that flowed from their eyes said it all. They are so surprised, yet so pleased to meet each other again. Fr. Murphy guides them into a large reception room that overlooks the garden where he had arranged armchairs close to the front bay window. Leaving them for a moment, he calls out to one of the nurses on duty to bring a large pot of tea and a plate of ham and tomato sandwiches.

"Peg dear, I've so much to tell you, but first tell me about your life and what has happened since we last met," delighted Fr. Murphy, but, he certainly wasn't prepared for the springboard reaction from Peg.

"But shur Father, where did ya get to? Ya never told me that ya were leavin'. They just gave me a ticket for England and that's how it was. What went wrong? What did I do? Why didn't ya write? Ya'r sister Kate in America kept in contact and sends parcels but she has never mentioned ya," called out Peg in one breath.

The questions just continued to flow and flow and then there was a lull as Peg's sobs echoed throughout the room.

"Ohhhhh....my child...ohhhhh...hush....now...it's okay," sighed Fr. Murphy as he tries to calm her down.

Jim leaves the room, as he feels uncomfortable with Peg's sobs of surprise, wonder and grief. This personal moment belonged to Peg and Fr. Murphy and out of respect for both of them he felt he should allow them that privilege.

Fr. Murphy explains what happened and they soon catch up on past events and memories. He talks about his sister's child Geraldine and how she is now attending a Catholic high school in New York and hoping to attend university in Washington once she graduates. Peg is happy to talk about the past as now the missing links of the chain come together for her. For years, she could never understand why Fr. Murphy left for the missions so quickly and especially without saying good-bye to her and also why his sister never mentioned him in her letters from America. He apologises to Peg for letting her down. Peg tells him about Johnny and Sean Og and the life she now shares with them.

"Jim's a wonderful man Father, he's so kind and carin', he provides well for us all. We've a lovely home outside Glenbeigh. It's a farmhouse with a few acres of mountain land that Jim's uncle left him when he passed away. Ya're welcome there anytime," she said taking a hold of Fr. Murphy's hand.

After a meditative walk in the gardens, Jim returns and is relieved to find both of them in good heart and cheer. Their reunion seems so fitting and right. He is happy that he has made the right decision, after all, they had shared many happy days and Peg looked upon Fr. Murphy as a friend from the past who had mysteriously disappeared from her life.

During the afternoon, visitors start to come and go so Fr. Murphy decides to take both of them to his bedroom as he felt that it would be more private there. In the privacy and tranquillity of his bedroom, they get engrossed in chatting about the abuse that occurred in the Industrial Schools.

"The Catholic Church has a lot to answer for," insisted Jim pointing to the picture of the Pope that was hanging on the wall. "Terrible stuff have happened to children under the guardianship of the Religious Orders. Mother of Christ….why…..did…..it happen…..Father?"

"It happened because they were allowed to get away with it. Well, putting it mildly, there were more hawks than doves amongst the Religious Orders," replied Fr. Murphy shaking his head in disgust. "Religion is easy, as people can be control in a religion but it's Faith that counts. Faith in oneself. faith in life, but above all the faith in the higher Being who is God."

After a few moments to recollect his pathway of thought he continues in a reflective tone of voice.

"The leaders of the Catholic Church instilled fear into their followers to make them believers, turning them into God fearing people. But if the gospels tell us that God is understanding and kind, why then would someone fear goodness, surly that's a contradiction to the teachings of the main gospels. It has taken Buddhism to show us what Christianity is really about….."

"Interestin' emmm I see," replied Jim taking off his jacket and hanging it over the chair next to Fr. Murphy's bed. "I never thought of it like that, but hearin' it the way ya've put it Father, it all makes sense now."

As the hours pass by, Fr. Murphy tells them of his experiences on the missions and what his experiences have lead him to believe.

"Too many Priests, Christian Brothers and Nuns just wore the suit and habit but failed to abide by the Christian understanding behind the cloth they wore. I guess Martin Luther had the right idea, that all Christian men and women should be responsible for their own fate of their Faith. At the end of the day, a Priest is only the middleman between a believer and God. Take out the middleman and you'll have direct contact with God. We must go with our consciences and to ignore it is neither good nor safe, for it's our consciences and not the Priest that really lets us know what's right or wrong," he said standing by his bedroom window that overlooks the laneway at the back of the Rest Home.

Jim is very impressed by Fr. Murphy's understanding of the Christian faith for he himself had often questioned the teachings of the Catholic Church. Not in any way that he disrespected the teachings but more so, doubted the practically of it with regard to living and the rearing of a family. His past thoughts were inline with that of what Fr. Murphy had just related to him. He felt safe and comfortable with this religious man, for the first time in his life, he saw a priest as a person who was human, and not as someone he had to respect because of the cloth and position, he held.

As Fr. Murphy looks out his bedroom window his attention is drawn to the evening sky.

"What a miracle of wonder, nature is, a miracle that we take for granted each day of our lives. If we're to be truly Christian, we need to honour the truth and unless we're able to do that, we'll never confront the wrongdoings in our daily lives. I guess allowing a cloud of silence to develop over any wrongdoing enables evil to succeed and the same can be said about what went on in the Industrial Schools in Ireland all those years ago....."

Peg sat quietly in the corner, just looking on at the two men in her life that made a difference and who were engrossed in deep discussion. She noticed that from time to time, Fr. Murphy would look to her as if he wanted to say something but time and time again he resisted. Each time their eyes met, they just smiled and nodded. Lost in the moment were two people who in their hearts knew that the past had to be put to right. She trusted this man, for her, he was her guardian angel that took care of her and made her feel so wholesome and safe in the past. Peg's eyes wander around the tranquil yellow and green bedroom that is graced with a few lemon geranium plants and photos of his family and friends from the missions. In the corner of the room is a little picture of his sister's daughter. As Peg focuses on the photo Fr. Murphy feels a little uneasy. Jim notices Peg's intense stare and takes a closer look at the photo himself.

"My niece....Geraldine...as a baby," muttered Fr. Murphy as his watches the two focus on the photo.

"Amazin, emmmmm," mumbled Jim. "She has the look of our Johnny.... that's amazin'.... but... I guess all kids look the same at that age."

"Maybe so," muttered Fr. Murphy as the guilt of deception of the past surge through his veins while he eases the photo from Peg's hands and places it on the bedside locker.

His heart throbs, for here standing in front of him, is the real mother of this child. But, how could he tell her that such an injustice had been done to her. His heart now throbs with anxiety and he throat tightens as the guilt emerges from the inner core of his being. All those years ago, Peg had entrusted her confidence in him regarding her firstborn and how the nuns had told her that the baby had died. He had comforted her during her sadness but never told her the truth. His niece Geraldine was Peg's little baby. Now, he had to confront his past and unravel the demons that wronged Peg. Justice had to be done and he always believed that justice delayed, is justice denied and truth behold, this was one case where it certainly was.

Peg makes her way out of the room and glances back at Fr. Murphy and Jim as if to say, "somethin' ain't right." There is a silent and both Jim and Fr. Murphy look at each other and on shaking hands, they both knew in their hearts they were issues that needed to be sorted out.

"Ya're a good man and it's such a pity I didn't have the honour of meetin' ya before this," said Jim.

"Look after yourself and take good care of our Peg. She's a special person that deserves the best," replied Fr. Murphy patting Jim on the shoulder.

"Supper in five minutes," echoed a voice from the dining room at the end of the hallway.

"Sometimes, I find it difficult to understand the ways of God," Jim muttered to Fr. Murphy on their way down the narrow hallway to the entrance porch.

"I guess many of us mightn't understand God at all times, but it's good to feel that God understands us. There're even times when we say that we're not God's friend, but it's nice to know, He's always ours," grinned Fr. Murphy amused by Jim's doubting Thomas's attitude. The two men bid their farewells and promise to stay in touch.

"I've my own demons and wrongdoings to sort out," thought Fr. Murphy to himself as he watches Jim's car pull away from the entrance gate.

As we grow from childhood to adulthood too many of us become trapped in institutionalised thinking which can often pollute our minds, we need to learn to think for ourselves and take responsibility for our own choices. In life, all of us have to make choices, some big, some small. But it's not the choices we make that haunt us, but it's the way we choose to make them. For many of us when it comes to making choices we take the easy path and choose the choice that suits ourselves so that we don't complicate our lives. That doesn't mean that we choose the right one. To make the right choice, we need to get in touch with our conscience and that was what Fr. Murphy needed to do. For years, he too, had followed the escape goat pathway in life of suitable choices but not necessary the right ones. But tonight, he had to consult his conscience so that he could do right by himself, by Peg and by God. After spending some time in the chapel praying for guidance he returns to his room and writes a letter to his sister Kate in America and asks the night-nurse to post it on her way home from work.

Dear Kate,

It was good to hear that your health is much better and you're getting back on your feet. The flu can certainly take the best out of a person, especially if they're not in the best of their health. I myself, are recovering slowly from my own illness but meeting up with Peg and Jim gave me a great lift. I know that we've spoken over the years about telling Geraldine about Peg and something in my soul tells me that the time is right. But I wonder whether it's the right time for you. I'm aware that Geraldine is curious to whom her birth mother is, but she is also aware that she'll never take your place, Kate.

Are we doing an injustice to both of them by keeping them apart? This is something I asked myself in the chapel tonight and prayed to God to send me the answer. I truly believe that Peg has suffered a lifetime of grief due to the injustice that was inflicted on her. It was from that same injustice that a wonderful little gift came into our lives. We've had the pleasure of enjoying the love and happiness that a child can bring into a home but maybe it's time to give back a portion of this love and joy to Peg, the rightful mother. I haven't spoken to Peg about this situation and won't until I've your blessing to do so.

Words, I feel are difficult to write to express what I need to say but I know from our closeness that you don't need me to write words for you to understand what needs to be done.

Kate, you've a difficult decision to make and I can only pray that it brings happiness to all involved. Tell Geraldine I said hallo and wish her well in her upcoming exams.

God bless and I'll keep you in my prayers.
Your fond brother,
James.

The following morning, he returns to the chapel and prays in gratitude to God for giving him the strength and courage to do right and request that justice will be done. During the day he telephones Kate about Peg's visit and tells her a letter is on the way. Kate is aware that her adopted daughter Geraldine is curious about her birth mother and believes that maybe Peg's visit to him is a blessing from the Gods. But she does request that Peg isn't told about the truth until she herself tells Geraldine.

He now feels a weight lifted from his soul and hopes that when his time comes to confessing to Peg that

God will grace the moment with joy and happiness and not with resentment and grief.

Chapter Seventeen

Official Mail

The postman drops off two letters for Jim, one from the educational department and the other from the Southern Health Board that states that Johnny would be better off in a special school for handicapped children. Peg refuses to co-operate and insists that she will take Johnny to England rather than send him away from a loving home. Jim confides in Doc regarding the matter. Doc keeps an ear to the ground and finds out that it was the old Parish Priest from Glenbeigh who had words with Jim a while back, lodged the complaint concerning Johnny's well-being and up bringing.

Doc believes in his heart that the bond between a child and a parent is like a golden cord that's deeply rooted in the subconscious. This special cord shouldn't be severed and if done so, the end results can have a detrimental affect for both child and parent. But more so in the case of Jim and Peg, for the love and support that they had parented Johnny with over the years was a unique example of what family life is all about.

"I tell you the man to sort this out, is Patrick from back yonder, the local councillor. He's well known for his determined nature to sort out injustices and even children in the local town-lands are accustomed to reciting the cilice, 'Patrick's ya'r man'. He'll certainly get to the core of this issue. He has good contacts in all the political parties and is well respected by them for his stamina. He's always ready to help the marginalized and the people less well off. He also has relatives high up in the legal and medical professions and for that reason alone, he'll be able to get information regarding the running of these schools that wouldn't be readily available to the public. He'll certainly put an end to this and put your minds to rest," insisted Doc when he met up with Jim in the local pub one evening.

"I don't know about that. Ach shur, ain't he Fine Gael and we've always voted Fianna Fail," sighed Jim as in his heart he felt it might be a little hypocritical to bring his problems to a person that he didn't vote for.

"Yerra Jim, I don't think that matters to much to Patrick. He's a good man and one that's out to fight injustice. He had it tough himself. I canvassed with him when he first went for the Kerry County Council. That May, we both crossed the bogs and sloughs with our bikes on our shoulders, I'll never forget it. He went into places I never even knew existed. He showed me the isolation that aul people have to put up with. He showed me the meeker existence and the poverty of families behind the scenes. He vowed that he'd make changes if elected. True to his word he has been, for he has brought roads to places the Kerry County Council probably never knew existed and houses for families who were living in wet damp, cold bothans or hovels for the want of a better word," replied Doc.

"Do ya think in ya'r own heart that sendin' Johnny into the educational system in a special school would be good for him?"

"Schooling and its choice of subjects can do much harm to the health of certain children and especially when it comes to Johnny. Children at a young age learn through senses, there's a strong inclination to touch and handle everything in sight. Modern education that's confined to the classroom is such, that instead of educating children through their natural senses, it has a tendency to teach them the knowledge from books or by parrot style repetition of knowledge. Young children's heath will certainly suffer from it, as they're unable to apply themselves to long periods of concentration. Any learning that acquires attention should be done over short periods of concentration times. This applies especially to the very young child under the age of eight. Any difficult learning should be carried out in the morning when the mind is alert and not in the afternoon when the natural course of the body is to relax and rest. At night the minds of children under the age of twelve, shouldn't be burdened with longs hours of homework, as this will affect the natural flow of sleep that's required for a healthy growing body…"

"Is that so," mumbled Jim biting into his lower lip.

"Maybe Johnny could flourish from more child company of his own age, but shur, we can arrange that by introducing him to the local children or maybe to the children from the Foilmore Parish where you go to Mass and hopefully get him involved in child community events, but other than that, I'm ain't worried about the learning patterns of Johnny. On the whole, he's a very alert, inquisitive, happy little boy," replied Doc.

"Ach shur, we'll leave it in the hands of Patrick so. And as ya've already said, he's the man to sort it now," replied Jim now feeling a little more content with himself knowing that they aren't holding Johnny back in their eagerness to care, love and protect him.

Over the coming week Doc makes it his business to have a quiet word with Patrick who arranges to meet up with Peg and Jim on his way back from one of his Council meetings.

"Howya Patrick?" asked Jim opening the door and guiding Patrick into the kitchen.

"Doc asked me to drop in, It seems you're in a wee bit of bother, Jim," said Patrick shaking hands with Jim.

"Before we'll discuss anythin' Patrick, I think we'd need to be honest with each other, ya got no vote in this house in the last election. Ya see me family have kicked with the other foot all our lives. We've always been true Fianna Failers since the civil war. Patrick, ya've every right not to want to help us."

"Jim, my dear man. I've no right in not helping you. I was elected to help people and not to assess who voted for me. So, if I can be of any help at all, I'll certainly will," smiled Patrick. "Appreciate your honesty though."

While they were chatting and explaining their circumstances and concerns Sean Og returns home with Johnny on the crossbar of his bike.

"So this is the young man himself?" asked Patrick holding his hand out to Johnny.

Johnny stands back and shyly cuddles into his mother while giving Patrick a smile with his little blue slanted eyes.

"Woo tat Ma?" asked Johnny.

"This is Patrick," replied Peg wiping the ice cream and chocolate from Johnny's face with a wet corner of the tea towel that was tied around her waist.

"Howya Patrick?" asked Sean Og as they shook hands.

"Yerra Christ, grand, just grand," said Patrick. "Sean Og, you're a busy man, like a March hare, always on the go,"

"Haha, well it's like this. By Christ, if ya rest ya'll rust," chuckled Sean Og dancing around and pretending to punch Johnny on the chin, who readily returned the gesture with a playful punch into Sean Og's stomach.

"Indeed you're right," chuckled Patrick "Is trom an t-ualach an leisce."

"Indeed ya never spoke a truer word Patrick. Laziness is in deed a heavy burden…"

"Just back from the caid?" asked Patrick.

"Yeah," nodded Sean Og.

"How did the local lads play?" asked Patrick, as he himself was football crazy.

"Well truth behold, it was very tuirseach, very tuirseach in deed, ya'd have got better results out of a few aul hens scrapin' and scratchin' at that bloomin' heap of dung in the backyard. Ahhh shur, they never got into the game at all. The Killorgin lads were all over them. But anyway, Johnny didn't mind as long as he got his ice cream and shur, the fresh air and the ride home on the bike did him grand," replied Sean Og taking off his coat and pouring out a mug of tea for himself.

Patrick smiles as he watches Johnny chase the cat off the kitchen table and hush it out the front door. Nothing wrong with that young lad, he thought to himself.

After an hour of listening to the issues that needed to be dealt with, Patrick sets on his way and assures them that he will investigate the matter but in the meantime not to let the worry of it all get in on them.

That evening, after Patrick had attended to his farm work, he writes a letter to the relevant departments and explains that it would be a grievous mistake and miscarriage of justice to remove the child from his parents and send him away to be schooled. He explains that Johnny has an endless sense of curiosity, love and affection that couldn't be achieved in a school. For his age, he displays a good common sense of his surrounds, his physical co-ordination and general disposition is that of a good happy healthy child. He goes on to say that the letter of complaint that was received by the educational department was out of resentment rather than out of any goodwill and it would be to everyone's' advantage to simply ignore it. However, should any of the educational inspectors or social workers wish to visit with Johnny's family they were welcome to do so.

On receiving the letters, the educational department and health board put the matter to rest. Patrick makes it his business to pay a visit to the old Parish Priest and lets him know that in his eyes Christianity is about helping people and not upsetting them. The Parish Priest has a good idea of what Patrick is talking about. He tries to degrade Patrick with intellectual words but Patrick brings him back to earth.

"Father, behind that collar you're just simply a man, just like me, no less or no greater, so don't think you can down trod me, it'd be more in your line to off load that begrudging camel hump you're carrying around and get back to being a priest...."

"That ain't a very Catholic manner," grunted the Parish Priest with a scornful look across his brow.

"Maybe, if we were less Catholic and more Christ like, the world would be a better place," snapped Patrick sternly.

"I'd my reasons for doin' what I did," muttered the auld Parish Priest.

"That I can accept," grunted Patrick. "Your actions where simply the antics of a desperate man but I dare say beneath that collar of yours, there's no great evil, maybe frustration and desperation but no great evil…"

"Hmm hmm," grunted the old Parish Priest and with that he turns on his heels and struts back into the church in a right strop, leaving Patrick standing alone in the frustration of the moment.

Patrick is determined to search out any information regarding educational files concerning the Industrial Schools of Ireland. During his investigations he is made aware of the Cussen Report and the Kennedy Report. Both intensive investigations carried out on behalf of the Irish State into the care of the children in the Industrial Schools of Ireland.

The Cussen Report had been shelved since 1936 and totally ignored. He has a gut feeling that something unchristian did go on in those Industrial Schools but meets with a brick wall when he asks questions amongst his colleagues in the Dail. Patrick, who is a member of the Health Board, turns his investigation in that corner but once again meets with a cloud of smoke, seemly whatever is known about the schools, everyone is of the opinion that it should be kept in the archives and allowed to dissolve silently into the past. This attitude only makes Patrick more determined to get to the bottom of the matter.

Two weeks later, while passing through Glenbeigh he meets up with Sean Og who tells him about a young boy named Joseph who attended the Industrial School with him and who died after receiving a severe trashing from a Christian Brother. The young lad received the beating because he wouldn't eat his bread and dripping. Joseph happened to be frisky little lad by nature but suffered from bronchial problems. When he refused to finish his supper the Christian Brother caught a hold of him, trashed him with his leather strap, and continued to do so until Joseph collapsed onto the floor. Then in a moment of frustration and anger the Christian Brother continued to kick the young lad until there was no more movement left in his body. The other inmates who stood by and watched on in horror were ordered out of the dining hall and the next time they saw this young lad was in his coffin. A coffin, that Sean Og and some of the inmates helped to make.

The following Tuesday while on a visit to the Dublin, Patrick searches out this young lad's birth and death certificates in the hope that he might be able to trace down some living relative. Returning home from a Council meeting he drops off to have a chat with Jim and Sean Og. Sean Og examines the death registration certificate and is adamant that Joseph died from a beating and not from what was recorded on the certificate. They are both taken back to find out that Joseph's surname is spelt differently on his death cert. His surname on his birth cert is recorded as Pike after his mother's surname yet on his death cert it was recorded as Pyke. This alone, frustrates Patrick, for he is now aware that should anyone bring legal action against the Christian Brother regarding the death of this young lad, there is a chance that the case would be thrown out of court. Is this another one of the Christian Brother's conspiracies and cover-ups? Patrick thought to himself.

"Patrick, what actually happened to the children that were handicapped that were in the care of the Religious Orders?" asked Sean Og.

"I believe, once they left the Industrial Schools they were committed to the County Homes or to Mental Institutions and left there 'til they died," shrugged Patrick taking another glance at Joseph's certificates.

"The Christian Brother that beat young Joseph to a pulp, what has happened to him?" asked Sean Og and the more he thought about the injustices, the more he could feel anger and frustration building up in the pit of his belly.

"Well, believe it or not, seemly he's alive and well and walking around without a care in the world. I made it my business to track him down and it turns out that he was transferred from school to school during his teaching time as he was well known for his notorious bullyboy antics," replied Patrick.

"So, ya're tellin' me that he's gettin' away with murder," insisted Sean Og now really frustrated with the thought of this man walking around without a care.

"Yep, it'd seem so. You see in the eyes of God, he's guilty. But in the court of this land he's innocent 'til he's found guilty and with a cock up like this on Joseph's death certificate, there's very little chance of getting justice for your friend unless we get the grave dug up. Even with that, you don't know what you'd find down there. If, there're more than one body, we'll need a DNA test to identify Joseph's remains and where do we go to find a relative? You probably find that his mother, whose name was Teresa Pike, was one of the Magdalen Laundry girls and there maybe no trace of her whereabouts once she left that place," sighed Patrick shaking his head in dismay.

"Ahhhhh Christ, there must be some form of proper justice here in Kerry?" insisted Jim.

"Jim my dear chap, the justice system in Kerry is a strange one and something tells me that there's something going on behind the scenes. It seems to be protecting the Christian Brothers and other abusers. But, hopefully in time we'll get a straight honest court of Law and justice will be served," replied Patrick.

"What about the Gardai, can they do anythin'?" asked Jim biting into his lower lip.

"Other than take a statement that's as much as they're prepared to do. I've investigated into that and they say that their hands are tied 'til they've enough statements to take proper action," shrugged Patrick.

"But surely to Jaysus, wan statement should be enough to take action?" insisted Sean Og.

"Well, you'd think so, but seemly it ain't enough according to the Gardai," replied Patrick.

"Patrick, are ya tellin' me, they're corrupt as well?" asked Jim.

"Jim, I ain't saying that, but there's something there I can't put my finger on, but I'll get to the bottom of it, I assure you. As Charles Dickens wrote in his novel Hard Times, 'what I want is facts'. Facts alone are wanted in life. And, that's what we need to get our hands on if we intend to expose the abusers. We need hard facts, facts documented and recorded in archives. Ones they can't dispute. That's what's needed to prove that the abuse did occur," insisted Patrick putting his hand into his pocket, taking out a pound coin, and handing it to Johnny. "Get yourself some sweets. You're a great wee garsun. You must be very proud of him, he's a credit to you all…"

Johnny grabs the money and happily scrambles off out to the farmyard with Sally.

"We'll need to search deep so, if ya feel the Gardai ain't inclined to help ya," said Jim.

"Well Jim, for some reason they're shy in coming forward when it comes to exposing the abuse in the Industrial Schools and to me that ain't a good sign. When, you get a gutless Garda in the force or one that's hiding skeletons in his cupboard, that ain't a good thing. Gutless Gardai breed bullyboys and germinate an unjust system. And in an unjust system, there'll be no fairness for victims of abuse and other less fortunate people who find themselves at the mercy of the Gardai."

"Geee Patrick, ya're right there," grunted Jim putting on his jacket and walking out to the farmyard to milk the cows and feed the animals for the night.

On leaving the farmyard, Patrick reassures Jim and Sean Og.

"Leave this issue to me and I'll get to the bottom of it. You see lads, if you want to find out about the workings of a hive of honey, it ain't the queen bee that'll give you the answers, it's the worker bees and that can be applied to the Industrial School. You ain't going to find the answers in the system that ran the schools. You'll find your answers from the lads and lassies that were reared in them. And I assure you both, if you investigate the registrations of births and deaths in each county, there'll be plenty of fodder for thought. You see the greatest secrets are buried in the graveyards. I dear say, that a few hours investigating the deaths of children while in care of the Religious Orders will tell you all you need to know. I'll track down some of the lads and lassies that attended these schools and see if they're willing to go public. Public exposure will fish out those evil abusers. It's well known that when a ship is sinking the rats will run and if we persist long enough these evil abusers, which are no more than rodents within our society will run as well and that's the time to catch the fuckers. At present, they're carefully protected and shelter by their own flock. That flock is residing in the Catholic Church. I'll need to keep my research under my cap for the moment for if the Religious Orders find out, they're sure to cull records or remove them from the archives, so please stay stump for the moment 'til I come up with some evidence...."

"By Christ, we will. Take care Patrick, and all the best," Jim called out as Patrick sets on his way eager to throw out his rod into the public arena of investigation to see what limp fish might bite into his bait.

Three weeks later, Patrick returns with a large envelope containing a detailed report, it's a copy of the 1936 Cussin Report.

"Howya Patrick, Jim ain't here at the moment," said Peg greeting him at the front door.

"Shur that's grand Peg, I'm just on my way back from a meeting in Tralee and just wanted to drop this in," replied Patrick handing her the large white envelope.

"Fancy a cuppa Patrick, I've just popped a few scones into the oven."

"No Peg, I won't, the kids are in the car and we need to get back to milk the cows. The kids have some schoolwork to catch up on as well."

"They're big now and growin' up to be grand responsible kids," said Peg waving to the four kids in the back seat of Patrick's car.

"They're growing up quickly all right, I guess we only borrow our children for a short span in life. The eldest is sitting her exams this year," said Patrick getting back into the car.

"Education is a great thin', all children should've a decent education nowadays," replied Peg.

"Times are different now. I myself, only had a primary education and learned the rest from the school of hard-knocks," chuckled Patrick. "If I take the mountain road, Peg, will it take me back onto the main road to Cahirciveen?"

"'Twill indeed…yeah 'twill… if ya follow the road down to the junction and then take a left you'll be back on the main Cahirciveen Road. As ya drive over yonder, take it ayezee, for Mickey's sheep are usually wanderin' around. And, I don't think he'd be too happy if ya took wan of his rams on the bonnet. He's hopin' to sell them off at the fair in Cahirciveen next week," chuckled Peg.

"How's Mickey doing? I haven't seen him lately," asked Patrick revving up the engine of the car.

"Ach shur he's grand, still loves the aul sup of whiskey and the odd flutter on the gee gees. He wanders home after a night in the pub and he'd try and convince ya that he ain't drunk but only intoxicated. Mickey has never been too upset with the worries of life, he's just himself. He's a great man for his age, still has all his wits about him," replied Peg.

"Yerra Christ, he must be touching four score and ten years by now," sighed Patrick settling into the drivers seat. "And beneath that aul peaked cap and crinkled face there must be so much hidden wisdom."

"That he certainly has. The yanks were home in the summer cerebratin' his birthday. He contributes his stamina and health to his spuds, cabbage, mackerel and carrageen moss diet," giggled Peg.

"Well whatever the fuck it is, he has the memory of an elephant, the eye of a hawk and the ear of a terrier," grinned Patrick.

"Shur, the locals would've ya know, that he has such keen senses that in the midst of a summer evenin' he'd sniff out a fairy and probably the odd strayin' mountain leprechaun as well. Hopefully, we'll be as healthy as him if we're fortunate enough to live that long…"

"God willing," smiled Patrick.

"Grand evenin' now, hopefully the rain will stay off. Thanks Patrick, I'll give this letter to Jim when he returns. He'll be disappointed to have missed ya," said Peg taking a look into the brown envelope.

"Tell him, I'll be home on Sunday, do call down and we'll have a chat. Bring the young lad and he can spend a few hours with the kids. And while you're down you can take a few bags of turf back with you. I see you're running low and I've plenty of it back yonder to keep me going. Take care and God bless Peg," called out Patrick as he drove off down the boreen.

Peg is anxious to see the report herself and on opening it, she finds that Patrick has marked sections that he thought might be of interest to them, there is also a letter, which reads,

Jim, Peg & Sean Og

With reference to what we were talking about, a colleague of mine found this 1936 state report in the archives of the educational department in Dublin. On reading it, I believe that the State gave the Religious Orders and the Christian Brothers in particular a licence to abuse. Now, I've a better understanding as to why the Christian Bothers saw and continue to see no wrong in what they did and continue to do so.

The very fact that this Report into the Industrial Schools was shelved, gave a license to members of Religious Orders to abuse and germinated a safe haven for the infestation of abusers between 1936 and 1960. If, the recommendations of this report were adhered to, many children would've been spared the emotional pain of the horrific sexual and physical abuse they suffered while in care.

Even though the report found fault with the schools regarding the care and education of the children under the Religious Orders, it agreed that the schools should continue to function but under close supervision. Between 1930's and the 1960's on average 150 children per year were sentenced by the courts to the Industrial Schools throughout the length and breath of Ireland. I believe, once children were placed into care, the Irish State by effect become the guardian to those children and had an obligation towards their welfare and education.

According to the 1936 Report, 87 percent of the children placed in care was due to poverty and not due to criminal reasons as many of us were lead to believe.

In 1970 another State report also verified that the environment in residential schools was unhealthy and unsuitable. This has now brought about the closure of the Industrial Schools and a provision for a safer and healthier environment for children in care.

The 1936 State Report was an in-depth investigation into the care of the children in the Industrial Schools. It questioned the transfer of the children in the court system. The report refers to the food and the silence during the meals, stating that it was unhealthy and should be discontinued, in their opinion it was a harsh and unnecessary disciplinary measure that should be abolished.

It goes on to say that meals were to be of a high nutritional standard supervised by the medical officer in charge of the schools. Standard recommendations were to be given to the schools. No variation to the meals was to be carried out unless recommended by the medical officer. This is a far cry from meals of bread and dripping that many of the victims of abuse have reported!

With reference to the military style drill that took place in the yard, it states that it was unhealthy and should be stopped. The report referred to the use of children as child labourers in many of the Industrial Schools, especially in the ones run by the Christian Brothers and insisted that children should not be used to replace farm labourers. It expressed that the education of the children should be of a recommended standard seen that the Irish State was guardian to the children sent to these schools.

Other recommendations were; that on a quarterly yearly basis the children should be medically checked out by the doctors assigned to the schools. All deaths were to be recorded and any sudden death or violent death had to be inspected by a medical officer. If a child was injured or sick, the parents of that child or the close relatives were to be notified. The school journal was to be inspected by the Inspector from the Educational Department during his visits to the schools.

I also found out from a relative of mine who is now a retired Medical Officer that in 1939, a female doctor was appointed medical inspector of the schools. In one of her reports, she states that she was appalled by the conditions in most of the schools. In 1944, she reported the bread fed to the boys in the Industrial Schools was "mouldy" and some of the children were in rags and barefooted. It'd now seem to me that her reports weren't acted upon and in many cases probably ignored and binned. To date, many of the survivors' memories of their time in care in the Industrial Schools comply with her reports.

Seemly according to a Fine Geal colleague of mine that in 1946 a Monsignor visited Ireland from America. During his visit he was horrified to discover the widespread use of severe physical punishment carried out in the Industrial Schools. Representatives for the two major political parties in a meeting in Dail Eireann criticised the Monsignor's comments. Seemly support for the government objections appeared in the Press in 1946.

In the meantime, I've carried out some research of my own and discovered that the research into the deaths of the children in the Industrial Schools indicates that many of the children in care died from neglect. Survivors of abuse remembered boys who went missing from the school were surprised to hear that these boys had died while in care. The survivors remembered these boys in good health just before they went missing. One survivor who was at Letterfrack Industrial School informed me that his mother wasn't told of the death of his brother or of the funeral 'til it was all over.

Children in the schools were dying of childhood illness such as whooping cough and measles yet no child residing outside the schools were recorded of dying of the same illness. Surly it's a well-known medical fact that these illnesses are contagious. The question now needs to be asked, did the children in the schools die from medical neglect or were these illnesses put on the death certificates to cover deaths from abuse or violence as in the case of that young Joseph Pike in St Joseph's Industrial School for boys in Tralee.

Medical people who knew and witnessed the neglect and abuse of the children in the Industrial Schools and who stood by and did nothing to prevent it, in my opinion broke the Hippocratic Oath.

Truth behold, the people responsible for the running of our Irish State did know the truth regarding the neglect and abuse in our Industrial Schools. Their repeated silence and cover-ups show that they condoned the abuse. Whether we want to accept it or not, the fact is that the Irish State gave the Christian Brothers and other members of the Religious Orders a license to abuse our children.

Questions also need to be asked, why was the 1936 Report not acted upon? Why did our politicians sneer the Monsignor and Medical Officer's reports? Surly if action was taken then our children wouldn't have been abused?

After tracking down some of the people who attended these schools, it would seem, that while some of them didn't encounter any abuse, many others detailed their horrific experiences. It seems to me that it was the children who had no kin that bore the blunt of the abuse.

I've come to realise that things were a lot worse than I thought, I guess only time will tell if the 1970 Report that was carried out in 1967 and presented to the Government in 1970 will make a difference. I guess closing the Industrial Schools is a beginning and seemly the Health Boards are now making a commitment that all children will be looked after in a safer and healthier environment. But I dear say, only time will tell, the outcome of this will only show up in years to come but I desperately hope that we won't have another, out of the frying pan into the fire saga.

The goal of the medieval thinker wasn't to enlighten but to control and the same can be said about the Religious Orders that ran the Industrial Schools in Ireland in the 40's 50's and 60's. But on saying that, it was nothing short of criminal expectation that the Irish State should sent young boys into Industrial Schools and expect Christian Brothers to care for them as replacement parents. During those years it was women who cared for kids, men had no understanding of the emotional needs of young kids and certainly not the Christian Brothers, for many of them were only kids themselves when they were taken from their homes and ordered to join the profession. So, with that in mind, no wonder abuse went on.

Under any pressure you're going to have bullying and abuse and that's human nature. I know it's wrong, but those were the times we lived in. It was an era where women looked after kids and men brought home the bacon!

Well, truth behold, I feel during these decades, many innocent children were sentenced into the belly of the beast.

Sincerely,
Patrick

After reading and emotionally digesting the contents of Patrick's letter, Peg amidst her sadness of the injustice of what happened to her in the past, at this moment in time feels good in some strange way because now she holds written proof of what happened, did really happen. And for the first time in her life, she feels rid of the burden of trying to prove it. Now, people would and could believe her and Sean Og. Now, they both could put the past to rest and get on with their lives. For her, justice has been served, for all she ever wanted in life was, for people to believe her about the abuse that did happen in those awful Industrial Schools in Ireland.

The following Sunday after twelve o'clock Mass, Peg and Jim visit Patrick and his wife Maureen.

"Maureen, ya've a right gala goin' on here today," chuckled Peg making her way into the kitchen and threading carefully over the flagstone floor scattered with toys, books and shoes.

"These are Kitty's kids from across the water, they always home for the summer. Shur, the freedom and fresh air are great for them," replied Maureen clearing up after the Sunday lunch. "Patrick's family remind me of the swallows, they always return to the homestead in the summer time...."

"Com'ere, Johnny," beckoned the kids.

Patrick's kids were having their own fun and games in the cowsheds and Johnny the extra spectator would only add to the excitement of what they were up to. They had set up a betting arena for two legged hen races. They had tied two hens together by the legs and had them racing up and down the shed. There were great shouts of laughter and glee as the hens raced round and round in a small constructed arena made out of hay and straw. They had eight pairs of hens, all racing around at any one time. Odds were given and bets were placed using stones for money. The English cousins just watched on in amazement. To them the antics that their Irish cousins got up to were beyond their wildest dreams and only what they read about in mystery stories. They themselves had never imagined that children really could get up to such mischief in reality. For them, playtime was a skipping robe or bouncing a ball against a wall. But their Irish cousins found fun and joy in the wilderness of the countryside.

Johnny got great mileage out of this fun and insists on racing around with the hens. This of course only adds to the excitement, as Johnny would fall over the straw on his way around the arena.

"Hip, hip hurray for Johnny," the kids yelled out.

"Yaaaa, yaaaaaa," screamed Johnny holding onto his little specs as he races round and around the stack of straw and hay.

Meanwhile, back in the house the adults are enjoying a cuppa and a light-hearted chat about the comings and goings of the local neighbourhood. As the clock ticks away, issues of the past, present and future are discussed. Jim stands up from the table to stretch his legs and while looking out the kitchen window to see if Johnny is anywhere in sight, he spots a grand reek of turf piled up against the west gable of the cowshed.

"That's….a grand aul…..reek of turf….. ya've there," he remarked resting his elbows on the windowsill.

"Indeed it is, the children helped me to get it out of the bog. We had some great harvesting weather last year, had it saved and out of the bog in a matter of a few weeks. Can't do without the turf for the winter. If you're fortunate enough to get a dry batch, it's like money in the bank. Nothing beats a warm glow in the long winter nights," replied Patrick.

Just then he remembers that Peg and Jim didn't have their own bog and they needed to buy in the turf from the local supplier, Tom Morrissey. He is also aware that things weren't too good for the family since Jim was let go at the local creamery.

"Have you got a few days on your hands, Jim? Maybe over the next few weeks or so, I could do with a hand taking the rest of the turf out of the bog. If you have, I could see you right with a trailer of turf in return. How about it?" Patrick asked.

For Jim, this was like a blessing from the Gods. Turf was scarce and the price was certainly to be high this year as most of the farmers were selling it to the Deelis Power Station.

"Yerra Christ that'd be grant, Sean Og will give a hand as well, the turf would be much appreciated this year of all years," replied Jim.

Patrick knew what Jim was referring to, how tough life had become for him since he has tried to find justice for the victims that were abused in the Industrial Schools. Patrick's eldest daughter, who was listening in the background is alerted to the fact that her father is only trying to help Jim by seeing that they have fuel for the winter months, calls her Dad aside.

"Dad we're able to manage the turf, shur there's no need for him to give his time," she whispered.

"Ahhhh shur, I'm well aware of that. But there're times in life when people need help but they're too proud to ask for it or even accept it. That doesn't mean, you turn a blind eye to their needs and not help them. There's always a way around helping people while allowing them to hold on to their dignity," whispered Patrick.

Smiling at her Dad she replies, "ya're the best, love ya," and after giving him a quick peck on the cheek she happily returns to the fun and games in the cowshed.

In his heart, Patrick knew that his children could out manage any farmer in the locality. He always knew that the farm was safe in their care when he was attending the council meetings and dealing with other political issues. They could stack hay, tackle a bog of turf, sell cattle at the local fair and milk cows better than any of the neighbouring farmers. They were always happy and willing to go that extra mile to help others and that was what made Patrick proud to be their Dad. But, he knew also that when it came to mischief his children were certainly to be found right in the middle of it. On the other hand, when it came to responsibility each and every one of them would act in an adult manner and do their best.

Patrick and Maureen were both firm believers that a good education stands to a person in life but they also felt that if they could teach their children to turn their hands at anything then their children could travel anywhere in the world and not fail life. From their own experiences they came to realise that life does not fail people but people fail life by not learning from their mistakes and by hiding or running away from their problems.

Meanwhile, Johnny is overcome with the excitement in the cowshed and runs in to tell his mother.

"Ma, Ma, kum," he yelled, leaping up and down with excitement while tugging at Peg's sleeve.

With that, the adults are curious to find out what excitement beholds Johnny and follow him out to the cowshed. On opening the shed door Patrick couldn't believe his eyes on seeing what he saw.

"Hop out of there the lot of you," he yelled out. "Into to the house to your mother and see what she has to say about all of this."

And with that, there was a scattering of children, hens, straw and feathers from every corner of the shed.

"Kids will be kids," chuckled Jim as he helps Patrick to untie the hen. "I dare say ya ain't be getting' too many eggs over the next few day after this ordeal."

"Well, we never get any eggs to tell you the truth. I just like having the hens around. My mother always had a few, God rest her soul," replied Patrick setting Betty the big brown hen free into the farmyard.

Jim takes a look around the farm. At the farmyard gate the herd of cows had gathered and were waiting to be milked just as they were accustomed to doing so every other evening.

"I see, ye've wan grand-girl in their midst," remarked Jim as he walks amongst them checking out the flow of milk in their udders.

"That's White Horn, she's the grand aul lady of the herd. She has served us well over the years, through good times and bad with her offspring and always guaranteed us a pay cheque every month from the creamery. She has come to her day and now it's our time to look after her," chuckled Patrick as he pats White Horn on the head. "I won't have it any other way, you see Jim, it's amazing how fond of animals a person can become and over the years she has become a cherished member of our family."

"Kids never change, no matter what. Their antics remind me of when I was a young lad meself," Jim said to Patrick making their way back into the kitchen where the kids were trying to justify their innocence with their mother.

Each was trying to out-claim that it was the other one's fault and when that didn't work, then came the usual plea for mercy. "But I only did it 'cause the others were doin' it....."

"A good brisk game of football on the strand will soon sort this gang out," grinned Patrick winking at Maureen. "Come on the lot of you, on with ye'r jackets and boots and get the football for we're off to the White Strand. Shur Jim, why don't you take Johnny along as well and we'll leave the ladies to themselves."

And with that, it wasn't long before seven heads were bobbing up and down in the back seat of the car with Jim in the front passenger's seat and Johnny on his knee. The two men couldn't get a word in edge ways with the chatter and racket from the back seat.

As they drove over the bridge that leads out of Cahirciveen, Jim notices the old railway bridge on the right.

"It's a cryin' shame that the train doesn't come this way any more," remarked Jim.

"Indeed it is Jim, it was a great loss to the area around here. In years to come, I dare say, we'll regret it a lot more, for it'll only be then we'll truly understand its loss. There's going to come a time when the youth will want to live here in Cahirciveen while working away in the outside counties and the rail transport would've been a great asset to them. But I guess like many things in life we've to go without it to appreciate its value," replied Patrick slowing down to acknowledge a few of the town's children who are happily playing football on the roadside. "During the Second World War, the train was certainly God's gift to the locals. There was a great demand for fish, cattle and sheep and the local people were able to source out markets further a field because of the railway line. The railway was a gathering place of sadness and joy. Sadness when people left to find a new life abroad, a place of joy when the fortunate ones returned at Christmas and at hay making time..."

"Yep sadness and joy, that's certainly true," butted in Jim as he points to a large field in the distance. "Ye've hare coursin' up yonder. What do ya think of the coursin' yourself, Patrick. Truth behold, I ain't too gone on it, meself..."

"Well, any sport is okay if it's just and fair to humans and animals and neither are abused. But when the greed to win takes over, it seems that some type of beastly influence beholds the attendees and they become greedy bloodthirsty savages wallowing in the glory of the on slaughter of innocent worn out hares. Now, that to me is very wrong and cruel. Strict laws and regulations will have to come into force to protect the rights of the dogs and the hares. But, for some strange reason the bloodier it is, the more people it attracts, seemly they come from as far as England, Wales and Scotland to attend the coursing here," yawned Patrick wiping the window screen to get a better view of the road ahead.

"Well, when it gets to the bloodthirsty stage I think it should be banned," insisted Jim trying to keep a hold of Johnny as he was up to his usual impish mischief and trying to get into the back seat of the car. "What about the drag hunt, ye've wan of those around here as well."

"Yeah, that's right, it takes place not far from were we live, up the Bachaghs Road in actual fact," replied Patrick looking in the rear view mirror to see what the kids were up to in the back of the car. "I like the drag hunt. I think it's a nice clean sport. A man sets out on the morning of the hunt and he drags a large hunk of rotten meat around after him. As he drags it around over the marshy land and terrain it leaves its scent on his trail. He takes the route that takes him into the forest, across the bogs and back home again. When he returns the hounds are left off to source out the trail and the first hound home wins the prize. It's lovely to watch them source out the scent. Every now and again, one of the younger hounds would take a wrong turning and that'd upset the rest of the pack and take them off the scent. The yelpin' and barkin' of their frustration would be heard far and wide as they try to sniff out the trail once more. But no matter how long it takes, they'll always find their way back home. On the whole it's a nice clean sport and a nice hearty family day out. No blood and no abuse of animals…."

"Except to the poor misfortune fucker who has to pull that great aul hunk of rotten meat," laughed Jim.

"Ach, he doesn't mine, he usually gets a fiver and a few pints of ale for his trouble. But believe it or not, it's said to be an honour to pull that hunk of rotten meat," joked Patrick winking at Jim. "And a member of the same family have done so generation after generation."

"Jim…Jim…Jim," called out one of the kids from the back seat, "I know a poem….. about a hare…..do you want me to recite it for you?"
"Indeed, I would," exclaimed Jim as he entices Johnny to sit up and pay attention.

With that, there was no holding back the young lassie as she recites her poem in all her glory.

The Hare
"So nimble and fearless he hopped through the moor
With such freedom because there was no closed door
The sun shone through the windows of the clear blue sky
And he thought to himself, 'Tis far too good a day to lay down and die.
Such peace that surrounds him makes his little heart ring
In tune to the song that the mockingbirds sing

The fragrance of the flowers makes his little nostrils run
But not before long his long ears pricked up to the bang of a gun.
When he saw some dogs and hunts men come in sight
The aul hare's heart almost stopped with fright
Such screams could only come from the human race
That'd terrorise an innocent aul hare at his early morning pace

His memories of mankind were far from good
Only place left for him was straight to the wood
The howlin' hounds thundered in around him
While the road ahead seemed so dim
Darkness drew around him, yet it was still only day

The mocking bird's song was not very gay
Mighty mouths tore him apart.
While glee was expressed by each human heart

If from the above one lesson could be learned
That God's creatures on earth are here to be loved and not
to be slain
Are human's souls and hearts so empty that they can't find
empathy?
For an innocent aul hare at his early morning pace!"

As she recited the verses one by one in her poetic tone, Johnny listens attentively with his little slanted eyes peering over his specs and a big beaming smile plastered across his bonny face. Just as the last word was recited, he gives a hearty clap and encourages Jim to join in.

"I can see ya're ain't just a pretty face, ya're a clever lass as well and a very clever wan indeed," chuckled Jim looking back at the young lassie and winking at her.

"Well, my Daddy thinks so as well, ya do, don't ya Daddy?" she giggled shyly.

"That I do," winked Patrick as he looks at her in admiration through the rear view mirror.

"I see our rebel boys are out in force again," said Jim resuming his conversation with Patrick.

"Ohhhhh yeah, you're referring to the big sign up at Mountain Stage," replied Patrick waving to one of the locals as he pulls in to the side of the narrow road to let a tractor pass.

"Indeed I am. They've IRA plastered across the mountain cliff and rocks and BRITS OUT across the railway bridge. They're determined lads and will get the message across at all cost. Do ya think, we'll ever have peace up there." Jim was referring to the Northern Ireland troubles.

"Not in my life time. You see, the war in Northern Ireland is unique in itself. It ain't like many other wars that were fought around the world. Many a war is fought because of riches and wealth but this is a war about a belief. A belief, that's inbred into the blood of Irish men, women and children from generations past. Every August a group of blue shirt supporters from South Kerry go to a memorial service for Michael Collins back in Bealnablath. Year after year, the same questions are still asked after the ceremony. Was it friend or foe that shot him down, but more important who was right and who was wrong? I guess the answer to that, Jim, we'll never know. But, from looking at the situation in Northern Ireland his plight has certainly been passed down from hand-to-hand, from father to son as well as from mother to daughter. And many a gunshot has haunted the lives of many an innocent person. When one believes what they're doing is just and right they'll never give up until their mission is accomplished.

We may have agreements, but deep in the heart of some of the people that're involved in their quest for justice in Northern Ireland, there'll never be peace or contentment. Take alone, the conviction of the lads in Long Kesh, look at the strength and honour they feel they're upholding and with a whisper of a hunger strike in the pipeline that alone should tell the British government that these lads can't be silenced and when one is knocked down another will arise in his footsteps. The British government may call them murderers and many others may do so as well, but the IRA see themselves as political prisoners and that's why they see no wrong in bombing or knee capping. It's wartime in their eyes. And they're willing to fight to the bitter end until they achieve what they believe is rightful theirs, In thirty years from now we'll still have agreements signed and argued about…"

"By Christ, ya might be right," muttered Jim biting into his lower lip.

"Jim my dear man, the other thing to remember, where there's war, there's money to be made. You'll always have the person out to make a quick bob out of somebody else's misfortune. Take for instance the money that organizations and bullyboy groups demand from innocent business people as a form of protection. There's big money to be made in crime and for that reason alone some bullyboys who up hold no honour will never want peace in the North," insisted Patrick.

"God, ya're right, ya've somethin' there. I never looked at the situation like that. Do ya know, ya're right, so right Patrick," responded Jim as he tries to hold on to Johnny who is determined to get into the back seat of the car with the rest of the kids.

"Johnny lad, we haven't too far to go now. Look, there's the strand in the distance and look at that big castle in the field," called out the kids in the back seat. "And look over there, do ya see that big mount of stones, that's a fairy fort and fairy ring, that's where the fairies live."

"This place must be steeped in history," said Jim looking around at the local countryside.

"Indeed it is, some of it forgotten and it's such a shame 'cause that's our heritage," replied Patrick stopping at the strand entrance.

"By Christ, there's some amount of small farms around here, ach shur, the average acreage must only be twenty or so," said Jim getting out of the car and looking around at the vast number of small fields that stand out because of the stone fences that separates each one off. "How do ya think we'll fair in the Common Market, will it be of any benefit to us at all?"

"Well it's like this, the Common Market will offer us the cream of the wealth when we join it. Then, when we've settle into our membership, we'll be offered the curd, but when we get too settled in and have practically sold off our Irishness and look upon ourselves as Europeans, all will be left for us is the whey and that'll be the true test of our entrance in the Common Market. We'll then, need to ask ourselves as a nation were we sensible to give way to the aul times for the new and can we afford to live on the whey after having up to two score years of the taste of wealth. Hopefully, all will go well, but only time will tell. But, there's one thing for sure, the aul breed of farmer is dying out and will never be seen again. In 1966 the farmers walked from every part of Ireland to Dublin to be heard and speak out in one voice. It took some of the

Kerry and Cork farmers up to twelve days to get to Dublin and yet when they arrived they waited for days on end, cold, hungry and worn out while sleeping on the footpath outside the gates of Dail Eireann determined to get their story and grievances heard. All this was done in the name of a few extra pennies for a gallon of milk," replied Patrick as he kicks the football across the sandy White Strand and with that the children are off chasing it as their screams of delight out pitch the gullies in the distance.

It was just a few minutes after seven when the gang return home from the strand just in time to milk the cows for the night.

"We'll surely have rain tomorrow, so we'll need to make sure that the ducklings and the young chicks stay in the shed. I think they're far too young to be left out in the yard to survive on their own," Patrick said to the kids as they happily get out of the car one by one eager to attend to their evening chores.

"How do ya know it's goin' to rain?" asked Patrick's eldest daughter.

"Well, it's like this, if the sun goes pale to bed, it'll rain tomorrow it is said. That's what your Grandad always believed and he was never far wrong. He had the gift of looking into the sky and forecasting the weather," chuckled Patrick.

"I'll tell ya another," said Peg. "Wan of the nuns in the Industrial School would say, a mackerel sky means twelve hours dry."

"The aul folk were more in touch with nature, it's such a pity that the wisdom of their ways ain't passed down to the younger generation," said Jim handing a teddy bear to Johnny who at this stage is well worn out from his fun and gallivanting on the strand.

"We'll get on the road," Peg called out to Jim.

"Don't forget your coat Peg, it's hangin' on the banister of the stairs," Maureen called out. "It's a beautiful wan. I often admire your style and fashion."

"Well Maureen, I get all me clothes from parcels from America and I restyle them to suit me figure. Ach shur, ya know ya'rself I'm handy with the aul sewin' machine."

Jim and Peg return home that evening both very satisfied with themselves.

"Maureen is very nice, so down to earth for a councillor's wife," Peg yawned. "God, I feel very weary, aul age must be catchin' up on me."

"They're nice honourable people. I'm glad we made contact with them. Patrick's a trustworthy man. I'm lookin' forward to spendin' a day in the bog with him. The turf will be grand for the winter. He's got great time for his kids. Doc told me last week that Patrick brings them to the Council meetings with him during the summer months. Seemly the kids would happily play in the park just off the Ash Memorial Hall in Denny Street in Tralee while the meetings are goin' on. At lunchtime ya'd find him sittin' in the park with Maureen and kids enjoyin' a flask of tea and sandwich. Now that's what family life is really about. Appreciatin' each other while enjoyin' the simple things in life."

"Life's comin'....together for us....ain't it Jim?" yawned Peg once again as she looks back at Johnny sleeping peacefully in the back seat. "I'm a lucky woman. I've got it all."

"Emm," nodded Jim as he looks back at Johnny through the rear view mirror.

There was a harmonious silence between them for the rest of the journey home. Every now and again Jim would ease his speed as the setting sun clouded his vision of the road ahead. The countryside is in full bloom, which is to be expected for this time of the year. The tourist buses are full to capacity touring the Ring of Kerry. Some of them have pulled in to park on the stretch of road between Darby Bridge and Mountain Stage. This is a popular stopping off spot for the tourists as there is a wonderful view of the Dingle Peninsula. This evening the scenery is spectacular and the view across the bay is truly amazing, for with a pair of binoculars you are able to see the farmers working in the fields along the Doonmanagh and Inch coastline. The mountain sheep mingle amongst the tourists. Cameras are clicking and binoculars are held high. The Americans, whom for their own reasons are all determined to claim their Irishness, exhibit smiles and wave the traffic on. Some would have you believe they were more Irish than American or Canadian even though neither their mothers nor fathers ever stepped on Irish soil. But never the less, if what they believed in their hearts made them feel at ease in the surrounds of this beautiful Irish countryside isn't that all what really mattered?

Sean Og greets them just as they pulled into the boreen that lead up to their home. On seeing Johnny fast asleep in the back seat of the car he remarks,

"I see me squireen is gone to slumber land."

Jim and Peg gave a hearty laugh.

"Had a good day?" he asked, bending down to put the leg of his cream trousers into his sock so as not to get the oil from the chain of the bike on it.

"Yeah, great wan. Off to the pub?" asked Peg.

"Naaaa, off to the village to practice for the tug-of-war, our lads are goin' to beat the shit out of the Cahirciveen buckos this time round. This year it'll be like putty in our hands, we've a great chance, Patsy Bowler is on the team. With muscles like his and a net weight of twenty stone on him without the drink, ahhhh shur, the poor Cahirciveen teams won't have a chance. I can see us now, Patsy on the fallback with his two hefty heels firmly grounded into the soil and his body nicely angled back, half hoisted from the ground, motionless like a drugged up pregnant whale. Then the rest of the team puttin' a nice steady strain on the rope encouragin' the Cahirciveen buckos to build up a sweet sweat and then when they're nicely knackered, we'll stagger them across the line. Leavin' them puffin' and pantin' like shagged out long distant runners. And the crowd all jeerin' and cheerin' hup there ya boyos," giggled Sean Og acting out the strain on the rope.

"Ach shur, I've me money on the Over-the-Water lads, they've the three O' Shea brothers on the team this year. They're well aware that the winnin' of a tug of war ain't about how much weight ya've on the strain of rope but that the stamina and technique of winnin' is in pullin' as a team in harmony with the lad at the back of ya," heckled Jim giving Sean Og a fun loving punch. "Ye could do with an injection of new blood into that crew of yer's. Yerra by Christ, ye'r blood has gone sluggish and it needs a jump start."

"Yerra be whist, keep ya'r money in ya'r pocket and not another word just in case ya puff out bad luck. Peg, what did he gulp yonder in Patrick's for he has the power to turn honey sour. We're on a winnin' streak. I feel it in me waters," jeered Sean Og in his macho cocky form.

"God bless ya'r imagination and optimism," smirked Jim. "Shur, even without Patsy, ye would've a mighty chance any year if ye bothered to stay sober."

"Shur, it's the bloomin' ale that gives ya the strength," giggled Sean Og acting out the pull on the rope once again. "Well anyway, back to more serious matters, I milked Daisy and she's up yonder in the field at the back of the meadow. Buttercup is up there as well and she's certainly gonna calf in the next day or so. Ahhhh, I reckon she's due on or just before the summer solstice. We'll need to keep an keen eye on her, as it's her first time. Peg, the hens are in the shed and Henny Penny is still refusin' to leave the nest even though I've thrown out the glugars, maybe we'd try her with a few fresh eggs. She's very broody, she might hold on and hatch out the next batch, shur, what harm is there in givin' her a second chance…"

"Grand so," nodded Peg. "Shur, we'll do just that."

"Aul Goosy Lucy is sittin' like the Queen Mum above in the hay barn, she was due to hatch out yesterday. I don't think there's anything yet. Shur Peg, ya might need to take a closer look. It's a brave wan that'd take on that bitchy rip. Gee, she gets a fair hump on her if ya try to get near, " chuckled Sean Og and with that he throws his leg over the crossbar of his bike and peddles off into the evening whistling the tune, "A Nation Once Again."

Johnny has no hesitation in going to bed this evening but insists that he kneels down by his bedside to say his night prayers. Johnny takes great pride in reciting the little prayer that Fr. Murphy had taught him during one of his visits and would always insist that Peg sat by his side and recite it aloud with him.

"God bless me home from thatch to floor
While the twelve apostles guard the door
Four Angels glide over me bed
While Gabriel stands at the head
With John and Peter at me feet
All to watch me while I sleep
Now, as I lay down me head to rest
I pray the Lord me soul he'll keep
And if I die before I wake
I pray the Lord me wee soul he'll take..."

Once he is safety tucked in with a good night hug and kiss he is contently on his way to dreamland.

Before Peg settles down for the night she looks in on Goosy Lucy. And to her delight and amazement the goose is off her nest and parading around with nine little goslings. She hisses at Peg as if to say, "these lot ain't for the pot, these nine are mine." Peg approaches the goslings to take a closer look, but Goosy Lucy is having none of it. With a hiss and a flapping of her wing, Peg gets the message and steps back. What Goosy Lucy was really telling her, "ya can gawp but ya can't touch."

"Ayezee does it, my dear lady, I understand. But wait 'til Johnny feasts his investigative eyes on ya'r gaggle, won't he be the happy wee garsun tomorrow mornin'," chuckled Peg.

As she returns back into the kitchen she thought to herself that she must scatter some of the herb valerian that's growing in the back garden around the out-sheds, as she certainly didn't want rats attacking the young goslings. And a compound of sunflowers seeds powdered down and sprinkled around where there is evidence of mice should hopefully kill them off as well.

Chapter Eighteen

Jim And Johnny Return To See Fr. Murphy

Their male bonding sessions give Jim a realisation into the understanding of a priest's life. They build up a deep friendship and Fr. Murphy awakens Jim's interest in spirituality. Jim now understands that you don't need to be religious to be spiritual.

During one of the visits Jim asks Fr. Murphy if he was tempted to have a sexual relationship with a woman. Fr. Murphy tells him that he is a man in priest's clothes who on many occasions grieves the loneliness of his calling and his moments of no longer wanting to be living in the cracks of other people's joys and sorrows. He explains to Jim that it is the power of prayer that gives him the strength of his calling and that he is happy now that he remained loyal to that calling, the calling from God and not that of his church as he puts it.

"Jim, my dear fella, the calling from the church leaves many questions unanswered and many answers that need to be questioned," insisted Fr. Murphy as he strolls around the rose garden with Jim. "Also during my time as a missionary. I've questioned the rulings of my church and its leaders but now realise that many of these rules were made by men and not by God. You see Jim, God doesn't make life difficult, people do."

He goes on to tell Jim about the love he had for a nurse during his time on the missions and how it broke his heart to tell her that nothing could ever become of it.

"Many members of the Religious Orders were a bunch of Pharisees and hypocrites who believed that a loving relationship between two consenting adults was so wrong in the eyes of the Catholic Church yet the abuse of an innocent child was accepted and shunted when someone was brave enough to bring it to the ears of the leaders," he grunted with scorn and resentment in his voice. "Was it, that the life and dignity of a child played such an insufficient role in the Church or are we still engrossed and entwined in pre-Christian satanic rituals, that's a question I often ask myself. The church isn't all about priest and power, it's about God and people embracing life. Too many members of the Religious Orders abused the power that was entrusted upon them by their calling into the church. I now know that power in the right hands is a gift from God but power in the wrong hands can be a dangerous weapon."

"Did ya ever have a sexual encounter with a woman, I mean a real wan, not just a peck on the cheek?" Jim asked as they relax on the garden bench near the water fountain.

Fr. Murphy laughs in amusement.

"I was a lad before I become a priest, and truth behold, a right scamp of a lad some might say. The night before I left for the Seminary, I never slept. I was out on the town all night with a girl called Joan Connor. She went to school with me and as children we shared every dream and fantasy and vowed that we'd marry and have a baker's dozen of kids. We were as thick as thieves through good times and sad ones and would go as far as telling devilish lies to cover up for each other if our parents caught us out in a wee bit of bother. I guess that's what childhood friends are about…"

"Indeed it is," chuckled Jim.

"Well to cut to the chase, that night she tried her utmost to convince me that the priesthood wasn't the road for me. She wanted us to gallivant off to England and get married. Even though, my heart was telling me that she was right, my head told me that I'd to honour the promise my mother made to his Lordship the Bishop. You see, my mother promised that she'd have one of her sons in the priesthood and it happened that I was the youngest and there was no place for me on the family farm. My eldest brother Jack, was allotted the right of becoming heir to that and my sister Kate was to train as a nurse in the Mater Hospital in Dublin. Ach shur, you know yourself, in those days we'd no say in our futures," said Fr. Murphy taking a few short deep coughs to clear the phylum from the back of his throat. "Our fate was at the mercy of our parents and in my case the Bishop who happened to be a distant relative of my father. Well anyway, Joan my good loyal friend was determined to break me into my manhood and that night we both lost our virginity at the back of the public toilets. Looking back now, it certainly wasn't the most purist place to lose one's virginity but it was there the unity of hearts took place. I don't regret it, both of us got lost in a moment in time and I guess it was meant to be. That was my first and last time I had a sexual encounter with a woman. But I guess if you asked me did I masturbate and I answered no, then I'd be lying…"

Jim just nodded and smiled.

"In the Seminary the lads were lads, some of them had intimate moments with each other and in later years some of them reluctantly admitted to having gay tendencies. That never appealed or enticed me. I never had the urge to get intimate with another man. Some of them would even go as far as flagellating themselves. When I took my final vows, I still had the urge to look at beautiful woman but I stayed loyal to the cloth. Well, that's if you don't consider sexual fantasies, I'm human under my collar after all. And, if that doesn't count, I've indeed stayed loyal to God and myself. Although, I don't think asking a priest to abide by his vow of celibacy is necessary a good thing. I think if Priests, Nuns or Christian Brothers were allowed by the Catholic Church to get married, you'd certainly have more contented members in the Religious Orders. But maybe in time, the Church will see its way to granting such a privilege to its chosen few but on saying that, I guess it'll never happen in my lifetime…"

"Would ya say that demandin' celibacy and chastity within the Religious Orders had somethin' to do with the abuse of young innocent kids in the Industrial Schools?" asked Jim, now caught up in this intimate conversation, "Could it be that they took out their sexual frustration on the kids that were placed in their care?"

"Good God no," replied Fr. Murphy in horror. "That abuse that went on, was just pure evil and malice, that had nothing to do with celibacy or chastity, that had to do with the actions of a few evil men and woman. No excuses can be made to cover up the horrific wrongdoings of those evil people. The abusers are shameless Godless people who hide under the umbrella of Catholicism and who by their evil actions alone condemn and insult the spirit and morals of our Church. They'll be the cause of our Church falling apart. And they'll tear it down stone-by-stone if they don't put their wrongdoings to right…."

"Would ya not think that maybe the Church needs to fall apart to out-root the evil and start afresh?" asked Jim straightening the peak of his cap.

"You might be right. Maybe it's time for the church to be less Catholic and more Christian, I don't know Jim, I don't have the answers for they lie in the hands of the next generation. I guess time will tell," muttered Fr. Murphy picking a three leaved clover and sapping out the juices between his fingers.

During their visits, Johnny grows very fond of Fr. Murphy. While working in the Congo as a missionary, Fr. Murphy had learned to be a ventriloquist and this fascinates Johnny, as he honestly believes that the puppets that Fr. Murphy kept in his bedside locker were talking to him. One of the verses that the puppet of Pinocchio recited that really grips Johnny's attentions is,

Happiness.
Happiness is a gift from God.
If you look you'll find it near.
You'll can find it in the swimming cod.
Or in the bright eyed passing deer!

Happiness is the song that the
Early bird sings.

It is a smile from a child.
A scream of glee!
Happiness is there for you and me.

Happiness is the seed that makes love grow
It energises a rainbow as the sky dips low
It is the contentment that helps men rest
Happiness is the root of every life's success.

Happiness germinates in the hearts of all men.
Just as it flourishes in the clucking hen!
It is a flowering meadow at it's best.
Life without Happiness can be such a pest!

And when Fr. Murphy recited each verse time and time again Johnny would sit there with a great big grin imitating the actions of the puppet as Fr. Murphy guided it around the room. The Nurses and patients also grow very fond of Johnny and give him little treats. During their visits Johnny has some challenging questions about God and the Holy Family for Fr. Murphy to answer. Fr. Murphy finds the curiosity and the imagination of a child's mind both educational and amusing.

Chapter Nineteen

Bees Swarming

"My dear laddie, ya're in top gear this mornin," Jim called out to Sean Ogwho is happily whistling to himself while kicking Johnny's deflated football around the farmyard.

"Ach shur, I'd a grand aul supeen of ale in me belly last night and me head and me heart are high on it still," giggled Sean Og to himself as he picks up Sally by her two front paws and in rhyme to his whistling takes her in waltzing sweeps across the yard. "I supped a aul mug of strong coffee with a half a lemon and three teaspoons of honey just as the dawn chorus was startin' up this mornin' and that has kept the hangover in toe and now a good swift cycle should set me in top gear for the day."

"Was there some cerebration in the village last night?" asked Jim.

"Naaaa, just a few of the lads and meself went a wee bit crazy for the heck of it. The Killorgin fellows were hither and we'd a right bit of craic amongst ourselves and that was good enough reason for me to enjoy the antics of the moment," chuckled Sean Og wiping his brow with his back of his hand. "Gee, me head still aches from laughin' me cacks off with the craic that was goin' on..."

"If Peg finds out that ya've spend all ya'r hard earned cash on ale she'll have somethin' to say about that," smirked Jim.

"Ach, even thought I still gummin' for wan pint to cure the hangover, I'll be well out of it before she cast her naggin' eyes on me. I'll need to look in at the bees over the next few days and clip the queen's wings. I don't want them to swarm, for it'd be a pity to lose them. There's a good strong hive up in the back meadow and hopefully with the summer we're in for, God willin' we'll get a good larder of honey this year, " said Sean Og while patting Sally on the head as she bounces off in the direction of Johnny.

Jim looks up into blueness of the June sky and the high altitude of the clouds tell him that the day ahead is going to be a scorcher. For as the old saying goes, clouds that float high will soon run dry.

"They may come out today, I'll keep an eye on them in case they'll swarm. Have ya a hive ready to nest them should they decide to take flight?" asked Jim taking off Johnny's jumper and asking him to take it into the kitchen.

"I've set wan up in the orchard. But hopefully they won't. I'll give the frames a good goin' over tomorrow and knock off any queen cells. That'll keep them at bay," muttered Sean Og strapping his flask and sandwiches to the carrier of his bike and off he peddles in the direction of the village.

Jim is to keep an eye on Johnny for the day as Peg has planned to go over yonder to Tom Kelly's to give a hand with the meals. Tom has a few lads building an extra wing onto the hay shed and with Tom's wife due to give birth to their tenth child any day now, all willing hands are greatly appreciated. Peg would normally take Johnny across with her but he is for some unknown reason going through one of his impish moods and he is sure to get into a bit of bother. Today he is in a right minx so Jim felt the way to handle him is to keep him busy. Feeding the hens, gathering eggs, taking Sally for a walk and getting him to help out with the weeding of the front flower patch should be enough to keep him occupied or so Jim thought.

At mid-day, Jack, the next-door neighbour drops in to borrow a shovel. But Jim knew in his heart that it's really only a chat he has come for. He is still grieving for his wife Siobhan. She had passed away just over a year ago. Over the years of marriage she had become his life and soul. Jim gets lost in conversation with him. Now Johnny being as glic as a fox, knew in his gut feeling that this is his opportunity to slip away with Sally and it isn't long before the two bosom companions bonding in each other's existence make their way through the farmyard and up into the back meadow. Sally and Johnny have a true understanding of each other and over the years looked out for each other with their instinctive eye. Sally was just a puppy when Johnny was born and she would sit by his pram and bark if a stranger dared to come near. If Johnny was to get into mischief over the years, Sally had a way of informing you by her strange whimper. Johnny's first words were not Mama or Dada but woof, woof. As the old saying goes, a dog is a man's best friend and this was certainly true in Johnny's case.

Johnny's greatest joy on a summer's day was to run through the wild flowers that grow in the meadows with Sally barking at his heals trying the catch the odd butterfly in flight. When the daisies were out in full bloom, he would sit for hours making daisy chains for Sally and also for Nancy the goat and should Betty the big brown hen or Goosy Lucy happen to cross his path, they too were honoured with a daisy chain. In Johnny's world, the animals and poultry were creatures to befriend and he had an amazing insight into understanding their ways and temperaments. It wasn't unusual for him to lie down among the daisies and buttercups searching for the ladybirds and grasshoppers.

From Peg he had learned that nature takes care of the garden and vegetables in its own way. She is a firm believer that one could have a wonderful productive garden by introducing certain creatures and insects into it to eat up the invaders or what she herself would call, the non-desirables. She maintained that frogs would eat the slugs and other insects. A hedgehog would take care of millipedes and slugs. The ladybird, which is her favour of all insects, would eat the aphids that greedily fed on her brassicas and the birds would see to the slugs and snails that embedded themselves under her lettuces. She would grow onions beside the carrots and it wasn't unusual to get the odd sniff of stale stout around the rows of the young onions and leeks. Every year the spring cabbages were surrounded with a row of onions and foxgloves as Peg's mother was of the belief that this would keep rabbits away. And in between the rows of young seedlings she would lay layers of newspapers and as the slugs gathered on the papers she would destroy them with salt. So, from watching Peg gardening and becoming acquainted with her ways it isn't unusual for Johnny to gather ladybirds, spiders, frogs and even the odd hedgehog to support Peg's psychology.

After spending some time filling his pockets he is suddenly alerted to a noise that is strange yet familiar to him. As he perks his head above the meadow grasses he could see a dark cluster hovering over him. Sally was now barking as if to tell him that danger was lurking. For a moment he is blinded from the glare of the sun as he looks up into the sky trying to make out what the dark shape hovering over him, really was. In the excitement of the moment he loses his little specs. As he crawls his way out of the long grasses searching for them, his surroundings are overcome with the buzzing that brings him to his senses.

"A twom...... a twom," he yelled and with that he is up on his little legs and running as fast as his little feet could carry him. Sally is in his footsteps barking and jumping around in circles trying to release the stings from her tail.

Jack is just about to leave and from the distance he hears Johnny bawling.

"Da, twom. Da twon."

"Jim me good man, I think Johnny's in a wee bit of bother," insisted Jack pointing up yonder to the meadow. With that Jim dashes up towards to Johnny.

"Good lad, take it ayezee, I'm here now," hushed Jim as he tries to comfort Johnny and ease his sobs and gags of fear.

Johnny continues to bawl out, "twom, twom,"

"It's okay son, no harm done. I'll sort it out, but ain't ya the clever bucko to spot it," grinned Jim as he continued to reassure Johnny. "And what've we got here?" Jim was referring to the grasshoppers, daddy-long-legs, ladybirds and a small frog in Johnny's pocket.

"Pa.. pa..tents for Maa," replied Johnny now feeling more at ease and recovering from his ordeal in the meadow.

How am I goin' to manage this wan, Jim thought to himself. Collect a swarm of bees while keeping Johnny happy and occupied in such a way that he won't have time to get into mischief. If he left him down in the kitchen he was sure to get into trouble. If he left him with Sally there was no telling what the pair of them would get up to. And if he brought him to collect the swarm he was sure to get stung.

God, he thought to himself, this predicament reminds me of the story where the farmer had to cross a river with a fox, a goose and a bag of corn. The boat was only big enough to take one of them across with him at a time. If he brought the goose and bag of corn across and left them on the bank while he went back to collect the fox, the goose was sure to eat the bag of corn. If he brought the fox and goose across and left them on the bank the fox was sure to eat the goose. Now, Jim was left to solve his equation. Haha, he thought I've the very thing, a packet of jelly. Peg usually kept one at the back of the cupboard just in case they were going to have visitors on a Sunday afternoon. Custard and jelly was a sure hit with most people and Peg's custard was so thick that you never went home hungry. If Peg needed to get some knitting or sowing done in the afternoon, a section of strawberry jelly was sure to keep Johnny content and chewing for an hour or so.

"Johnny, me good fella, com' with me, I've a lovely treat for ya," grinned Jim fetching the packet of jelly from the back of the cupboard.

Then hand-in-hand they both ramble off up to the meadow, each contently knowing in their heart they were both winners. After all, Jim was going to get his swarm and Johnny his fill of jelly. Having tied Sally to a bush and given her a bone from the Sunday roast to chew on, he then settled Johnny up with his treat and sets off to conquer the swarm. Jim was used to attending to bees over the years and the odd sting or two didn't bother him too much. In a strange sort of a way, he welcomed the sting because an old farmer told him years ago that bee stings would keep arthritis at bay.

Johnny wasn't to bothered about waiting on his Dad while he attended to the swarm and once he had his fill of jelly, he was content to sit and wait, busily picking off sciotans and fineogs from his legs and arms that he had picked up while he was rolling around in the meadow grasses earlier with Sally.

The swarm had settled on the upper outer branch of the oak tree at the corner of the meadow. Jim is happy with this, as it would not create any problems for him. Turning to take one last look out for Johnny just to make sure that all is going as planned, he climbs up the tree and carefully bends across positioning the skep under the swarm that was made out of last years barley straw. And then, with a good firm toss of the branch he knocks the swarm right into the skep.

"Ayezee....does it....now," he mumbled to himself. The bees are buzzing around him, some pretty confused with the situation and more angered by the disturbance. Once he gets his feet firmly on the ground he upturns the skep and positions a stone at the corner of it to allow the confused bees into the Queen. The few remaining bees in flight around the branch soon make their way into the skep.

"That's.... a job...well done," Jim thought, chuffed with himself that all had gone to plan as he makes his way over to the other hives. The colony of bees seems to be content and the pollen flow is certainly to put a smile on any beekeeper's lips. It is a sure sign of the jingle of more coins in a homemaker's purse. It also indicates that more suppers are needed to keep the worker bees happy and productive. As he stands there for a moment listening to the bees humming, the croaking of the frogs, the birds chirping, the goats bleating and the sound of the stream as it ripples its way through the drain that separated the two meadows just up yonder, he couldn't help thinking to himself that he is one of the privileged few who has discovered nature's orchestra.

After collecting Sally and Johnny, he happily makes his way back to the house. On the way back he gives Johnny a firm warning that on no account is he to go near the bees. Settling into a nice cup of tea and a slice of apple tart he recites the verse to Johnny

"A swarm of bees in May is worth a cock of hay
A swarm of bees in June is worth a silver spoon.
But a swarm of bees in July ain't worth a fly."

Jim patience is put to the test, as he wasn't prepared for Johnny's insistence to having the verse recited over and over again.

That evening, just as the sun is going down, Jim places a board covered with a white sheet at the entrance to the new hive that Sean Og had prepared earlier on during the week. Having collected his swarm from the meadow he shakes them out onto the board and stands back as they happily make their way up the board into their new home. Time and time again this action of the bees always fascinates Jim and brings home to him the miracle of nature. One or two of the drones hover around him in close flight as if to say, "ta, ta."

Before retiring for the night, Jim looks out yonder onto the valley and thanks God for the mild misty May and the calm warm June and as the old saying goes, mist in May followed by heat in June, makes the harvest come right soon!

Chapter Twenty

A Relaxing Day In The Bog But No Escaping The Past

Up in the bog in Gurteen, just a few miles out of Cahirciveen, Patrick has asked a local jobber to leave a trailer. All they have to do is fill the trailer with turf and the local jobber will collect it on route home from the Cahirciveen Fair on Friday and deliver it to Jim's doorstep.

There is a refreshing breeze stirring throughout the bog adding comfort to the heat of the sun. The three men had an early start for they knew that coming up to midday the sun is sure to be at its best and the more work they could put in before noon the less physical effort it would take to work in the heat of the afternoon. The bog beholds its own wonderland in summer time. The bog-cotton is out in full bloom and the heather with its rustic colouring compliments the blackness of the turf banks in the background. The reeks of slean turf stand proud and have greater architectural compaction than the sausage machine turf. Somehow, the farmers didn't take the same pride when it came to reeking up the machine turf, but then on the other hand, maybe that had to do with the length and compaction of the sods.

The corncrake can be heard in the background and the dragonflies hover around the water holes. Puffs of smoke from the small scattered turf fires that the farmers used to boil the kettle and maybe with the odd egg wanders off into the sky throughout the stillness of the day. For a lonely person, the isolation of the bog is no place to be, but for the contented man, woman or child it's certainly to compliment their aloneness. For it's one place on this earth that you are sure to experience an oneness with yourself and nature. Jim always had a fascination for birds and is surprised to see a kestrel hovering around the rough grasses in the distance. Throughout the morning, it would come closer and hover in flight around the trailer. In the distance the cawing of the crows disturbs the silence of the day. A fox stops to stare as it makes its pathway across the rough turf banks and isn't too disturbed by the human presence that invades his terrain. Scattered throughout the bog, stumps of bog oak stand proud adding an architectural profile to the surrounding wilderness. All in all, the man who has befriended nature would have you know that to him the bog could be classified as a wonderland that is enriched with a unique serenity in its remoteness. It is certainly a place where one can have the ability to eliminate thoughts from one's mind and yet be totally aware of the world around.

The heat of the day forced the men to strip off to the waist. Sean Og is somehow reluctant to do so. When Patrick suggests that he takes off his shirt and let the fresh air to his body he replied.

"Ahhhh Christ, I'm unable to let the sun to me back because it'll agitate me skin. After the trashin' I received from the Christian Brothers at the age of ten, shur Christ me back was never the same again. They lashed me to a pulp and it took months to heal. Truth behold, I don't know whether it was the beatin' or the iodine troubled me most. For weeks afterward, the nurse plastered me with zinc and iodine. God, it stung deep into me bones. Ya see Patrick, the Christian Brothers would take young lads from their beds, make them remove their clothin' and whip them with a leather strap. I happened to be wan of those misfortunate lads...."

"Fuck'in hell...... what?" exclaimed Patrick.

"When I was detained in that school I was accustomed to wettin' me bed if I was nervous or worried. It all happened on the day when the inspector called to the school. We'd had prepared for weeks in advance and everythin' had to be just right for his arrival. The clever lads were put to the front of the class and the rest of us were to stay stump in the background. I was huddled up in the back row and it was just me misfortunate luck that the school inspector asked me the question on sums. In the shock and dismay of it all, I was dumbstruck and was unable to answer the question. The inspector wasn't too bothered at the time. He stood by me desk and explained the answer. I was scared shitless, so frightened that I started to get flustered and began stammerin'. For the life of me I couldn't understand what he was tellin' me. All he replied was, ayezee boy, steady now. I didn't get to where I'm today because I knew all the answers. I too, had to be shown everythin' when I was a wee garsun, just like you. You do know Rome wasn't built in a day. When he left to inspect the other classes, the Christian Brother in charge came back into the room and gave me a wallopin' across the head. He left me in no doubt that I'd remember the answer forever more. All day, I knew I was in for a crucifixion...."

"Mother.....of....Jaysus," muttered Patrick under his breath.

"Ya see Patrick, waitin' for the lashin' was worse than the lashin' itself. And I'm in no doubt that the Christina Brothers were well aware of that. Young lads would bawl more durin' the waitin' of the beatin' than durin' or after the beatin' itself. Well to cut to the chase, it was about midnight when I heard the heavy footsteps come to the dormitory door. With the fright I pissed meself. As the footsteps came closer across the dormitory floorboards and echoed through the room, I shitted meself as I trembled and whined. I'd no control over the fear in me body at all. Ach shur, didn't I know well what was in store for me. Me mercy was now in the hand that controlled that almighty big leather strap. The Christian Brother grabbed a hold of me by the ear and dragged me out of me bed. All he kept roarin' was, 'ya dirty filthy swine, get out here ya dirty ignorant swine'. The other boys in the dormitory were instructed to follow. I can still hear the Brother howlin' at them as they cowardly shuffled out behind me. I was made bend over fully naked on the bottom steps of the staircase. Wan of the Christian Brothers stood over me with his feet on me out spread hands while the other lashed me from behind with his leather strap. The huddled inmates gawpin' on were asked to count the blows. Their tremblin' shriekin' voices still taunt me. The Brother who was holdin' me down by standin' on me hands roared at the huddled frightened inmates, 'louder, louder,' and the louder they yelled the stronger the lash I received. Seemly, I received fifteen lashes of the leather strap. Well that's what wan of the inmates told me. After the tenth lash, I was out of it and woke up in the sick dormitory the next mornin'. Me flesh red raw and I lay there whimperin' like an injured puppy. The scars never fully healed and if I happen to get the sun on them at all, they give me grief. There was that time in England on the buildin' site when the skin peeled off the scars and the Irish chippies would joke amongst themselves, here comes the Irish diulach from the concentration camp, which meant the Irish boyo from the concentration camp."

Patrick and Jim just stood with mouths opened and a look of horror on their faces.

"Fuck'in evil bastards," muttered Patrick. "They were bad evil bastards to do that to a child."

"Ahhhhh well, that was the past and I came through it. I'm here to tell me tale of woe. Many other lads weren't as fortunate. Thinkin' back now on me time across the water in England, I met up with a chap in a pub wan night and he too claimed to be reared in the Industrial School in Tralee. Seemly, he was wan of the specials who happened to be badly abused. He was transferred to the school when he was only a toddler. His mother absconded with another man and left the family in the care of the court. So I guess truth behold in those days both families and State were off loadin' kids into those schools and expectin' the Religious Orders to take over guardianship of them. I don't like speakin' about it 'cause they're memories I'd rather forget but it's hard to put them to rest when I've the scars to remind me. I guess, when the Christian Brother said 'ya'll never forget the answer again,' he certainly made sure of that," sniffled Sean Og and spitting the phlegm out onto the turf-dust.

"Mother of Jaysus, how did you come through it at all and come out sane?" asked Patrick picking up a piece of bog cotton and chewing on the stem.

Sean Og continues to load up the turf into the trailer and with head bent low responds in a quiet voice.

"Well, I don't like to feel sorry for meself, ya see when I start feelin' sorry I've me bad days. I do me best to look on the good side of life and after all, I've a lot to be grateful for now as I've found a nice life for meself with Jim and Peg."

"By Christ, aren't you entitled to feel sorry for yourself. I don't know if I'd have coped in your situation. It was well known that when it came to the Christian Brothers and discipline they were hard tough men. My experience with them hasn't left me with too many cherished memories either. We all feared the strap and getting our heads shoved into a trough of water, but other than that, I don't ever remember any of the boys been sexually abused. Although on saying that, you never knew what went on behind the scenes. There was a lot of blackguardly going on when it came to the less fortunate lads. I can tell you they'd one rule for the rich and another for the less fortunate. Your fate all depended on your parents. Who they were and what they had," said Patrick shaking his head and taking out a handkerchief from his back trousers pocket to wipe the sweat of the day from his brow.

"I'm beginnin' to think that they sent all the fuck'in crazzzzy Christian Brothers into those Industrial Schools," shrugged Jim firing a few more sods of turf into the trailer. "When I was talking to Fr. Murphy last week, he was sayin' that it seems that there was a sheltered paedophile ring within the Christian Brothers and that they'll continue to shelter it for years to come. I meself think that it was some crazzzzy pre-Christian ritual they were practicin'. What do ya think Patrick?"

"Well, if someone laid a hand on one of my kids the way the Christian Brothers handled the lads in the Industrial Schools, I'd have them hung, drawn and quartered and would happily do time for it. When I think back over my school going days and in the history classes they drummed into us that Ireland was the island of Saints and Scholars, how wrong…...they….fuck'in….were. Seemly, from what I've found out about the abuse that went on in the Industrial Schools and the Magdalene Laundries we were just an island of sinners and Pharisees lead by a bunch of hypocrites on bended knee," insisted Patrick spitting out the chewed stem of boy cotton. "The horrific hardships of your childhood must affect you now in your daily life, Sean Og. I think you're an amazing fella to have coped with what you'd to cope with….."

"Did ya ever confide in a Priest at the School regardin' the abuse?" asked Jim.

"Well, truth behold, I did, actually it was in confession and that very same night I was dragged from me bed and given another wallopin' with that big leather strap from a Christian Brothers for tellin' horrific lies and committin' a grievous mortal sin in the holiness of the confession box. I was ordered to kneel naked at the end of me bed in front of the other inmates and recite ten decade of the rosary for me penance while beggin' God for forgiveness. The Christian Brother who gave me the wallopin' stood over me and told the lads that I was a sinful evil boy who'd meet my damnation in the eternal fires of hell for me terrible lies. In me heart, the only sin I committed was that I told the truth but nobody would believe me…."

"Fuck'in……hell," muttered Patrick.

"Years later, when I spoke to a lad that attended the school with me, he told me that he was sexually blackguarded by that very same priest," sighed Sean Og sitting up against the reek of turf and taking a sod in his hand and breaking it bit-by-bit. "I don't know if I'd honestly say I'm copin' with the past. I guess I've managed to push it to the back of me mind. I'm only truly glad that

Johnny will never experience the MARK. There're nights I suddenly awake from a deep sleep, all cold and clammy. Me heart throbs with the feelin' that I'm goin' to die while strugglin' to get me breath. It's the flash backs from the past that taunt me. I keep a night-light burnin' throughout the night. I don't trust the dark. I guess somewhere in me head I fear that somewan will come and sexually abuse me. Night in and night out, I never close the curtains in the room as the light of the night sky gives me peace of mind. Doc has me on tablets for the anxiety and depression. I take them every day and I feel they help me to look on the sunny side of life. He's great. I feel I can talk to him about it. Of course Peg's experience was just as horrific as mine. But on the whole I suppose, as the years pass I've found great peace in nature. I love workin' out in the openin' air. I don't like to be confined. Emotionally, I feel trapped indoors and always need an escape hatch. That's why I've the half door on the house. Havin' it opened gives me a sense of security of an access to an ayezee get away. I don't know what I'm runnin' away from but it gives me peace of mind anyway. Doc says if it gives me ease of mind, then it can only be good."

Sean Og went silent for a while and the sound of the corncrake could be heard in the distance. The gentle breeze that now gave coolness to the moment gently disturbed the stillness of the bog cotton. Sitting erect and looking ahead into the distance he continues in a disturbed tone of voice.

"Everythin' about those fuck'in men that abused us was horrible because they wanted only for themselves. We were there in their eyes to be used and boy-o-boy did they do just that. They stole our integrity and our childhood. They broke us down rib-by-rib and nerve-by-nerve until we were of the belief that we were no good. It took years for me to accept that I was an okay fella. Actually, it was Doc who helped me realise that. Because of me days in that Industrial School and the abuse I suffered, I've developed a fear and hatred of the Christian Brothers, Doc calls it xenophobia. He tells me that it's natural under the circumstances of me experiences. To think back now, me name became a whisper in the schoolyard while I became accustomed to respond to the call of a number. I guess if the lads and I didn't keep our names alive by whisper our Christian names would've become a memory on some courtroom wall or in an aul file in an educational department. It's very hard for anywan who didn't experience sexual abuse to truly understand what it does to the core of wan's spirit. Night after night, on hearin' their heavy foot steps crossin' the dormitory wooden floorboards, me lips would quiver and me belly would tremble knowin' that the rottenness of their marrow was about to enter and infest mine…"

Once again there was a deep silence and Patrick was totally bewildered by what Sean Og just told him and how right he was, how could he truly understand what a victim of sexual violence feels or goes through when he himself had never found himself in that situation.

"What hardness of heart beheld them, but in reality they were cowards. They attacked the most vulnerable, the children. And they're still cowards today, skittering around and hiding away from the truth. A real man faces up to his wrongdoings. A coward is a sneak that will run and hide, lie and deny their wickedness and wrongdoings. These men seemly had an addiction for an obsessive self-passionate greed within their moments of wroth and relieved their anger and frustrations by beating and sexually assaulting children. You mentioned the word MARK, what's that?" asked Patrick spitting out the chewed stem of bog cotton.

"That's the name we give to what happened to us in the Industrial Schools. It stands for The Massive Abuse Regarding Kids. Anyway that's enough of those morbid memories for wan day, I guess I should count meself fortunate, after all, I lived to tell me story. Ahhhh shur, me good friend Joseph Pike wasn't so fortunate. The Brother responsible for his death beat the livin' daylights out of his sick body 'til there was no more life left to live. The Christian Brothers covered up this man's horrific actions. And Joseph is now buried with the secret conspiracy concernin' his death. The truth will never be proven and they fuck'in made sure of that. It upsets me when I think back over those days," sighed Sean Og walking toward the car and reaching for a basket in the back seat. "How about a sup of tea? Peg put in a flask and a few buttered scones. I think there's a nice piece of apple tart in the bottom of the basket as well. I've always been of the opinion that a good cuppa makes big problems seem small and I can guarantee ya that Peg's cuppas have sent many a trouble on it's way."

"Yerra Patrick, shur there was nary a wan the kids in those schools could turn to for help. Mother of Jaysus, it's hard to believe that so-called good quality people could be so evil," whispered Jim to Patrick.

"Much of the evil and malice that exists in our society today has germinated and propagated from above. Its roots have nothing to do with the common folk. It's like a stalactite in a cave, it's frozen hard to the core and deeply rooted from above. It has weaved its way into society from the minds of the so-called quality people in so-called respectable positions in life. And remember, just because they go about reading good quality newspapers that certainly doesn't make them good quality people. The common folk have often come out the worst for the conspiracies and cover-ups of these so-called quality people," huffed Patrick gathering up a few sods to make seats for the lads.

After enjoying the cup of tea and putting the world to right the three men decide it's time to be heading home to attend to the farmsteads. On the way home they stop off at Carhan Bridge, as Sean Og wants to look around the ruins of the birthplace of Daniel O'Connell. A man better know to the locals as the Liberator. Sean Og remembers how in the Industrial School the Christian Brother took great pride in informing the young boys that Daniel O'Connell was a remarkable man who through his own courage, perseverance and political knowledge took on the British and fought for the rights of Catholics in Ireland. As the three men stand gazing at the wonders of history that bestrode this stone ruin, they are in one agreement that it's a shame to allow it to fall down as year-by-year and stone-by-stone the memories of this noble man were drifting off into the past.

"Looking back on our heritage, Daniel O'Connell was truly a remarkable man, born here in 1775 and who went on to be a lawyer and stood alone to lead the Irish people in the fight for their cultural identity and their right to claim back, their right for their Irishness, to be Irish. He was one of Ireland's greatest sons and one might say that he'd the sharp wit of a razor blade, the heart of a dove and the strength of an ox embodied in the courage of a lion. He was certainly a man that feared no one when it came to fighting injustices. He strived to rejuvenate the spirits of many an Irish man, woman and child by restoring dignity and knowledge to them after so many years of being downtrodden by the English who'd reduced them to a beastly state of existence...."

"A... wonderful... son.. of Ireland," mumbled Sean Og.

"That he was indeed and he'd have you know," sighed Patrick biting his lower lip. "Tír gan teanga, tír gan anam."

"Byjoe, ya certainly right there," nodded Jim. "A country without a language, is indeed a country without a soul..."

"Yep, that's what Daniel O'Connell believed. In 1847 he breathed his last while dying of a broken heart. It is said, that doctors attending him couldn't cure him and on his deathbed his final wish was that his heart should be parted from his body and left to rest in Rome while his body was to be returned to Ireland and buried amongst the dust of his ancestors. Sadly thought, truth behold 'twas his own people that left him down as they were influence by bribes of money and false promises of noble titles from a crooked English Parliamentary Minister," said Patrick picking up a stone from the ruin and holding it in his hand. "It's amazing to think, so many years ago, a mother gave birth to a most prominent man and yet, it all started out in this humble natural surrounds. There you've, the small mountain Bi na Ti to one side, Cnoc na Tobair mountain in the distance and Carhan River rippling its way through the marshy countryside. And while she laboured, little did she realise that she was to give birth to a son that'd change the course of Irish History. I guess we all have a purpose in life, it's just that so many of us fail to listen to that purpose as we pass through our adult years….."

"Ya're probably right Patrick, too many of us run and scramble through life and don't ever accomplish what we're meant to do," replied Jim strolling down to the river to see if there are any fish jumping. "Would ya catch the odd aul fish in here, Patrick?"

"Ach shur, you might catch the odd one alright," nodded Patrick dipping his foot into the water. "But you'd have to go up yonder to get a salmon. A few of the locals would quietly do the odd bit of poaching every now and again…."

"I'd say, that wouldn't go down to well with the river bailiff," grinned Jim.

"Indeed it doesn't, but they've their own way of working things out, let's say they've an unwritten understanding," giggled Patrick to himself stooping down to test the coolness of the river with his hand.

"Sheeeee, whist," insisted Sean Og looking over yonder. "Ain't that the cuckoo? God, believe it or not, this is the first time I've heard it so close this year…"

"Byjoe, that's right," said Patrick listening attentively with squinted eye and head erect. "That's the cuckoo right enough and it's coming from the oak tree over yonder."

"I remember in the Industrial School we learned a poem about the cuckoo and we'd recite it out loud. Ach shur God love us and save us from all harm, we got great mileage out of that poem. Yerra, I must have been only seven years old or so," chuckled Sean Og to himself.

"Did it go like this?" asked Jim, "Cuckoo, cuckoo what do ya do?"

And before he could recite another word Patrick and Sean Og joined in,

"In April, come I will.
In May, I sing all day.
In June, I change me tune.
In July, I get ready to fly.
In August, go I must."

And with that, the three men were overcome with fits of laughter.

"Be Jaysus, maybe the Christian Brothers did teach us somethin' useful after all," laughed Sean Og.

After a few minutes of boyish antics they revert back to the their historical conversation of local politics.

"There's a famine workhouse around here as well Patrick," said Jim picking off the petals of a large daisy and allowing them to float off down Carhan River.

"Indeed there is, not too far from here, just up the Bachagh Road. Its ruin still stands proud. It's hard to believe that as far back as 1848 when Ireland was doomed with the Great Famine, hundreds of men, women and children died on their way to the many workhouses that were scattered through length and breath of Ireland. There's a small narrow road leading up to it and it's known as the Paupers Road. It's said that during the time of the Irish famine the corpses of starved bodies were to be found along that roadside, day in and day out, many of them with grass stained tongues. It was a time when the strongest of the Irish set out in their throngs as exiles across the ocean in Coffin Ships to America, hoping for a new life and intending to rebuild Ireland from abroad. Those that were fortunate enough to survive the horrific voyage stayed faithful to their word and sent dollars back home to their loved ones they left behind struggling to make a meeker existence on the Irish sod," said Patrick picking up a handful of soil. "How many of us take time out to appreciate the fact that this soil had fed, so many mouths in the past and will continue to do so long after we've died. But ironically, we become a part of the soil and all its history when we pass over to the Divine after our death…"

"Byjoe….ya never spoke……a truer word," nodded Sean Og. "Very few of us realise that or should I say even care to realise that."

While they are there, a bus load of American tourists stop to take a photo or two of the ruins of this historic place, each and everyone of them anxious and eager to find out as much history as possible from the three local lads. After all, they too had a secret admiration of Daniel O'Connell as many of their ancestors had come from Ireland to find a new life for themselves in America. Ironically though, yet after so many years of American living they still claimed their Irishness.

Chapter Twenty-One

Jim's Worst Nightmare Returns

No menu is complete without a side dressing and the same may be applied to any so-called love affair. Lies, deception and contempt are the main ingredients to the side dressing of an extramarital affair. Jim had a taste of the lies and deception and due the bad taste they left in his mouth after having his fill he wasn't too incline to wait around for his mouthful of contempt. But Mary O'Sullivan on the other hand had acquired a taste for all three and Jim was to become another one of her victims that just happened to fall into her honey pot. He too, like many other decent chaps was confronted with his own demons as they unravelled and returned back to taunt him. Day in and day out, he spent most of his time ducking and dodging Mary because of his guilt and fear of his out of marriage relationship with her.

Mary had acquired a reputation for herself that certainly would not do her any favours on her curriculum vitae. Deep in the pit of her belly the aching sensation to the fact that she had worn out the soles of her shoes and welcome in Iveragh and destiny was somehow telling her that it was certainly time to set her life's compass towards another land. Over the years, America had its attractions and there she would hopefully make a fresh start and become a new woman. But, like any venture, money is one of the foundation stones and without money, dreams can often remain just dreams. With no credibility in the local community or in the bank, she sets out to use Jim as bait for the price of her mail ticket, blackmailing him by demanding a ransom for the secrecy of their affair or she threatens to tell Peg about it. She demands that he pays her fare to America plus a wad of quinines to dissolve his guilt dowry or Peg will know the truth about her good Catholic husband. Jim tries to scrap up the money by betting on the horses but Lady Luck doesn't befriend him.

One evening, Jim's confides in Doc for guidance when he calls in for a chat and a cuppa on his way back from visiting Pat Connor's wife who hadn't been feeling well for a number of weeks now. But Doc also wanted to make sure that Peg was still taking her tablets that the Consultant from Tralee Hospital recommended. He asks Jim to bring her to his clinic in the next few days so that he can take more medical tests and monitor her health. He isn't too happy with the test results that came back from her appointment in Tralee General Hospital, the X-ray showed up a tumour in the lower section of her large intestine and this is of grave concern to him. But this is news that he feels he will keep to himself until he meets up with Peg.

"I ain't gonna ask you, why you did it, or tell you that you're a foolish stupid buccaneer to get involved with that wan, 'cause that's something you already know yourself," said Doc on hearing what Jim has to say. "But I'll ask you, how do you intend to overcome the end revelation when Peg finds out, and believe me find out she will. Having an affair with Mary O' Sullivan is like standing with a grenade between the cheeks of your arse. It'll all end in disaster once the explosion fucks off. And then you'll end up like the Humpty Dumpty saga."

"Yerra Christ, I know Doc and I know it pitiful cryin' over spilled milk when me conscience tells me what I did ain't only foolish but also unjust and especially when Mary has no intention of spreadin' any ceilmheas on me behalf or in other words goodwill," replied Jim and Doc could tell from the tone of his voice that he was seeking out an escape hatch for his taunting demons.

"Well you've certainly landed yourself arse over tit this time around my dear chap," giggled Doc finding Jim's misfortune comical.

"Maybe, if I pay her the money, she might leave well enough alone," replied Jim looking down the boreen and yelling out "Home Sally, home Sally…"

"No Jim, you'll pay her effin' all, for once you hand over a penny you sign your own guilt warrant, Tell that rip, of a wan to fuck off to Hell and that you intend to come clean with Peg. She won't expect that and hopefully she'll back off. I dare say that wan has done this before. She's a wolf in sheep's clothing or to put it in another way, she's simply just a tart without a heart that has left you like a cock skittering about holding on to a explosive fart," chuckled Doc wiping his wind chilled nose on the back of his hand.

"But if I come clean with Peg the outcome is sure to be a fuck'in disaster. How will she cope with it, especially now that she ain't feelin' her best?" asked Jim not expecting to hear those comforting words from Doc.

"Ahhhh mother of Jaysus, don't think too less of Peg. She's an intelligent woman and anyway I'd say she has some idea that something did happen. Women just have an instinct for things like that. I being a betting man myself, would bet that she knows about the affair but is playing her cards close to her chest," insisted Doc.

"Byjoe, do ya really think so?" asked Jim feeling like a puppy stuck in a corner confronted by a tomcat.

"Yeah," nodded Doc looking at Jim over his specs and repositioning his tweed hat on his head. "I'll have a word with Mary, that'd put her off the scent and hopefully she'll ramble off and prey in some other poor fecker's patch. She certainly won't have expected you to tell me."

"Would ya, maybe that might give me time to sort out things here on the home patch."

"I don't think time is going to do you any good," smirked Doc. "You'll need to pray to God that Peg's in an understanding and forgiving frame of mind when the shit hits the fan….."

"Be Jaysus if it was as ayezee as that, life would be grand," muttered Jim patting Sally, all this time she had been sitting patiently wagging her tail with her paw held high.

"Emmm.." nodded Doc.

"That's me girl, hey fetch," said Jim throwing a small stump of wood down the boreen and with that Sally is off on the chase.

"Jim, there's nothing wrong with life, it's just you, like many others before you and I dare say like many more that'll come after you, you've been a foolish buccaneer and now you've to pay the price for sowing your wild oats," giggled Doc giving Jim a fun loving punch into the belly. "And simply that's all. Maybe now you'll appreciate Peg for Peg, and not hope and fantasise for something that only exist in your vivid imagination...."

"Ach shur, men are very weak when it comes to the fairer sex and maybe it wasn't a rib that God took from Adam but his backbone to create Eve," mumbled Jim to himself.

"Well one thing for sure, woman have a better way of coping when it comes to life's struggles," replied Doc taking out his pipe and filling it up with tobacco.

"Eve was certainly the clever wan, for didn't she tempt the foolish Adam in the Garden of Eden all those years ago and God knows, things haven't changed much, women are still makin' fools of men, they're still throwin' out their fishin' lines and reelin' us in like eels, allowin' us to wiggle and waggle, patter and prance until they've us in their clutches," smirked Jim still trying to justify his stupid actions.

"My dear chap, you've to be foolish to be made a fool of and it doesn't take a clever woman to make a fool out of a foolish man and especially one that's suffering from a bad dose of dickitis, if you get my drift," joked Doc tilting his head to one side and winking at Jim while making a clicking sound with his tongue against the roof of his mouth.

"I suppose...... it's the temptation...... that makes people have affairs," shrugged Jim.

"No it ain't, my dear man. Affairs have nothing to do with temptation, that's the hopeless plea of a guilty man. Affairs are to do with willingness and that's just simply it," replied Doc puffing away on his pipe.

"Did ya ever have wan?" asked Jim and in his mind wondering if he's the only fool to make such a taunting mistake in his life.

"You mean an affair?" puffed Doc.

"Yeah," muttered Jim.

"No, but if I did, it wouldn't be classed as an affair for me, for my Betty has passed on. You've to be in a committed relationship to have an affair," giggled Doc knowing in his heart that Jim is from his buttocks to his heels deep in a cesspit of guilt.

"Yeah, I guess so, there's no two ways about it, but I'm in deep shit and sinkin' fast, no matter which way I turn there's gonna be a shitty fall out," sighed Jim still wondering which direction he should take in solving the equation that life was challenging him with.

"Just fuck'in tell that wan, to go to Hell the next time you see her and I myself will have a firm non negotiable word in her ear. That one must have had a morality bypass done at some stage in her life, you see Jim my dear man, as my grandmother used to say, God rest her soul, 'when need must, the devils drives'. And that's certainly so in that fuck'in wan's case," insisted Doc getting into his car and driving off down the boreen towards the direction of the village.

The following evening, Doc calls into the Shebeen for a quick pint and to make it his business to have a word in Mary's ear that hopefully would stop her on her tracks and dissolve her from Jim's anxiety picture. If the two lads had played their cards right, this might be Mary's Waterloo or was that just wishful thinking on Jim's side? Doc didn't offer any olive branch to Mary and what he had to say really stunted her pride, in such away that for days afterwards she was prancing around like a nervous young rabbit suffering from myxomatosis. A woman's scorn is like a sharp knife but more so in the case when there is no self-honour to uphold and truth behold this was certainly so in Mary's predicament.

The following Monday night, Mary makes it her business to approach Peg after an ICA evening meeting that is held in the backroom of the Shebeen and her mission isn't one of goodwill.

"Peg, I need to talk to ya about somethin' that has played on me mind for sometime now. As ya know I'm leavin' for America in the next month or so but I can't leave without apologisin' for the affair I had with ya'r Jim a while back. I don't know if ya knew about it but I'm so sorry for steppin' into ya'r marriage and probably stirrin' up a hiccup or two," she said with a twinge of narcissism in her voice, as she stood there all dressed up in her multi-coloured acrylic frock.

With that, Peg stops her on her tracks.

"Of course I knew," she sternly replied.

Mary is stunted for a moment or so as this is certainly not the response she was expecting.

"Did...he...tell....ya?" asked Mary in a hesitant tone in her voice.

"No," responded Peg abruptly. "I'm a woman, a mother and above all as ya're fully aware I'm Jim's wife. Wives just simply know when their husbands are havin' affairs, but ya wouldn't be aware of that for ya're neither a mother nor a wife. A woman, who's a wife can feel it in her marrow when somethin' like that's goin' on..."

"I'm sorry for causin' ya such bother and grief. Ya see it was just somethin' that got out of hand. Were ya annoyed with him?" asked Mary trying to raise her voice so that she might have some hope in belittling Peg amongst the ICA members.

"Indeed I wasn't, but annoyed that ya thought, ya'd cause trouble for him by informin' me now after all this time," snapped Peg with a shrug of her shoulders. "Off with ya'rself and póg mo thóin."

"I'm…so…....sorry," said Mary meekly knowing now she is making a fool of herself and hanging herself with her own egoistic loop.

"My dear Miss O'Sullivan, byjoe, sorry ya'll be if ya don't get out of me feck'in way before I wallop ya wan. Be off with yar'self and crap yar obnoxious shit in somebody else's camp," sternly but proudly replied Peg looking around to see whose ears were close to the floor in search of gossip. For she was well aware of the fact that Mary O'Sullivan's nocturnal antics were always a source of interest to the local gossipers.

Peg was proud with the way she handled the situation, as she was well aware of the begrudging gossipers' eyes and telescopic ears that were focused on her. Peg is a small slender pale skin woman with red long hair and all her power and strength is in her tongue when it comes to getting out of an argument. One never knew, whether it's that she was inspired by a fiery Spirit Guide or it was just the nature of a red haired woman that empowers her words, but somehow she has the ability to knock someone right out of their six inch stilettos and have them arse over tit on the floor with only a few lashes of that tongue of hers.

This was what she had learned to help her survive the tough times in the Industrial School when the older girls would bully the young ones. She had also learned from her time in the Magalden Laundry that keeping your fists in your pocket, your backbone erect, powered on with a stiff neck followed by a sharp lash out of the tongue was a sure way of keeping an argumentative hound in its place when an non-negotiable argument was about to erupt. The other principal that she soon became acquainted with in the school was that SOS didn't necessarily stand for Save Our Souls; it also stood for Stretch Or Starve. A principal that came into action when the nuns were not around to supervise meals, as courtesy and manners took a back seat when hunger infested the pit of their bellies. Anyway, in many cases it was survival of the fittest. She has a unique Irish beauty about her or as the Americans would say, she is a true Irish Cailin. And indeed she is, but somehow she was born with Scottish blood in her veins.

"Good night to ye all, I'm off home to cook up a nice mixed grill for me Jim, he's usually hungry when he comes home after the IFA meetin'. Shur Christ, he loves me home cured rashers with the wee bit of fresh liver and onions on top of a thick crust of me homemade brown bread," hailed Peg to the women standing around as she walks off with her head held high like a proud peacock. But in her heart, it's not a mixed grill she wanted to give Jim but a good lashing to bring him to his senses. But She certainly wasn't going to let the gossipers know her feelings.

"Just wait until I get me hands on that fella when I get home," she muttered to herself getting into her car. "Havin' high jinks with that skinny whore of an aul wan. God knows, haven't I enough with Sean Og and his wanderin' eye not to mind Jim now with the virus of the wanderin' willie. A good dose of castor oil should put a stop to that fella's frisky antics. Mary O' Sullivan of all women, ach shur, what ailed that eejit of mine? Sweet Jaysus, I suppose there's some truth in the sayin' an achin' willin' willie blurs a man's vision...."

But deep in the core of her spirit, she knew that she herself wasn't too willing when it came to the sexual side of their relationship and felt more at ease with herself to let the whole situation rest in silence rather than to confront it at this moment in time. She is well aware that she has come to a stage in her life where in a Sunday tabloid newspaper she would certainly qualify as a candidate for the Born Again Virgins' column rather that for the Bouncing Sexual Beings that usually appeared on page three. And anyway, Jim's selected amnesia used to irritate her at the best of times, not to mind that mule wayward spirit that would possess the core of his marrow every now and again and more than likely he is sure to suffer from a bout of both of them if she confronts him regarding the saga with Mary O' Sullivan.

Hopefully, time would sort the matter out she thought to herself as she drove home from Cahirciveen, but a good dose of castor oil he certainly would get. Ach shur what harm would come of it, other than clearing him out, but this alone would give her some satisfaction and in some strange way a little victory in her heart. And it certainly would have him skittering about for a few days holding onto himself in a right stump of a strut, you know the stoop, here's me head and me arse is comin' syndrome.

She was often angered and saddened by the fact that all Sean Og would ever have in life is a wandering eye or a kiss and a cuddle. Because of that horrific lashing that he experienced in the hands of the Christian Brothers, fate would never allow him to have a sexual experience with a woman. They had destroyed his manhood but that was a secret that Sean Og and Peg kept close to their hearts. After all, he has his pride and is still restoring his lost childhood dignity. She is well aware that this is one of the reasons why Sean Og never had a girlfriend and why he would joke that bachelor's way of life was the life for him. And when Johnny would question his reasons for not having a wife, he'd recite the rhyme, time and time again,

"Scissors and string, scissors and string
When a man's single he lives like a king
Needles and pins, needles and pins
When a man marries his troubles begin."

But regardless of his flippant excuses, Peg knew that in his heart he would've loved the company of a woman in his life.

Meanwhile back in the hall, Mary wasn't prepared to admit defeat to having a chip knocked off her egoistic rump.

"Did ya hear that rip of a wan called Peg, with her airs and graces and I only tryin' to put things right," Mary muttered to Peter Mc McCarthy's wife, Teresa.

But, Teresa had the measure of Mary and was well aware of her purring cat antics she used to mystify her husband Peter, night after night in the pub. Shur, the poor man would've restless nights thinking about her. There were even times he went off his food just like a troubled tomcat. She was in no doubt that her Peter was a right hobo before she married him and that was one of the reasons why her parents didn't give the marriage their blessing. But over the years, she had learned to tame him but knew that he could never be cured, for after all, wasn't his father one of the Coffey's from Caragh Lake and the hobo nature was in their marrow. And having that Mary O' Sullivan, sniffing around was certainly not going to do Teresa any favours for one night alone with her was certainly to undo years of taming. Deep down Teresa herself, had the personality of a female robin, willing to allow her husband the honour of taking the senior role in their marriage but now that she herself, was in the autumn of her life she was eager and ready to protect her own territory and make sure that her say was heard.

"Ahhhh, ya silly lass, once again, ya missed ya'r opportunity to keep ya'r big aul gob shut. Ya're only a rabbit and she a vixen. Ach shur, don't ya know by now, that a rabbit doesn't prance in front of a young vixen. Keep that in mind me dear lass and ya'll do just fine in the big USA," replied Teresa in her own sarcastic way as she continues to pile the cups and saucers into her basket. "Is minic a bhris béal duine a shrón…"

"Haaaa," shrugged Mary with a puzzled frown across her brow. "What's that ya said…"
"As the aul say'in goes in irish," huffed Teresa under her breath. " 'Tis many a time a man's mouth broke his nose."

Mary now knowing that she wasn't going to get her way, throws her eyes up to Heaven on leaving the hall and mutters to herself.

"The sooner I get me arse out of this effin' place the better. Shur, those aul country nags, God love them, are as useless as tits on a bull."

She was referring to the women attending the ICA meeting. With head held high, she whistles her way back into the pub.

"Right lads what'll it be," she yelled out drawing attention to the thirsty punters. "Let's get some spark back into the night, it's like grab a granny night in the backroom with those auld hags walkin' around. Wan thin' for sure I don't intend stickin' around here waitin' to become bone-meal for the maggots in the local bone-yard. I intend to live me life before I die and ain't becomin' a weathered up aul prune like that lot out there in the backroom...."

The punters just give a quick glance up from their pint glasses and smile for they're in no doubt that someone has just pulled a tail feather out of Mary's egoistic rump.

"I don't think too many would be inclined to borrow a garment from that wan's laundry to keep themselves warm on a frosty mornin'. Ach shur, there must be more material in me Pat Joe's handkerchief than in that bit of a guna she has on," whispered one of the ladies as Mary rushed by.

But Teresa kept a close watch on Mary leaving the hall and was certainly not too impressed by her whistling. For she herself was reared to the belief that when women whistled, evil spirits were near. Her grandmother had reared her by the philosophy, "a whistlin' maid and a crowin' hen are neither fit for God or men." And to top it all, Mary had a crooked mouth, when one took the time to focus on it for a moment or so, you'd notice that it went up on the right side, sunk deep in the centre and had a downward slant to the left. That was a good indication of a crafty, sly person and a villain for gossip. As the old saying goes, "a good shaped mouth speaks honourably but the crooked mouth strives to cause scorn and grief..."

Chapter Twenty-Two

Jim Confesses While Fr. Murphy Stands By His Convictions

Jim returns to see Fr. Murphy and confesses to him about his love affair with Mary O' Sullivan and how she is now trying to blackmail him. But to Jim's surprise his good friend isn't too perturbed and takes it all in his usual Christian stride.

"My dear chap, we'll all have to answer for our mistakes or they'll taunt us until we do. Mistakes are lessons that God sends us and when we learn from them and put them to right, then and only then can we move on with the rest of our lives. I guess mistakes are a way of finding out who we really are in life and how we react and cope with the ups and downs that we experience as we grow from day-to-day," said Fr. Murphy on hearing about Jim affair.

"Is there any way of avoidin' mistakes in life?" asks Jim.

"Indeed there is, if you consult you inner voice which is your Spirit Guide, then you can often do the right thing. But I guess too many of us are unaware we've an inner voice to consult and make Hell on earth for ourselves. You see, my dear friend, confession in the Catholic Church is a quick way out of wiping the sinning slate of our conscience clean. The right confession is to face the wrongdoing or the person we've caused an injustice to and ask them for their forgiveness. That's the true Christian way of doing a Godly confession, but no doubt, many of us would prefer the regular penance that consist of the three Hail Mary and the Our Father thrown in for good measure, for all-in-all, it saves face, would you agree?" replied Fr. Murphy.

"Ya might be right there," said Jim grinning and thinking maybe they are some normal priests in the Catholic Church after all.

"Jim, I need to see Peg for I've something to confess to her. Would you tell her to come and see me sometime in the near future? Somehow, I think what I'm about to confess will come as no great surprise to her. You see Jim, she was grievously wronged in the past and things need to be put right. I was unable to talk to her about this issue before now 'cause it affected so many others. I think the time is right for justice to be done. There can't be any more lies or deception, matters must be put to right, Peg must know the truth," insisted Fr. Murphy and Jim could tell from the tone of his voice that whatever was playing on his mind, it was serious and a cause of grief to his good friend.

"Ach shur that ain't any bother, I'll do that for ya," replied Jim wondering what could his friend have to confess to Peg, after all, he was the one person that was caring and kind to her in gone by years.

Just as Jim is getting ready to leave for home Fr. Murphy remembers he has something to tell him.

"I know I'd something to tell you Jim, I was talking to a friend of mine last week. He's a retired civil servant and he gave me some information regarding those Industrial Schools. He was able to get into the archives in the educational department and put his hand on it. Seemly, during the 1950's the Religious Orders were unhappy with the Probation Act that was set out by the Courts. The number of children sent to the Industrial Schools was dwindling and this was a cause of concern to the management of these schools. You see, at the time each school received a capital grant for every child that was sent there and the fact that the number of children were slowly falling, it was affecting the income made from these capital grants. In other words, their income was suffering and they saw children as commodities that'd raise an income for them...."

"Ya.... can't be..... serious," exclaimed Jim.

"Indeed I am. The Religious Orders were also unhappy with the fact that the Vincent de Paul and other charitable organisations were more in favour of fostering the needs of needy families than sending kids into care. These organisations were more family orientated and believed that the way forward was to build up and support the family unit rather than breaking it down by tearing it apart. The courts were also in favour of this, as they themselves never intended those Industrial Schools to become long-term detention centres. Since the Religious Orders needed to reclaim their revenue, they then targeted the misfortunate single mothers in different communities. Seemly, they went ahead and drew up a financial plan and programme which stated, if children born out of wedlock were to be given over to them and reared in the Industrial Schools, it'd be more financially favourable for the Irish State. The local authorities supported their proposal and as a result of this, the Industrial Schools were able to remain open...."

"We'll never get to the end of it, the more we tap away at the injustices the worst they get," replied Jim shaking his head in disgust.

"Now, there's a letter here I want you to see as well, I know I put it in a safe place as I thought it might be of interest to you. Since your first visit, I've done my own research into the different Industrial Schools and seemly there's a story to be told about each and every one of them. The abuse didn't just apply to the Christian Brothers it was wide spread across the boundaries of all the Religious Orders involved in the running of these schools. Last Friday, I received a letter from Sr. Dominic who's a good friend of mine from Dublin. She was one of the nuns who worked in the Magdalene Laundry in Cork. In her letter, she writes that she remembers in 1943 thirty-five young children and one elderly person died in fire in an Industrial School that was run by the Order of the Poor Clares in

Cavan. The remains of the charred bodies were buried in a mass grave. On the night of fire, the door to the dormitory was locked and the nuns insisted that the children get dressed before leaving the burning dormitory. You see these order of nuns were of the belief that it was immoral and immodest for girls to be seen in public dressed in their night attire. As a result of the delay in getting the children out, thirty-five of the kids burned to death and those that survived suffered severe burns and other injuries…"

"Mother….of…..Jaaaysus," exclaimed Jim in horror.

"Seemly the locals noticed the smoke coming from the school and tried to help but they weren't familiar with the layout of the school as the Poor Clares were an enclosed order and they had very little contact with the outside community. Over the years, the locals had questioned the local Parish Priest and members of the Irish Government regarding the suitably of having children in their care as they felt the isolation wasn't healthy. Sr. Dominic's research shows that in the departmental files the children that died were referred to as numbers. Up to ten of these kids that died that night had no living relative and were sentenced to the school by the courts at a very young age…."

"Christ…almighty," mumbled Jim shaking his head in disbelief.

"Seemly the Irish State and the nuns in question played down the background to this tragic event and even though there was an investigation regarding how the fire occurred and why so many children died, it showed great leniency towards the nuns in question," said Fr. Murphy handing Jim the letter.

"Where will it all stop?" muttered Jim biting into his lower lip, "I think we've stumbled upon a den of rats, no matter which way ya look, it seems that youngsters' rights were molested in all quarters and there seems to be fuck'in cover up after fuck'in cover up…."

"Emm," nodded Fr. Murphy.

"So ya're telling me that these youngsters were literally charred, buried and now forgotten. Their memories just a name and a number in some forgotten file in a Births and Death Department. Yerra Christ, does anywan give a care or a fuck'in thought about these youngsters at all," grunted Jim and there was anger raging in the pit of his gut.

"The way I see it now is that, denial and guilt are very destructive, retarding emotions. The abusers and victims mustn't live with such emotions. Denial is a false sense of reality, while guilt can become a dark cloud of rejection. There's no two ways about it, abusers need help and victims of abuse need help. Abuse, whether physical, emotional or sexual, has to be culled and gutted out. We'll always have victims if the core of the problem isn't sorted out. The Irish State needs to help the abuser to stop the abuse. As long as there are abusers left untreated, we'll always have innocent victims suffering, many suffering under a cloud of silence. Society has to stop turning a deaf ear to all types of abuse," insisted Fr. Murphy searching through his files looking for a letter he received from a survivor of abuse who was sentenced by the courts to Daingean Industrial School in the late forties, all because he stole a loaf of bread and a packet of matches.

"But the abuse of innocent children has taunted the victims into their adult years. Shur the good God himself knows that I've see that with Peg and Sean Og," said Jim sitting on the edge of the bed reading the letter.

"You're right on that account, many victims of abuse have turned to drink to find an emotional dumping ground for their past. Self-dislike and self-punishment ain't uncommon among the victims. Many have become the victims of broken marriages 'cause of their inability to build up personal trust with people. Low self-concept has resulted into an emotional and physical handicap that has prevented many of them from reaching their full potential in life. Depression taunts many of them. Many live with the struggle of coping with coping. Other suffering daily from bouts of anxiety and sadly have felt that life could offer nothing to live for, so the hand of suicide was their only escape from the emotional torment they've to live with. And all this because of the abuse they suffered and Jim it goes on and on and on….."

"How do ya go about treatin' abusers, for instance the Christian Brothers? Do ya simply lock them up and fuck'in throw away the key?" asked Jim biting into his lower lip.

"Well, as long as the Christian Brothers deny the abuse, they'll never accept treatment. There's no doubt each and every one of them who has abused must be made accountable for their actions and be punished accordingly. Their counterparts must stop hiding and protecting them. Even though many victims only expect an apology from them, I fear, that ain't enough. The word sorry frothing from hypocritical lips is like pouring hot water on snow. Firstly, each one of them must be identified, defrocked and stripped of their collar. They must be stripped of their title. I feel the man who is the abuser is hiding behind that collar and title. Then and only then can they be treated for their horrific crimes, too many of them are hiding behind their counterparts and under the umbrella of Christianity…"

"Ya're certainly right there."

"Their horrific evil malicious actions have degraded the Catholic Church and everything good and Holy that it stands for, but above all, those evil people are an insult to Christianity. They're malicious controllers, who used innocent youngsters to fulfil their own insecurities. They became overtaken by the love of power rather than by the power of love. In the treatment, they'd have to follow an in-depth programme drawn up especially for abusers. And they should strictly adhere to such a programme. Victims of abuse may feel that their abusers need to be named and shamed and brought before the criminal court of this land and answer for their crimes. However, truth behold, many of them will never face the court of this land but they'll have to answer to the Court of God on their deathbeds and I guess that alone should be of some reassurance and consolation to the victims…"

"Maybe so," mumbled Jim.

"You see Jim, if we fail to put right our evil actions we'll have to pay for them in our next life. But the most important thing that's urgently required to protect our kids for the future, is a list of sex offenders to be drawn up and their movements and whereabouts monitored," insisted Fr. Murphy closing his files and placing them back into the drawer of his dressing table.

"Byjoe, ya don't pull punches Father, do ya? Deep in me gut, I don't think the Christian Brothers will ever apologise for their wrongdoings, for that alone would be the first step in admittin' to their wrongdoings and they're too cowardly to do that. Would ya agree?"

"That maybe so, but don't get me wrong Jim, there're only a few bad apples amongst the Religious Orders and Christian Brothers that're intent on taking the Catholic Church down with their evil malicious actions," replied Fr. Murphy walking to the window and opening it to let a wasp out. "We need to listen, understand and recognise that there're good people working in the name of God in our Churches, Convents and Monasteries. It's up to these good people to come forward and help the nation to stop any more abuse from happening. We can all work together and give a firm commitment that such abuse won't continue and another innocent life won't be destroyed by premeditated evil actions...."

"Peg is unable to forgive her abuser, I guess it's very hard to forgive an abuser."

"Jim, my dear chap, too often when the victims of abuse come forward and look for help, they're told too readily, to forgive their abuser. Forgiveness is very difficult to give when your abusers ain't willing to repent for their wrongdoings. Before someone can repent, they've to admit to their wrongdoings and if the Christian Brothers and other members of the Religious Orders are unwilling to admit to the hurt and the horrific sexual abuse that occurred in those Industrial Schools to so many children that were placed in their care then it's very difficult for the victims to forgive them," huffed Fr. Murphy.

"Shur, the families of these abusers will suffer in their own way when all this abuse is exposed in the public arena, Father."

"Jim, we shouldn't have scorn for the families and friends of the abusers. They didn't cause the abuse. But they too need to stop finding excuses and scapegoats because they're afraid of their self-image. As long as they deny or prevent the abusers from getting help, the abusers have the potential to abuse again. By helping the abusers to come forward, they'll allow victims to free themselves from their inability to live life to its fullness. The family, friends and the religious counterparts of the abusers can play a major role in justice. They need to get the abusers to put their actions to right and take responsibility for their crimes. Victims of abuse need to be released from the nagging concept that it was their fault. Victims of abuse were innocent, trapped in a silent cloud of doubt," demanded Fr. Murphy banging the table with his fist, forced on by his rebel nature and convincing himself and Jim that the slate of abuse has to be wiped clean and that's his final word on the matter.

After bidding farewell to Fr. Murphy, Jim sets out to collect Johnny from the rose garden where he is contently chatting with the elderly patients.

"Right me little macin og, ready for the road? Ya'r Ma will be wonderin' what happened to us. We should've been home well over an hour ago," Jim shouted across to Johnny.

"Kan mee ket ite keam?" called out Johnny wiping his snotty nose on the sleeve of his sweater while happily leaping up and down with his shoes on the wrong feet.

"Indeed we can and maybe a few bulls-eyes as well if ya hurry up. Johnny, me dear squireen, would ya ever use that hankie ya'r Ma put into the top pocket of ya'r britches and while ya're at it, put those brogs back on the right feet," chuckled Jim to himself in amusement with the thought that no matter how many hankies Johnny had, he'd always resort back to the sleeve of his sweater to clean his face or wipe his nose and whatever it was, he always felt more at ease with his shoes on the wrong feet.

With that, Johnny gets his teddy and jacket from the nearby bench and after giving farewell hugs and cuddles to his elderly friends, they both set off on the road home to Glenbeigh.

Chapter Twenty-Three

Puck Fair

Puck Fair is one traditional Pagan festival that holds many a happy memory for Irish folk. It's the time of the year where logic and common sense take a backseat in life and a member from the animal kingdom comes to town to rein over the local inhabitants. The week before this traditional festival the town's folk wander off into the Kerry Mountains in search of a Billy goat. Once found, he is brought back down to Killorgin, where he is scrubbed, groomed and paraded through the crowded streets before he is honourably crowned King of Puck. Then, to his dismay and to that of the hordes of visitors that attend the fair, he is hoisted high up into the air onto his rightful throne and expected to remain there for three days and three nights, reigning over the town of Killorgin and the surrounding town-lands. And while he is allotted the privilege of doing so, the local inhabitant bestow upon themselves the privilege of acting the goat as they mingle amongst the crowed streets, wheeling and dealing and wallowing in porter and song.

Year after year, familiar faces would appear, each and everyone with a story to tell. The eve before Gathering Day the Fair Green comes to life with the return the hawkers, the barrel top wagons and benders while caravan after caravan line the streets bedded down with satisfied children with jam and ice-creamed faces.

No visit to Puck is complete without a visit to the "bean feasa" or fortune-teller and sure enough they were here again this year, all lined up in the local streets each and everyone of them claiming to be the seventh daughter of the seventh daughter of Madam Rose Lee. And who ever this special Madam Rose Lee was, you certainly had to give her some credit for having so many seventh daughters! There is one thing for sure though, fortune telling and inflation have a way of going hand-in-hand because it was the only commodity that had a hundred percent mark up on its price tag year after year. But that didn't perturb the inquisitive fortune thirsty souls, for no matter what it cost, you still were sure to find the faithful lined up outside the caravans as they eagerly await the good news that fate beguiled them with over the year ahead.

Coming through Killorgin on his way back from a health board meeting and following a visit to some of the County Homes is Patrick who happens to meet up with Jim and Sean Og both enjoying the excitement of the fair while relaxing in the heat of the August sun.

"What've you got there?" Patrick asked Sean Og, he was referring to a piebald pony that Sean Og had tied up in a small cattle trailer.

"Yerra, it's a present for Johnny. I'm gonna get him into the ridin'," replied Sean Og and he was very proud of his new purchase.

"Ach, mother of sweet Jaysus, Sean Og, that one's frick'in wild, shur you'll kill the child if you put him up on her," laughed Patrick at the innocence of Sean Og and the naivety of his good-hearted intention.

"Ahhhhh shur, it's only leapin' about a wee bit, it'll calm down after a while," insisted Sean Og, determined not to be put off by Patrick's comments.

"I'll tell you Sean Og, the only one that'll be leaping about when you get that piebald home will be you, Peg will run you and your present out of the yard," giggled Patrick reaching out to rub the piebald on the belly and with that it gives such a leap that it shakes the whole trailer. "Ayeze now lass, ayezee Ayezee   now..."

"Ahhhh, ya of little faith. A few days groomin' and calmin' down should've this wan eatin' out of the palms of me hands. Horses are like women, treat they ayezee, treat them kindly, treat them well and they'll behave," laughed Sean Og amused by the antics of the pony.

"I don't know about that," chuckled Patrick shaking his head and walking across to Jim who is contently eating a great big ice cream cone with a fine piece of chocolate stuck in the centre of it. As he approaches Jim who should be coming up along the footpath but the old Parish Priest from Glenbeigh in the company of the Canon from Cahirciveen.

"Welcome to Puck, Patrick," he said with a husky tone in his voice reluctantly taking his hand out of his trousers pocket and offering it to Patrick.

"Thanks Father," sternly responded Patrick but didn't return the handshake, "Canon, grand day for the fair."

"Indeed it is," replied the Canon and with a nod of recognition they set on their way.

"Howya Patrick," greeted Jim.

"Yerra grand, shur grand," replied Patrick.

"What…was…all….that…about," remarked Jim nibbling at the end of the cone. "I couldn't help see that ya refused to return the handshake…."

"Well Jim, put it like this, that wasn't intended to be a welcoming or a good wish handshake but an publicity stunt for the Canon's sake. I could see there was no welcome in that dead fish gesture and I certainly wasn't going to be a hypocrite and partake in the antics of the moment. A welcome germinates in the eyes of a person and reflects in the hand, but more so, the expression of the eyes speak the unspoken words. When I looked into that man eyes, all I saw was coldness and resentment," muttered Patrick taking off his tie and opening up the buttons of his shirt to cool down from the heat of the day.

"Byjoe," replied Jim. "Was that so?"

While the two men sit on the shop windowsill they get engrossed in conversation and Patrick tells Jim that he fears that there might be abuse of the elderly going on in the County Homes. He is determined to follow it up and research into what's going on behind the scenes. He plans to make an unofficial visit himself and see what's really going on behind closed doors. He feels, that each town and village in Ireland should have their own local scheme and support network to look after the elderly. This may mean building small-contained homes and flats that would allow the elderly their independence while being supervised by a medical team. His aim is to get the health board to sponsor a grant to cover the needs of community assistants that would help in information centres and skills training for people to care for the elderly in their own homes.

That evening after milking his cows and sorting out the farmstead, he telephones Doc at the surgery and discusses his plans. Doc is very impressed and offers to give any assistance that is needed to get the scheme up and running.

Meanwhile back at Peg's, Sean Og is trying to convince her that all is wrong with the piebald is that it needs a little kindness and attention. But Peg isn't convinced and thinks to herself, if a red hot poker was to be stuck up that pony's rear end, it wouldn't leap around as much. But once Sean Og had given his word that he wouldn't put Johnny up on the pony for a week or so or at least until she has settled down, she reassures him by saying, "ach shur she has a nice nature, it's just that she has too much spirit in her marrow but I'm sure if any wan can train and tame her, it'll surely be ya." Deep down she knew in her heart that once again his intentions are honourable but not very sensible.

Over the coming days, Sean Og spends every waking moment with the pony. Rubbing her hindquarters with potato Hessian bags to firm up her hind muscles together with daily grooming of her rough neglected coat and carefully clips her overgrown hoofs. He treats the gashes at the back of her front legs and dusts her off for mites and sweet itch. Abiding by the rule, that the way to train a pony is by kindness and common sense but above all, you have to show her who is boss. Each morning he would carefully slip a bridle over her head and with a long reins he gallops her around and around the paddock with two bags of sand on her back. But every time he attempted to throw his leg over her, she would give a mighty leap that would land him arse over brow back on the ground. But he is determined not to allow her get the better of him. From the two bags of sand he ties two wellington boots half filled with sand and hangs them down alone the girth strap line. Then leading her calmly around the field he slowly encourages her from a trod to a steady canter. To his amazement after a few hours of this she is willing and ready to take him for a ride. With a good gallop around the meadow and down the boreen, Sean Og has assured everyone that the piebald would be ready to take Johnny for a short ride in the next week or so.

By the end of the week he had even convinced himself that the pony was a good purchase, after all he had only parted with ten guineas for her. If he could manage not to kill off her frisky spirit by his kindness and if he could get on the right side of Lady Luck who would hopefully give him the thumbs up and send a wee bit of good fortune his way then he could enter the pony into the Cahirciveen Races. Now wouldn't that be grand, he thought to himself.

The following week, Patrick and the local Fianna Fail councillor meet up and organise a meeting that is to be held in the back room of the local hotel. There is a good turn out and all present are eager to find out what changes Doc and Patrick have for the care of the sick and elderly. Peg and Jim also attend the meeting. Who should arrive late but the two Parish Priests, one from the Glenbeigh area and his shooting counterpart from Cahirciveen. Questions are put to Doc from the floor. Patrick requests that it's important that people are aware of the conditions in the County Home in Killarney.

"The way aul people are cared for in the institutional homes under the care of the Health Boards are in my opinion an outrage. It's nothing short of abuse. Institutionalising the elderly is in my opinion an insult to their ability for independence within their dependency.

Everyday their independence is slowly stripped from them, making them more dependent on care. Many of them, left naked under sheets, lying in dirty soiled beds and with no contact from the outside world. Many others, unaware of what day or time they have," insisted Patrick looking around at the crowd and he is in no doubt by the expression on their faces that they are taking this matter as serious as himself. After a nod of recognition to the local Garda who has just entered the hall, he continues speaking.

"Basically they've nothing left not even their dignity. Their freedom has been removed from them and we must recognise that freedom is one's right and dignity and as long as freedom is removed from any human being, a part of their dignity is robbed as well. Some of these people come to be in the County Home just because they've the misfortune of having no one to care for them. Following a short time in care, they find themselves following rules and regulations to fit in with an administrational work routine.

We should remember that it was these very people that worked hard to rear families without any assistance from the Irish State. They struggled through good times and held their heads high while struggling through hardships in their lives. These are proud people who deserve to be cherished and not dumped into some aul home that's walled off like a prison. These people ain't criminals, they're our heritage and we owe it to them and ourselves that they remain in the communities they once lived in. We should be lobbing the Irish State for financial assistance. We should be looking for community housing where the elderly feel happy, safe and at ease with their surrounds, but above all, where they're allowed their independence and left with they dignity. After all, that's their birthright...."

The crowd nodded in agreement.

"We must also remember where people are cared for behind enclosed walls neglect and abuse can occur. Evidence of that went on in those Industrial Schools throughout Ireland. It's always the defenceless that are abused and neglected. We, as a community have two choices, we can turn a deaf ear and walk away to what's going on at present or we can stand together, take on the challenge and return these humble people to their rightful place, back to their communities. That choice is ours. But remember, we'll all have the privilege of growing old some day but hopefully we won't have the misfortune of finding ourselves in a County Home. Although, if we do intend to turn a deaf ear to the abuse and neglect of the care of the elderly and when we do land up in a place like the County Home then I don't think we'll have the right or the privilege to ask the younger generation for help."

The Parish Priest from Glenbeigh sat harking on every word and as soon as Patrick has finished speaking he was determined to up root Patrick's comment regarding the high walls and abuse.

"The Councillor made a point regarding abuse behind high walls. I'd like him to withdraw that comment. There're people here tonight, who're intent in demonising the Christian Brothers and other members of the Religious Orders. The Religious Orders have cared for children over past generations and in the hospitals, the sick and elderly are cared for to the highest standards. I'm appalled and grieved that he'd stand here to night and attack the people who care for the least fortunate and in many cases stopped children running amuck throughout the length and breath of Ireland. We, as a community can't change the system overnight and may have to do with what we've at present. Administration and nursing care is organised on a very tight budget and the people running the homes are better equipped to relate to whatever they themselves feel is best for those people in care," he said and you could tell by his tone and stance that he was intending to challenge this manner to the end.

Patrick was waiting for this man's attack and is back on his trail like a hound snipping out a rabbit.

"Now Father, I don't need to demonise the Christian Brothers, they've done that themselves by abusing young innocent boys entrusted into their care.

Their actions were nothing short of dehumanising young children. But the real culprit here is the State for it didn't insure the safety of its children. I make no excuses or apologies for exposing the abuse that went on in those Industrial Schools and the sooner you stop denying it, the sooner you and your counterparts can put these wrongdoings to right…"

"Here, here," muttered Jim under his breath.

"And Father, as for the administration and so-called experts you're referring to, they're the very people who hide blindly behind bureaucracy and I can assure you all here present tonight, it's this same bureaucracy that's the cause of neglect of so many less fortunate than ourselves. Bureaucracy is a polite way of silently saying to us, we don't give a feck'in damn. We need to cut through all this red tape and get to work. You see tonight, this meeting ain't about politics or religion. It's a human rights issue, the right of aul folk to be cared for in a Christian dignified humane manner and simply that's what it's about. It's about ordinary people like you and me taking responsibility for caring. What I believe is, we should be assessing the sick, disabled and elderly not on their inability to cope within their independence but on the ability to cope within their dependency. I'd like to sum up by saying that caring for someone is much more than surrounding them with four walls, a bed, a chair, a meal and a bedpan. There tends to be three marginalized groups in our society, these are the children, the disabled and the elderly. Strangle as it may seem, these are the essential human assets of any community for each in their own unique way have the potential to bring the best out of us."

Jim looks back at the Parish Priest from Glenbeigh and he could tell from the expression on his face that he was silently snarling like a terrier at a trousers' leg determined not to let go. And the stiff left over right leg position with his palm of his right hand firmly placed over the cheek of his left buttocks as if he was nursing a grumping boil left you in no doubt that he was certainly not a happy camper.

"Here, here," cheered Jim. "I agree with Patrick, lets stand up as a community and take responsibility for our elderly. If we continue to expect others to care for them, then we'll never have a say in how they should be cared for. We should keep in mind that the aul folk are dependin' on us the same way we'll depend on our children when our golden years come around. Wouldn't is be nice to look back in twenty years time and see our aul folk livin' happily amidst us and in daily contact with the youth of this community?"

"Very well put Jim," replied Doc.

"Coming from the Southern Health Meeting last week, I can see that the way the health system in Ireland is going, it'll be more administrational centred rather than patient centred and for that reason alone in years to come we're going to see rows of sick people on trolleys in hospital corridors awaiting treatment," insisted Patrick stand up as he addresses the crowd again. "Community carers will become the cornerstones of society and the vertebrae of the health system's backbone and for that reason alone without community carers the Health Boards will collapse. Every Community Health sector will need to appreciate their reservoir of carers and will need to recognise that carers will save the exchequer, millions of pounds each year. If Heath boards could be more foresighted regarding the huge obligation that carers freely and willingly give, day in and day out, I think it'd be less likely to take them for granted."

"I agree with you there, Patrick," responded the Fianna Fail Councillor. "But like many situations in the health Board, we only wake up to the problem when people's lives are put in danger and when many others die in vain. We're livin' in an era, where money speaks and when it comes to care and treatment, the health system is no different. It certainly needs radical change..."

The Fianna Fail Councillor is very interested that Patrick's motion regarding the transfer of the elderly folk in the County Home in Killarney be passed and proposes that a vote be put to the floor for support. When the vote is carried through there are no objections to the motion.

Once again, there's another hearty clap of appreciation and after another short period of questions and answers, Doc thanks everyone present and wishes them an enjoyable night.

It isn't long before the room is deserted and it reminds Patrick of the story of the Pied Piper and how all the children were enticed from their homes down the streets hypnotised by the sound of the music and tune of the Pied Piper. But in this case, the crowd are enticed by the sound of Ceili music as it hails them one-by-one into the dance hall next door. Throughout the remainder of the night, neither aches or pains, ailment or weight, age or gender seemed to matter for they all danced in one rhythm to the sound of the McCarthy's Ceili Band. The healing power of music is truly amazing or maybe some would have you believe, miraculous.

There in the midst of the excitement is Dave Lyons from Valencia Island who managed to convince the Social Welfare Officer in the Dole Office just there last week, that because of his bad back he'd never again be able to do a day's work and for that reason alone maybe he'd be better off on a Disability Book. Yet, when the McCarthy's Ceili Band reefed up, he was out on the floor hopping and leaping, twisting and turning in harmony with Mary Murphy from Over-the-Water as they danced the Kerry Polka. Not to mention Maggie Malone, who stumbled in with a walking stick because her rheumatic hip was giving her a wee bit of bother, she too was floating around the dance floor like a butterfly arm-in-arm with Jack Foley as he gracefully glided her through the crowd.

Old aged pensioners, who only a few weeks ago, the local punters would've given them a month or so to live, tonight they too were dancing reels and jigs with the life and energy of a hyperactive six-year-old in their marrow. But, the most fascinating thing about Ceili music is how it can put a spring into the leap of an overweight man or woman. One thing for sure, no tablet or injection from Doc could get the same result. And, if the saying be true that the way a man dances determines his sexual drive, there was one thing for certain with all the hopping and leaping around tonight from the male species no wonder there were so many fatigued women walking around.

Throughout the night, there were claps and smiles, roars and shouts, whistles and winks while thirsty punters with sweaty armpits and brows embraced the waists of energetic women who had shed their stilettos and cardigans. Hour-by-hour, cares and worries were danced off and new friendships were made just as old ones were revisited. But in the corner in his rightful place with a whiskey in hand was the Canon, as he shepherded his flock with his anticipating slanting right eye.

There is no doubt about it, that the Man Above, had a great sense of humour when he set out to design the human race and looking down from Heaven, life must be one big long comedy drama for Him. Now, whether you were a biblical man or simply a doubting Thomas from watching the antics of the aged, disabled and the feeble, hand-in-hand hopping and leaping to the sound of a squeeze box, no one could blame you for questioning the parable regarding the raising of Lazarus for the dead and the healing of the crippled and sick. Was it really a miracle of God or did Jesus just happen to have a squeeze box in his possession?

But, no night out is complete without its gossipers and their "Pigeon Press". And sure enough, there they were at the back of the hall, the notorious Mary and Johanna and with the familiar gimps on them you certainly knew they were hissing and pissing in everybody else's what-a-bouts and where-a-bouts. Well truth behold, if you stepped out of line the whole town were to be well informed of it the following day. But everyone was well aware that funerals were their speciality, both of them were well known for their attendance and the fact they'd religiously bring a peeled raw onion wrapped in tissues to give nature a helping hand with their hypocritical tears of sorrow.

The money from the raffle tickets was gathered in and put with the Canon's generous donation.

"Canon, I suppose there's no chance of a miracle happening tonight?" asked Patrick in his familiar anticipating tone of voice.

"What're you trying to suggest or suppose, Patrick?" questioned the Canon.

"Well, I'm not suggesting or supposing or even wanting anything but what I'm saying is that it'd be nice for Mrs. Moran to win. It wouldn't only be nice it'd be fair and justified. I think she's the most deserving here tonight. It'd be nice to see the winnings put towards building up a home rather than breaking one down...."

"Breaking down a home I don't understand," frowned the Canon with a puzzled frown on his brow, taking off his thick-rimmed specs and wiping them on the lining of his jacket as if to get a clearer vision of Patrick's proposal.

Now, both of these men had an unspoken respect of each other's existence and had set personalised tagged boundaries for one another. They may not always have seen eye-to-eye but there were times when they both would put their grievance aside and quietly worked hand-in-hand for the betterment of the local community.

"Drink, I mean Canon, It'd certainly be wasted if the prize money was to be thrown away on drink and you of all people are well aware of the destructive power of a drunken man or woman on a home. Let's say I'm wishing and hoping for a miracle and I'm counting on you to do it. To give you a helping hand, we've put the names on the back of the tickets. Now, I'll leave the rest up to your good self and the Man Above, do you get me drift?" winked Patrick as he set on his way through the crowd to have a quiet word with Doc who is standing by the entrance door chatting with the local bank manager.

"Yeah, I get your drift right enough. Ye politicians don't make life ayezee for the people of the cloth, but give me a moment with the Man Above and I'll see what'll become of it," muttered the Canon with a grin.

The music and dance are brought to a halt by the announcement that the raffle is about to take place. And so that nobody could be in any doubt of the outcome, Tony, the local Garda is to hold the box containing the raffle ticket and the Canon is to pick out the fortunate winner. With that, the notorious two, Mary and Johanna are up on their hunches and with the sound of a drum the winning ticket is pulled out.

"Number forty-eight…..I do believe…..would you like to verify that…..Garda?" asked the Canon as he shows the ticket to Tony, "Joan Moran…… is that so?"

"Correct," called out Tony and with that Joan is rushing through the crowd to claim her miraculous winnings. The Canon winks at Patrick and Patrick gives him the thumbs up.

"Shur, what'll you spend your winnings on?" asked the Canon.

"I'll be able to make curtains for the me cottage and maybe with the couple of bob left over I'd buy somethin' nice for the kids. Now this will be grand and a great welcome blessin' it is at this time of the year. God bless ya Canon, " replied Joan giddy with the excitement.
There were claps all round except from the two pigeon press reporters. Patrick just happened to be standing in earshot of them when he heard Mary say to Johanna.

"Was….that…just… plain luck… magic or simply a miracle?"

"More like a bit of skulduggery to me," responded Johanna with a begrudging tone in her voice.

"Ladies," saluted Patrick tapping them on their shoulders. "Enjoying the night?"

"Begorra, howya Patrick?….it's yar'self that's in it," replied the two in one voice and the coy gawp on their faces.

"Begorra it is," smirked Dan. "'Tis meself alright that's in it."

As Patrick goes out of earshot the two huddle close.

"Ya'd wonder what goes on in that fella's head, He'd didn't get my vote in the last election. I always support Fianna Fail. Did ya vote for him?" Johanna whispered to Mary.

Now, Mary might have had a reputation for being a community gossiper and as the old saying goes, there's honour amongst thieves but it is well known that there's certainly no honour amongst gossipers and you certainly didn't want one of your own pitching up camp in your half acre and Mary was well aware of this. She herself would never vouch for her participation in the local gossip. She would have you believe that she was one of the concerned citizen brigades who had inherited a genetic curiosity for human nature. She certainly wasn't handing Johanna ammunition to shoot her in the back of the head at a later date. Moving through the crowed hall on her way back to their watchtower, she somehow managed to change the flow of the conversation to Murphy's bull and the destruction it caused when it happened to break into Jerry Coffey's pedigree herd.

Meanwhile, Patrick had made his way to have a gratifying word with the Canon.

"Was that a miracle of God or just another one of your magic tricks?" giggled Patrick.

"Ye politicians have a lot to answer for," grinned the Canon shaking hands with Patrick and feeling very pleased with himself.

"Ach shur, in all fairneeees Canon, didn't God send Jaysus to do his miracles for him and aren't you only doing mine," winked Patrick as they both wish each other an enjoyable night.

Patrick is an honest and courageous man but he is also mischievous by nature. As he stood alone watching the cheerful crowd, he thought to himself that he would give the notorious two in the corner something else to grief about. He comes up with a plan of how Joan Moran could win the major spot-prize of the night. Now, that would keep a gossiper's tongue wagging for a week. He is a wise man for he also knows that the way to sort out gossipers is to keep them at arms length, keep them sweet but keep them wondering while wallowing in the doubt of their own gossip.

Deep in his heart, he is also happy for Joan, for only a year ago she lost her husband James in a mysterious accident. The neighbours were in no doubt that he was an unfortunate victim of circumstances. A week before his death, he had tried to cut all ties with the IRA and a week later to the date of announcing his intentions to the local Garda he just happened to drive off the road on his way home from work. He was found dead in his car by one of the locals returning home from the pub that night. An investigation into the cause of his tragic death discovered that the brakes of his car had been tampered with. Questions were asked, no answers were found. The whole neighbourhood were in shock, his wife now left to struggle with five children all under the age of six. Over the months that followed, the neighbours rallied around and did their best to help. At the funeral there was an unusual worrying silence as he was laid to rest. But truth behold, it just happened to be another one of those situations where everybody wondered, somebody knew but nobody said!

After a short chat, Doc and Patrick come up with a way that Joan would qualify for the final spot-prize of the night that entailed a large food hamper and they were both in no doubt, it would also add fuel to the fire of the gossipers. Doc, in his confident macho self after a few whiskeys took command of the stage and the microphone and calls out to the chattering crowd.

"Right Folks, lets have the last spot- prize of the evening. Now for this prize, the person will have to prove that she went into hospital to have a baby and slipped out the back door of the hospital with an extra baby snuggled away in the carrycot. The community were shocked and amazed but the Gardai could do nothing about it...."

"Ach shur, how in the name of Jaysus, could somewan get away with takin' another woman's child?" grunted Johanna to Mary.

"Don't know about that. I didn't hear anythin' about that, did ya?" replied Mary.

Patrick conveniently happens to be standing by Joan and whispers in her ear.

"That's you Joan, you've twins in the family."

"Meeee.......don't understand?"

"Think about it. You went into hospital, thinking you were pregnant with one baby just before James died but you gave birth to twins, in actual fact.....it happened to you twice," nudged Patrick.

"Holy....Jaaaysus....Patrick....ya're right."
And with that, Joan is up on her feet, yelling and shoving her way up to the stage.

"Byjoe....that's meeeee......that's meeee....shur I had twins."

"Correct," cheered Doc as the crowd clap with joy.

"Good on ya Joan. Hurray for Joan. James is certainly lookin' down on ya tonight Joan. He too, is probably dancin' the night away in Heaven. Good on ya." Is all that could be heard from the happy crowd as they clap and cheer aloud.

Patrick looks across at the notorious two and the expression on their faces said it all. Patrick was well aware of the fact that the hand that rocked the cradle had the power to rock the system and he called that woman power, but these two biddies, somehow had the power to disturbed the harmony of a nation with just one wag of their sharp and twisted tongues. But one thing he was aware of, is that a twisted sharp tongue grounds the foundation stone to human destruction and can sow the seeds of mistrust and doubt in the minds of the listener. And these two had such sharp tongues it was a wonder how they didn't cut themselves every time they spoke.

But the real heroes of the night are Bridie Bowler and Charlie Cummins, both from Valentia, living next door to each other but haven't shared a civil word to each other for years. They had inherited a legacy of grievances from their parents that was passed down from one generation to the next. And to crown it all, neither politics or religion helped, as neither of them kicked with the same foot in either pitches. Somehow, in the Siege of Ennis they got entwined and in the midst of the jigs and reels of the commotion Mary happened to lose one of her earrings and as it was a family heirloom, it was a cause of great anxiety to her.

Both of them were brought to their hands and knees in search of this precious life long treasure. The dancing crowd weren't bothered and the band just simply played on. After a few minutes of these life long enemies rumbling around on the maple floor and placing their lives at the mercy of the on slaughter of hammering feet dressed with hobnailed boots and stilettos both emerged with the ear ring sharing a civil tongue. During the night, as they chatted they did bury their inherited hatchet. And nobody was in any doubt of this for they left the dance hall hand-in-hand. As the Canon bid them both good night, he smiled to himself for he knew from deep within the heart of his soul that this is what everyday miracles and victories are all about. Little things like burying the hatchet and living with the understanding that we don't need to allow our lives to be traumatised by the affects of disagreement. We can choose to live in harmony knowing that in certain matter of life it's okay to agree to disagree and to allow others the right to their own opinions. And this is what makes heroes out of ordinary people like me and you.

Chapter Twenty-Four

Harvest Time

Harvesting time is a busy and an eventful time in any farmstead and when it comes to Jim's farm it's no different. Over the coming weeks there is plenty to keep an energetic farmhand tipping. The honey needed to be extracted from the hives in the upper meadow. There was one hive in the orchard that was kept for honeycombs and these were put aside especially for Johnny's asthmatic chest. Next year's cabbages, curly kale and spinach needed to be sown in trays in the glasshouse. The winter brassicas that were good and health in the back garden were ready for mulching. The perennial plants needed to be protected with straw, seaweed and comfrey leaves. A scarecrow was brought to life with some clothes from the parcel from America and put in its rightful kingdom amongst the cabbages and brussels sprouts. The spuds, carrots and beet in storage had to be secured from rats and other hungry winter invaders. The upper field where there was a good crop of oats two years ago, needed to be tilled and got ready for next year's sowing. Haystacks and silage pits needed to be sorted out. The farm sheds needed to be whitewashed and sorted out for the winter housing for the cattle that grazed in the yonder pastures. So, nobody should be in any doubt that all of this was enough to keep a handy man tipping over for a few weeks or so. Jim found this type of work not only healthy but it also gave him time to think while working alone.

Then, there was that great day of killing the pig for the winter supply of bacon and hams. That was the day when sausages and puddings hung from the clothes' rack in the kitchen. Peg and Sean Og took great pride in curing the different sections. She would make her own special brine of herbs and spices and soak the pork in it. But year after year, she'd insist on smoking at least a few sections. She would hang the sections high in the chimney of one of the sheds adjoining Sean Og's dwelling. Over the coming weeks a slow burning oak and apple wood fire would burn in the small stove and nicely smoke and preserve the meat. During those weeks, a unique but pleasant smell would come from the shed as the smoked scented hams and fish mingled with the scent of maturing cheese. Hanging from the rafters were a mixture of different cheeses some goats, some cows, others made from whey that had chives and garlic mixed in, but Peg's pride and joy was the sheep cheese. Even though Jim and Scan Og were never too enthusiastic about it, that didn't put her off.

Sean Og would coat the larger joints of meat with a mixture of sugar, herbs, saltpetre and salt and tightly pack them away in an old oak barrel to mature over the coming months. Sally the dog would watch on eagerly throughout the day knowing that there was a reward for her if she didn't upset the daily procedure and ritual.

The next big day in the harvesting season was apple-picking day. This was the day for making juices, jellies, jams and cider. Peg would core some of the good quality apples, string them on a long string and allow them to dry slowly over the kitchen stove. When dried, she would store them in airtight jars. Over the winter months these were to become treats for Johnny when sweets were scarce. Apple picking day was a day for fun and games for Johnny. Peg would hang an apple from the kitchen ceiling on a piece of string and Johnny would spend hours trying to bite into it with his hands tied behind his back. Sally would prance around him and every now and again she would have a go herself.

Harvesting time was really a family time. A time for them to celebrate the rewards of a good summer and the enthusiasm for the hopes of having a well blessed larder for the winter. If there were a chance that Peg could gather up enough berries she would make her own special summer variety preserves and store them amongst her butter curds, pickles and candies.

But during the months of autumn, the Sunday nights were ones to cherish and remember for that was when the neighbours would go from house-to-house playing cards. They would not only play for money but also for Christmas hampers, bottles of whiskey, brandy and not to mention the turkeys, legs of mutton and hams. Mainly, it was the men who played the cards while the women would happily pass their time chatting and knitting Aran sweaters and caps for their families and friends abroad.

It's amazing how the old sean-nos or traditional customs live on from generation-to-generation and when it came to playing cards they certainly have left their mark. Some of the older men were of the belief that card playing was about luck and not skill and Sean Og was no different. He would always make sure that he never sat with his back to the fireplace as he believed by doing so, you were sure to instil bad luck into your hand of cards. While Paddy Coffey on the other hand, would religiously place his handkerchief on the chair and sit in it throughout the game, his father and grandfather were of the belief that this was a sure way of a winning strike. And maybe there was something in it, as he would always come up trumps in the major games.

When the card games were over, a few extra sods of turf were placed on the fire and everyone would gather round listening attentively to Jeremiah who was better know as the Seanchai from Mountain Stage as he recited stories of days of yore. The children would sit around totally in awe of his stories of folklore regarding people going astray in the fairy mist "an ceo siog" on their way home from the pub on dark stormy winter nights.

The farmyard creatures that were befriended were a source of amusement no matter what season you lived in, for they had developed human characterises of their very own. The two grey geese with white bibs would come to the back door looking for scraps of food first thing every morning. Peg had named them the Sisters of Charity. She would joke, that the nuns had come back to taunt and haunt her in the form of these two crazy geese. The two geese would remain at the doorstep for ten minutes or so, knocking with their bills and when they realised there was nothing to be gained in alms, they would crap on the doorstep and set off on their way. Peg maintained that they would do this out of spite and somehow they were aware that this would get Peg in a right strop for the morning. Throughout the day, they could be seen going from stable to stable to see what they could retrieve, side-by-side nodding in harmony like two nuns saying their vespers. Every now and again the four Aylesbury ducks would mimic the same antics of the geese and join them on their rounds.

Then there was Roger the Indian Runner drake who had the posture and attitude of an Anglo Irish Landlord. He would walk tall with his head held high, graced with a grandiose attitude as if he was expecting the other ducks to bow their heads to him. Peg would have you believe, what he was trying to say was, "I really shouldn't be dwellin' amongst these riff raff...." Every now and again, he would make a farting sound which would leave him with an undignified hop to his waddle. This was not only a source of amusement to Johnny but also to the other ducks. They would quack and quack amongst themselves with their little heads bobbing up and down as if they were overcome with fits of laughter.

And then there was Mrs Broody the big brown hen that demented herself, running and racing around looking after her chicks. And between her clucking and crowing there were times when she herself was in some doubt whether she was meant to be a cock or a hen. Last year, Sean Og changed her eggs while she was sitting patiently on her nest and when all her clutch happened to be born with broad bills and webbed feet there was some confusion. The other hens and ducks had a look and with all the clucking and quacking you could tell that they were saying, "ya've been had, ya've been had aul girleen...." But Mrs Broody knew, a mother has got to do, what a mother has got to do and that's simply get on with the job of rearing her clan. And over the weeks that followed she was in a right tri-na-cheile dragging and chasing them away from the puddles of water in case they might drown or so she thought. Well, that was one clutch she was happy to bid farewell to when they were old enough to leave the safety of her nest and bosom.

But, when it came to George, the big proud rooster, it was a different story. He certainly didn't suffer fools gladly. He would take no nonsense for humans, animals or fowl. According to him, there was one law and that was his law. And no matter how much you encouraged him to abide by the farmyard rules, he would always revert back into his own contrary ways. He demanded a six-foot personal zone around his presence at all times. And if you dare to enter that zone he would soon remind you with a sudden dart from his spurs and claws. Once you respected him and accepted his nature, he was fine. Peg was aware that the way to a man's heart was through his belly so if she practised the same philosophy on George then they might have an understanding. And sure enough, she found out that he was parochial to a fresh egg. So every morning without fail, she would bring him a token of her respect in the shape of raw egg from the henhouse. Peg maintained that he was the reincarnation of the cranky Parish Priest who had resided in Cahirciveen all those years ago and who was better known to the locals as Misery Miser.

Sally, the dog was a bungle of joy day and night, always ready to hear your joys and woes. She was cautious of people around Johnny and looked upon herself as his guardian. She got herself into the family way by Jack the greyhound mutt from down the road a few years back, but soon discovered after a few weeks of mothering that parenting wasn't really for her, she felt that she was more of a career girl. From that day on, any stray dog that happened to fancy his chances of charming her was politely given his marching orders. Peg maintained that Sally had human sensibility about her and many folk would say that she was right. But lyric music was Sally's speciality and whenever she heard it on the wireless, she would stand erect with her head arched into the air and howl as loud as she could in tune to the music. There were times when you would wonder if the ghost of an opera singer possessed her doggy existence. Every now and again she would insist on having one of her doggy days. On that day she would stretch out in comfort on the thick goatskin rug in front of the open fire and neither man, woman, child or beast could move her. Then, the following day she would be back to her usual attentive self, ready and waiting to be at everybody's beck and call.

Nancy the goat was a cross between a Victorian lady and a kitchen maid. There were times, she would stroll around the yard all high and mighty but when it came to feeding time she certainly forgot her table manners. Her milk was a God-sent for Johnny. It not only helped his asthmatic chest but also his eczema. She had no objection to Johnny humiliating her in front of the other animals when he would insist on dressing her up in Peg's old scarf and cardigans. He would then put her on a leash made for one of Jim's old leather belts and take her down the boreen with Sally for a stroll. You were assured that they were never too far away by the ding-dong of Nancy's bell. Sally and Nancy were kindred folk and maybe it was so because they shared a special friend, but whatever it was, when the family was away they would both curl up together at the back door waiting patiently to greet the family's return with a woof, woof and a maa, maa.

Chapter Twenty-Five

Challenging Moments

Peg visits Doc, as she isn't feeling her best and she tells him that she is so afraid of dying and wishes she were more courageous while coping with her illness.

"Peg, always remember courage ain't the absence of fear but the willingness to proceed in its presence," explains Doc as he tries to reassure her.

"Cancer, of all illnesses, I can't understand how it came to infest me," sobbed Peg.

"Cancer ain't choosy and its host cells will happily invade any organ of the body. I believe that cancer is the illness of the unlaughed laughter and the unshed tears. It germinates in the psychic and results in tumours in the physical body It's the illness of the suffocated emotions past and present. It's fast becoming an illness of our times. I guess one could say it's a legacy of western living. In another thirty years, it'll germinate its parasitic cells in one person in every three," said Doc taking off his specs and cleaning them with lining of his tweed jacket.

"Doc, I've so many mixed emotions these days. I don't know whether I'm comin' or goin' with meself. Me mind seems to take over me body and I can't seem to manage me emotions. I find meself lashin' out at Jim and Johnny for no apparent reason. I'm so angry with God, with life and with everyone that has somethin' to be happy about. I ask the question, time and time again, why me, ohhhhh Christ why me?" sobbed Peg aloud into her handkerchief.

"What you're feeling is normal, a natural response to a disappointment in life. One of the first responses or reactions to any form of disappointment in life and especially when it comes to terminal illness can be anxiety, fear and conflict with yourself and others," explained Doc with a sorrowful tone in his voice as it somehow troubled him to see Peg in such a state.

He goes on to tell her that the teachings of the Catholic Church tells us that to understand the ways of Christianity we need faith, hope and charity. But he believes to have a true understanding of life and what it has in store for us we need to have faith, courage and curiosity. Faith to become grounded in our own spirituality and not to allow dogmatic ways and teachings influence us into changing our inner belief. We need courage to live life while living with the essence of our spirituality. And we need a self-contained curiosity that will give us the ability to understand and reason out the mysteries that life holds for us. During our daily lives we are so disturbed by so many thoughts that are jumbled around in our minds that we find it difficult to focus on the here and now. If we could focus on what we are doing, we would get more enjoyment out of living.

"That's something you'll have to do, Peg. You'll have to focus on your ability to live in the present and not put all your energy into fighting and worrying about your illness. At present, like us all, you've potential for living and live that potential, don't knock it back. Accept your illness as a part of you. Befriend that illness and love it as you'd love yourself. Respect it as you'd respect yourself. But only allow it to take from you that which you're prepared to allow it to do. Don't let it take over your life or it'll taunt every breath you take. Disabling your ability to enjoy life," said Doc sitting on the edge of his desk holding Peg's hand as she sits hunched up sobbing away to herself.

"I see...I guess...ya're right...Doc, but...it's so hard," sobbed Peg finding it hard to get the words out.

"Peg, when you come to walk with your illness and accept it as a part of you, you'll find contentment with yourself and your illness. Then and only then, will you feel at ease with death, whatever you do Peg dear, don't lose your ability to laugh. When we lose the ability to laugh, we'll certainly experience an uneasiness that'll weaken our immune system. This uneasiness in us often goes on to cause disease in the physical and emotional body. The more ill at ease we feel, the more we allow ourselves to become separated from the world around us. When this happens, depression often hands us a lifeline, inviting us to go out on a limb and retreat from the merry-go-round of society, offering us time to rediscover and reclaim our lives through the help and guidance of professional people. If we could allow ourselves the privilege to find enjoyment in nature, we'd have a greater harmony between our bodies, minds and souls," replied Doc as he prepares to take more blood tests from Peg.

"That's interestin' for when I need to think, I go to the strand. I find great solitary with the sea and the sound of the waves lashin' up against the rocks. If I feel a rage within meself, I find goin' to watch the sea on stormy day tends to calm me emotional uproar that I can't put into words. I don't know why but for me it works. And then, when I'm happy I love to sit and look at the blueness and stillness of the ocean. I feel that water has great healin' powers. It....certainly....leaves.... its effect on me...Doc," yawned Peg now feeling more at ease as somehow the tears relieved her anxiety and crying wasn't something she felt she could readily do in the home as she feared it worried Jim and Johnny when she got herself into an emotional tizzy.

"Well, when you look at the ability and power of water and the life it beholds, it ain't surprising that it holds healing powers. It exhibits its gentleness in the lakes and its harshness in the sea. The rage of the sea can be linked to the torment that a troubled mind contains. Yet the gentleness of the lake resembles the contentment we feel within ourselves and with life. Simply, we're not in conflict with the elements when we're content within ourselves," said Doc standing up to take her blood pressure.

"Ya're so right, Doc," mumbled Peg letting out a long deep sigh. "Now come to think of it, we blame the weather for so much of our emotional upheavals."

"Peg, I thought I knew everything about health and healing when I left medical school, but the more, I practised the less I felt they taught us," sighed Doc writing up a prescription for more pain relief tablets for Peg.

"The body is a very complex creation and I guess we'll never truly understand the power that wan's spirituality has as it guides the human body through life," replied Peg sitting on the edge of her chair attentively listening to what Doc has to say about life.

"I've to come to understand that our bodies ain't just a great mass of flesh and boncs we carry around with us day in and day out, it's much more than that. It's the atlas to the human being. It's the nesting place of our feelings and emotions, our dreams and ambitions, our secrets and denials. It's the temple of our souls. It's the campsite of visited and revisited illnesses and conquered challenges. It's a reservoir of chemistry, biology and psychology. Each line, wrinkle, scar and wound revealing a page from life's story. It envelops our dignity and integrity with our individuality. It reveals to the world what we really are. And with all that in mind, I can't understand why we're so ready to treat it like a trash can," said Doc as he continues filling in Peg's medical chart and carefully puts the blood samples in a small envelope ready to be sent off in the evening post.

That evening while quietly sitting by the fire, Peg tells Jim about the seriousness of her illness. Even thought it upsets her very much she tries to keep a brave face and keep the conversation as light hearted as possible. As they memorise over the good times and the challenging times they laugh at the mistakes they both made and how it worried them so much at the time. Yet now, all those mistakes were only shadows in a moment in time and milestones of learning behaviours in character building.

Peg is finding it difficult to come to terms with her illness and is determined to fight it as she feels that maybe Doc is expecting the worst. But deep down, Jim has seen a lowering of her spirits over the past month and fears that Doc may have it right. Her weight loss is beginning to be noticed not only by him but also by the neighbours who asked about her well-being of late. As they talk about their innermost wishes and dreams she tells him that if she was given one wish from childhood she would wish to live Christmas through the eyes of a child. A special feeling and moment that was taken away from her when she was sent into care in the Industrial School.

Jim smiles at the simplicity of the wish but when he takes time to think about it fully, it's only then he truly understands the affects of the mystic magic that Christmas has on a child's mind. During his own childhood he had always taken this for granted, as he never questioned Santa, for Santa always came and on Christmas morning a little surprise was always to be found under the Christmas tree.

Chapter Twenty-Six

An Autumn Stroll

While out picking blackberries with Johnny, Jim meets up with Doc who is walking his dogs in the forest. They talk about death and the fears that we have around dying. Doc shares his wisdom with Jim on how to allow Peg to live life while preparing for her passing. Doc explains that if one loves life then there is no need to fear death and if we cerebrated the gift of life every day we would be prepared for death. He tells him how he himself confronted death when he attempted to take his own life after his wife's passing.

"Jim, I felt so alone and empty, I felt that I'd nothing to live for. I felt totally detached and isolated from this world of ours. But time and God helped me to heal from within and somehow life did come together for me. I've been fortunate enough to have some good times and now I'm able to find strength from the wonderful memories my wife shared with me while she walked this earth," said Doc.

As the two men get engrossed with chatting about life and death, Doc has some sensible words on how to prepare Johnny for the passing of his mum.

"Over the next few weeks Peg will to come to term within herself with the many emotions that taunt the terminally ill person," said Doc as he picks some of the fresh ripe juicy blackberries from the brambles on the nearby hedgerows. "You see Jim, too many of us kill off the terminally ill person before they die. People aren't dead until they've taken their last breath. And one of the greatest holdbacks in dying is that people look at you as dead while you're still living. Whatever life, we've in our veins we must be allowed to live it. There're many simple things we can do for terminally ill patients to comfort them while they're living...."

"Maybe so," sighed Jim nibbling at a blackberry.

"Often in my work, I liken dying to the labour of childbirth. In childbirth, the mother goes through pain but when it comes to death, it's the family and friends that go through the emotional labour pains for the person that's dying. But like childbirth there's also joy in death knowing that you've helped the dying person to achieve their goals while they were still alive. But the greatest joy of all is being aware that on their deathbed they've made their peace with themselves, peace with their God and with who ever else they needed to make peace with. And it's only then you yourself, can rest in peace knowing in your heart that their deserving Spirit can pass on to the next world and not linger as a troubled Spirit around the earthly zone. Death needs to be befriended and not feared. If we could allow ourselves the privilege of doing so, we'd live life to it's fullness and get the best from it. So you see Jim, birth and death are an essential part of living. We may try to separate them and pull them apart but they're joined together by only one fragile breath. It's that tender fragile breath that allows us to live or to die. We've the choice of dying while we are still living or living while we're dying. That choice...... is..... for us to make."

"I see," replied Jim looking around at the beauty of the autumn leaves.

Doc hands an unripe blackberry to Johnny and laughs aloud at Johnny's facial expression as he chews into it. As Johnny skips on ahead with Sally the two men continue their conversation as they causally stroll through the forest with the rust coloured leaves rustling under their feet.

"What's a child's reaction to death? Take Johnny for instance, what'll I tell him when he wakes up wan mornin' and looks for his Ma. In the honour of Jaysus, how on earth, am I gonna explain death to him and how does a child like Johnny cope with the death of his Ma? There must be times after a death when parents are so busy tryin' to put life back together again that they unconsciously ignore the grievin' and confused emotions of the kids involved," Jim asked nervously as if to convince himself he'd never have to face that situation.

Doc pauses for a while and picks a small twig from a nearby tree. Biting his lower lip and stripping the twig of its leaves one-by-one as if to recollect his thoughts.

"Jim my dear man, children have mixed emotions regarding death. I guess age and maturity in thought has a lot to do with it. A child under the age of five would see death as a long period of sleep in Holy God's house but every now and again would feel frightened and insecure if the person who's looking after them ain't close at hand. They may revert into their infant years, wetting the bed, looking for extra cuddles and may even want to go back on the bottle. While, a child from five to ten years may see death of a loved one as a punishment from God. They may blame themselves for the death. Again, you could've a period of mental recession where a child can go into their own little world. They may not want to sleep on their own or even demand a night-light while they're at rest. On the other hand, the child may rebel and lash out with temper tantrums. All-in-all, these feelings and emotions are normal under the circumstances...."

"Christtttt, is that so?" sighed Jim as he listened attentively to Doc.

"You'll have to explain that the death wasn't their fault and make sure that you're around to give them reassurance to see them through their good days and their not so good days. Usually in their drawings, the dead person is present for a period after the death but is often stood in the background. When it comes to explaining about death, you'll need to tell Johnny in a way that he understands that his Ma will always be near but not in the way he sees her now. If you involve him in the caring for Peg that in itself will hopefully prepare him as over the days he'll come to accept that his Ma will be leaving and you and him will cope in ye'r own way as life goes on...."

"Grand shur, I'll do that."

"Do mention the word dying and death in your everyday vocabulary and he'll become accustomed to what surrounds the meaning of these words. But Jim, when the time comes, you'll do right by Johnny. I'm convinced of that because of that special bond ye've with each other. He's wan lucky child for many other kids are less fortunate than him as they don't experience that same special bond with their parents..."

"What can I do to help Peg to die peacefully and not make her hold on to the feelin' of guilt that she may have for leavin' Johnny?" asked Jim as he heads over to Johnny and Sally who had been a little too adventurers and had climbed over a barred wire fence and are now in a little wee bit of bother as the wire is entangled in Johnny's sweater.

"Stay to the stiles, Johnnyboy, and ya'll be just grand," insisted Jim as he helps Johnny. "Sorry Doc ya were sayin'.."

"Yeah Jim, there's so much fear around dying that very often the terminally ill feel they've no one to turn to and as a result of this, they encounter a lot of silent anxiety and suffer inner torment regarding their moment of death. What they need most of all, is to feel at ease to discuss their fears openly. This will help them understand and reason out challenging moments that we're all faced with when it comes to dying. Where there's fear, there're always questions to be answered to ease that fear. If these questions are left unanswered, the person will suffer from unnecessary physical and mental pain. There will always be the natural worries and concerns regarding pain. Will there be pain? If so, will I be able to cope in a dignified way? If I'm unable to manage and cope, will I feel comfortable with the person I find myself at the mercy of? When it's time to letting go, how will my family and loved ones cope? Will they be able to accept it, so that I can die in peace? How will I cope when the people I love, can't cope with me suffering?"

"By….Christttt….so many questions….. and so many answers…..to seek out," muttered Jim under his breath.

"And then Jim, It ain't unusual for the person to be overcome with fear of the unknown, worrying about what really happens when a person dies? Is there an afterlife? Who can prove that there's an afterlife, maybe it's all hearsay, maybe not. They may even experience moments where they feel incomplete in their own life, feeling guilty for not achieving their life's goals. They may need to put personal grievances to right. Getting Peg to feel comfortable in her own spirituality will help her to prepare for the afterlife and allow her the freedom and dignity to make peace with herself, with God and with others. She'll need encouragement and assistance to write down her desires and wishes for Johnny and others after she has passed on. You, yourself will have the responsibility of organising the funeral, choosing a burial site and whatever type of removal service she'll desire. These are issues to discuss when Peg herself has come to terms with letting go of life and responsibilities and accepts the privilege to focus on the moments of passing on…"

"Christttt…..so much …to do," sighed Jim.

"What I always ask of the family and friends is to sit down together and write up a list of all the little accomplishments and achievements of the person who's dying. Something in the line of a written autobiography of the person, it doesn't need to be anything fancy. Put in some photos of past memories. Then, when the time is right, have a family gathering and let the dying person hear about their achievements. Let them know that they too have made a difference while living. This is often a good way of allowing them to say their farewells in the security and compassion of their family and friends. I guess you could liken it to the final farewell and a cerebration of the life they shared with us, not unlike the American Wake that the Irish cerebrated when a loved one was emigrating. After all, if we could look at death as a journey then there'd be less fear around it. And I myself believe it's a journey and a transition in one's life."

"A grand way of putting it," smiled Jim.

"Well, that's the way I've looked at it since my wife Betty passed on all those years ago with our little baby in her arms. I placed our little baby in her arms as she was laid to rest in the coffin. I feel their presence in my shadow everyday and there ain't a night I don't ask her to guide me through my working day. I guess in some strange way she has become my Spirit Guide. I believe she had the personality of the Mayfly, always living for today, for in her eyes there was no tomorrow. She loved life and lived every moment as if it was her last. She'd say that tomorrow is only a figment of one's imagination, a figment that allowed us the excuse to off load whatever we weren't willing to take on today. In some strange way, when her time did come to pass on, even though there was a great sadness in her parting, somehow, I did feel that she had achieved everything she had to achieve on this earth. God rest their souls and may they have eternal happiness in the arms of each other. For me Jim, Betty is my past, present and future. She was, she is and she'll always be,
The sun that brightens up my mornin',
The moon that brings me into my night,
The stars that flicker light through my darkness
And the air I breathe as I travel through life.. ".

"Christttt…..that lovely…simply…lovely," nodded Jim and his chin began to quiver.

"Peg will be to you, as Betty is to me. You never let go of a loved one for people in love never really die, as you'll always store them safely in your heart. They're so precious and dear when you feel so alone in your isolation of your emotional and mental confusing moments. If you love them when they're alive and cherish them when they pass on, you'll never lose them," sighed Doc as he wipes the tears from his eyes.

The church bell could be heard in the distance and the weather was on the turn as the heavy clouded sky had turned to drizzle when the two men bid farewell and each in their own way grateful to fate for granting them the privilege of sharing each other's companionship and friendship.

Chapter Twenty-Seven

Redeeming News From The Past

It's a wet Sunday afternoon in early October and Peg is pleasantly surprised with an unexpected visitor. It's her good friend Fr. Murphy. You should've heard the excitement from Johnny as he runs to welcome him. Sally too greets him with her usual welcoming yaps and wagging tail. And to add to Johnny's excitement Fr. Murphy has brought him a bag of toffees and an ounce of bull's eyes.

Peg had just put a match to the turf fire in the sitting-room grate and it isn't long before it's ablaze and they're all happily tucking into a nice cup of tea and a slice of apple tart with lashings of thick cream. As time passes, Jim notices that Fr. Murphy isn't his usual cheerful self and somehow he knows that Peg is aware of it also.

"I'm gonna take Johnny up the meadow to teach him a wee bit of dowsin' and we'll spend some time up in the spinney, Ach shur, ye might like to have a nice wee chat. I'm sure ye've a lot to catch up on," said Jim winking across at Fr. Murphy.

He anticipated that Fr. Murphy has something to confess to Peg and he feels whatever it is, it's in need of privacy. But he certainly isn't prepared for what Peg is about to be told.

"Dowsing?" replied Fr. Murphy. "Good God I haven't heard someone mention dowsing since I was a young nipper many moons ago. My Grand father had the gift...."

"Well, truth behold, it was me own father who passed the gift on to me when I was about Johnny's age so

I feel maybe it's time to see if Johnny can carry it on to the next generation. I've cut a nice 'Y' rod from wan of the apple trees and I'll start him out with that and see how he'll go. Hopefully we'll source out some water and that should entice him to learn more," said Jim beckoning to Johnny to follow on.

The spinney is the overgrown patch of wood attached to the farm and even though it's only an acre or so in density it is Johnny's wonderland. Sean Og and Jim had just finished building a tree house for him in the branches of the old sycamore tree. It is here that Johnny would spend many hours searching out rabbits, pheasants and other woodland creatures in the company of Sally. Many a time he would return home cold, tired and mucky with his little legs torn from the overgrown brambles and covered in nettle stings, but that didn't seem to bother him for it was all an essential part of his adventures with Sally.

"That'd be grand, Jim. Peg and I'll be on ye'r heels in a few minutes," replied Fr. Murphy winking back at Jim and relieved at the thought of being alone with Peg when he confesses what he has to say.

"Ach shur, Father, ya'll have another cuppa. Give me that wan ya've in ya'r hand. Ya've bein' nursin' that like a mother nursin' babe in arms since ya came in. Give it here to me and I'll put a hot sup in it," said Peg as she pours out another cup of tea.

"Shhhhh Peg, I'm grand girl, just sit down I've something to tell you. I don't know where to start," mumbled Fr. Murphy biting his lower lip, looking at her from under his bushy grey eyebrows, and doing his best not to allow the shakes of anxiety into his legs.

There is a brief silence.

"Yerra Father. What's botherin' ya at all, it can't be that bad. Ya're like somewan who's lost a pound and found a farthin'. Nobody I know died or committed murder or did they, but I must say, ya've been a little off colour since ya popped in," chuckled Peg trying to lighten up the silence.

"Nooooo. Peg, certainly not my child, but what I've to say affects us both. Emm, where do I start? Yerra shur, I'll start back at the beginning."

There was another awkward silence.

"Do you remember, when you worked with me in Cahirciveen all those years ago and a dark haired woman with a little girl came to stay with me for a week or two? Can you remember that far back, Peg? It was a lovely warm May. Yerra shur, I remember it well, the swallows returned in mid-April and the farmers were rewarded with a good harvest from the meadows and bogs," said Fr. Murphy.

"The woman that came to visit ya with a little girl called Geraldine. She had red curly hair, freckled skin and bright blue eyes. And I was so surprised at how different she looked in compression to her parents. Do ya remember Father? Both of the parents had brown eyes and dark hair. I remember the child was so happy with the rag doll I made for her," said Peg looking at him with a puzzled expression and wondering as to where the angle of the conversation was going.

"Yeah...the...very one," sighed Fr. Murphy as he feels an uneasiness overcoming him.

"Wasn't that ya'r sister Kate and her daughter? I remember at the time she spent a lot of time inquirin' about me family's background. At the time, this puzzled me but I thought that she was just simply interested in me. I remember wan evenin' I got very upset and told her about me little baby girl that I gave birth to and how she died. I could feel that she felt very uncomfortable with the conversation and she told me that ya needed me help with getting' the church ready for the evenin' confessions. The followin' day, on leavin' for America she promised to keep in contact with me and she was true to her word. Several times a year she sends a parcel to us. She never forgot us. Shur, ya had a photo of Geraldine on ya'r sideboard when Jim and I went to visit ya some months back. Do ya remember, Jim said that she had the look of our Johnny when he was that age?" smiled Peg as she sips the drags of her tea and rearranges the tea leaves at the end of her mug with her finger.

"I…certainly…do," replied Fr. Murphy. "Can you remember the day Kate took a photo of you and Geraldine?"

"I do indeed. I got me hair all done up and wore that lovely blue dress that Kate bought for me in the Irish House in Cahirciveen. I remember feelin' so excited 'cause Kate let me use her lipstick and powder."

Silence once again takes over and they both look at each other, each wanting to be rescued from the moment.

"I need to get something from the car. Fan linn," he said shattering the silence.

On his return he produces a photo in a gold frame. It's the photo of Peg and Geraldine.

"I'd like you to have this. The little girl in this photo ain't really Kate's birth-child. She was adopted when she was only four days old or so. You see, Kate and her husband were unable to have children and the nuns in Cork organised the adoption for them. So you see, Kate adopted Geraldine as a baby," said Fr. Murphy as he closely watches Peg's reaction and facial expression as she focuses on the photo.

"Good God…..wasn't Kate…..wonderful….to do that. Give a child the chance of a wonderful life," exclaimed Peg looking at the photo and she is overcome with tears, for at that moment, the past comes rushing back to her. "Ohhhh Christ Father, I'd give anythin' to think that me baby hadn't died and was somewhere safe and happy. How I've missed her everyday of me life. There ain't a day go by without I thinkin' of her. Ya know, I still light the candle by night to her memory. Strange though, I feel her in the shadow of me footprints."

Fr. Murphy embraces her in his arms, looks up to Heaven, and prays that God will guide him through what he has to declare. The silence around the secret of Peg's baby was a promise that he vowed he would never break until Kate granted him the permission to do so.

"Well, Peg my dear, Kate had every reason to be kind to you and look out for your well-being. All those years ago…..I found out…..that your baby….never died…. and …..she happens…to be the baby that Kate adopted. Kate was also aware of this but she was unable to tell you through fear and insecurity and maybe through selfishness. We kept it a secret up until last week when we told Geraldine about her birth mother, she's so excited and wants desperately to meet with you. Peg, forgive me for isolating you from this grievous secret that Kate and I've carried around in our hearts for so long."

Peg pulls away from his embracing arms.

"Whist…..what're ya sayin'….I don't understand… what're ya tryin' to tell me. There has to be some mistake, Father. The nuns told me that me baby died 'cause I didn't take proper care of her. Shur….that's what…they told me… all those years ago."

"I know Peg, what they told you and it was such a dreadful lie, you've suffered a grave injustice and I've taken an active part in it," sighed Fr. Murphy holding out his arms once more trying to comfort her in her moment of disbelief.

"But ya're tellin' me now, that she didn't die. And ya knew all along?" stuttered Peg in dismay.

"Forgive me Peg, all I can ask is for your forgiveness," gasped Fr. Murphy now stripping himself of his own dignity and feeling ashamed of intentionally wronging this innocent woman that stood in front of him.

"By Christ, nooooo Father. How can I forgive ya, how can I ever forgive ya when there's nothin' to forgive. I knew…..I just knew….. that I didn't kill…. me baby. I just knew it in me heart and soul. Somethin' in me kept tellin' me that she was alive. I always knew that she was out there somewhere. I…..don't know….why I knew that….. but I did. I guess it's a motherin' thing. God, ohhhh me God I don't believe it," sobbed Peg holding out her arms and embracing Fr. Murphy close. It's the closeness of a mother embracing her child.

"Ohhhh my child.... ohhhh my child," was all Fr. Murphy managed to mutter.

"Thank ya, ohhhh thank Father," she sobbed deeply with relief, grief and joy into the comforting embrace of his tightly gripping arms.

"But Peg, you're not angry with me?" he sighed as he tries to ease the tightness of his throat and steady his trembling hands and legs.

"Angry, I don't have time to be angry. Ach shur dear God, there ain't too much anger left in me. I've left most of me anger and grief in that terrible laundry in Cork. All I now feel is relief in me heart and soul. I can now rest in me bed knowin' that I didn't kill me baby. Whatever anger I've left would be wasted on those nuns that inflicted this horrific torment and life sentence on me. They'll have to face God on judgement day. They'll have to answer for their own wrongdoin'. I'm ain't goin' to punish meself by ponderin' to their wrongdoin' any more."

At this stage the tears shed by Fr Murphy and Peg join in unity with the closeness of their cheeks.

"Thank you Peg, for being so understanding of my selfish wrongdoings." muttered Fr Murphy.

"Ahhhhhh Christtttt, nooooooo Father, in all fairneeees ya'd ya'r own cross to carry and ya carried it well. It's about time ya were unburdened from that cross as I'm from mine. Ach shur, look at the terrible punishment that was inflicted on ya when ya tried to put things right all those years ago. Ya were only tryin' to help those who suffered terrible injustices at the hands of the Religious Orders. Ya were isolated from ya'r friends, ya'r parish and also ya'r family 'cause ya were courageous and honourable to become a whistle blower and let the world know about the sufferin' of victims of abuse...."

"That was a small burden to carry compared to the burden that was inflicted on you, my child," he whispered, sighing in a moment of relief.

His prayers were answered and once again he had so much to be grateful for, as God had befriended him and had listened to his request and granted it.

"But thinkin' back on that moment when the nuns told me that I'd killed me baby, it does make me want to yell out in rage. They made me feel so bad and guilty. I asked to go to the funeral and they said that the baby wouldn't want the mother who neglected her to be at the Mass or burial. They said that I was just as sinful as those women that were havin' abortions and that I deserved to be punished by God. Ach shur Father, at the time, I didn't even know what abortion meant. Were abortions goin' on in Ireland at the time, Father?" asked Peg wiping the glass of the photo frame with the corner of her apron as if to get a clearer look at her daughter.

"Indeed they were. I remember an uncle of mine, who was a doctor in Dublin in the forties and the fifties, told me that a midwife had her own nursing home in Dublin where she carried out abortions for the gentry. Doctors used to transfer pregnant ladies to her. Seemly a Mrs O'Reilly died in her care while she was carrying out an abortion and there was a right "ri ra and ruille buille" with the Law. As far as I can tell the midwife was charged with manslaughter...."

"Really?" butted in Peg amazed that the medical people would carry out abortions in Ireland for she always understood that women had to take the boat to England to have one in secrecy.

But in her moment of delight and realising the full extent of the good news that she had just received she cries aloud.

"After all these years, Jim and I've a daughter, Johnny has a sister and Sean Og has a niece, fancy that, sweet Jaaaysus, I can't believe it."

Her face now shone with a beaming smile from cheek to cheek. Fr. Murphy slips his hand into his inside pocket of his black suit jacket and pulls out another photo.

"This is your daughter Geraldine now. She has become a beautiful young girl not unlike yourself when I first laid eyes on you the day you got off that bus in Cahirciveen so many moons ago," he said handing it to Peg.

Taking the photo in her hand she looks at it in silence and then smiles with admiration.

"Me little Blathin, that's what I called her all those year ago. She's beautiful. Look at her beautiful long red hair and her bright blue eyes She even has me freckles. She's so beautiful. I can't believe it, lookin' at her, I feel that I've known her all these years...."

"But, you did my child, you kept her living in your heart. She's beautiful just like you. That's what Kate said the very first day she laid eyes on you, having found out that you were Geraldine's birth mother all those years ago," said Fr Murphy as he watches the mothering aura surround Peg.

"I remember it, like it was only yesterday. I can still see Geraldine playin' with that rag doll. I made it for her in the sewin' room at the top of the stairs in the convent. I remember the nuns got wan of the pupils to help with stitchin' on the clothes," chuckled Peg now shaking her head in total amazement.

"Well believe it or not, she still has that rag doll. Kate put it away safely as it was to remind Geraldine of you," chuckled Fr. Murphy as he eyes focus on the photo. "When I went to see them in New York last Christmas, I saw it on a rocking chair in Geraldine's bedroom. Kate and I laughed at how Geraldine had eaten off one of the arms when she was a toddler. We spoke about you and how we had so much to be grateful for....."

"Father, I'm findin' all of this so overwhelmin' It's somethin' I've wished for so long and now it has come true. For in me heart and soul, I knew she didn't die. don't know why, but I guess a mother just simply knows," said Peg holding the photo close to her bosom.

"Well the bond between a mother and child is something that's special and lives on forever. I guess one could say that it's the invisible string of eternity."

"When.....can.....I see.....me daughter?" exclaimed Peg with delight.

"Geraldine has known for many years now that she was adopted but it was only in the last week that she was made fully aware of the fact that you're her birth mum. She has asked to meet with you and is fair excited about it. Kate and I've spoken about it and we were hoping that Geraldine could come to Ireland and spend some time with you. If that's all right?"

"Mother of sweet Jaysus, of course it's all right. After all, she's family, wan of us. Johnny will be so happy to have a sister of his own to play with...."

"But.....what about.... Jim? How do you think he'll react to the news?" Fr. Murphy asked cautiously.

"Well I've told him about the nuns in the Laundry and how they said that the baby had died. He might find it hard to take it all in at once. It'll of course be a shock to him but a nice wan, please God," replied Peg walking around and around the room clapping and rubbing her hands with the delight of it all.

"Will it upset him? Maybe I shouldn't be around when you tell him. He mightn't be too happy with me when he realises that I kept the secret from you," muttered Fr. Murphy and one could tell that deep in his heart he knew that Jim wouldn't take the news in the same spirit as Peg.

"Ahhhh, don't let that bother ya. He'll be confused for a while, but in time he'll come to terms with it. He has a good forgivin' kind heart and after all, ya were only doin' right by ya'r family and Geraldine. He'd have probably done the same if he was in ya'r robes and shoes."

"You're an amazing, wonderful woman, you're a true symbol of Christianity. It's a pity that some of the members of the Religious Orders that made life so horrible for you and so many others weren't like you," said Fr. Murphy taking Peg's hands in his and kissing her gently on the cheek. "I sincerely hope all goes well for you and Jim. I'll be on my way and may God bless you and all those who dwell and visit here."

"Bless ya too, Father. And thank ya for bringin' such wonderful news to me. Ya'll never know how much peace and wellness I feel in me heart 'cause of this. I can die happily now knowin' that I didn't do wrong by God nor by me child," replied Peg as she slowly walks him to his car and waves goodbye as he drives off down the boreen.

In the far field, the cattle and cows were frisky and chasing each other around. That's a sure sign that rain is on the way, thought Peg to herself. Looking over yonder at Tom Coffey's farm she could see that the sheep had their backs turned to the wind and this verified her predication of the forecast. She could hear Jim with Johnny in the backyard sorting out the fowl and animals for the night. As she returns into the sitting room she decides that she will keep the news to herself for a day or so to let it settle in and she just wanted the privilege of having the pleasure and good feeling of knowing, what she now knew to herself for a little while longer.

"Everythin' okay?" Jim shouted out as he comes in from the yard with Johnny.

"Yeah," she called back and from the spark in her voice Jim could tell that Fr. Murphy had brought some good news.

"Fr. Murphy gone?"

"Indeed he is," chuckled Peg slipping the photo of Geraldine into her apron pocket.

"Had a good aul chat, didya?"

"Yeah, everythin' is just grand now, Jim," she replied trying to curb the excitement in her voice.

"That's….great," he called out. "Johnny me dear fella, lets get supper on and give ya'r Ma a rest."

"Weather's on the turn, don't ya think so?" called out Peg as she snuggled into her armchair.

"Ya might be right, ahhhhh shur, the mountains look very close," muttered Jim gawping out the kitchen window. "Emm….that….they do……that….they certainly do."

Just before going to bed, Peg lights the candle on the windowsill and in her silent prayer she thanks God for allowing Geraldine back into her life and prays that He will keep her safe until they both have the privilege of sharing some precious moments once again.

While they all slept peacefully in their beds, Peg creeps down stairs into the kitchen to enjoy a cup of coca and bond with her daughter in spirit. Her heart wants to shout from the rooftop, "me baby's alive. I didn't kill her. I've a daughter, I've a daughter." She aches to wake Jim and tell him but a voice from deep within nudges her to hold on to the feeling and cherish it. She holds the photo to her bosom and once again in her life she is totally overcome with the sensation that a mother experiences when she embraces her newborn for the first time. As she sits there in the stillness of the night, sharing those few precious moments with herself, she now has closure to a life long emotional and spiritual trial that she felt she was trapped in, for her, the jury had been out for so many years unable to come up with a verdict. Over the years, if only she had some evidence and acknowledgement of the death of her baby, a memory of a funeral, a burial site or even a death certificate but she had none of these to put her agonising mind at ease. Year in and year out, her mind was filled with so much doubt yet her heart and spirit held on to hope.

As she looks at the photo of Geraldine, she now has physical evidence that the verdict to her emotional and spiritual trial was, NOT GUILTY to the outcome of the life-long-charge the nuns from the Magdalen Laundry had committed her to, all those years ago. There is no anger in her heart nor bitterness, but relief for she could now focus her energy on coming to know her daughter once again.

As she sits there in her moment of reflection, her eyes settle on the photograph of Johnny as a baby on the windowsill and the more she looks at it, the more she could see Geraldine in him. Picking it up and holding the photo of Geraldine that Fr. Murphy had given her earlier that afternoon next to it, her mind wanders back to the births of both of her children.

It was just a year into their marriage when she gave birth to Johnny and after that, life changed for Jim and herself. She found comfort in her loving and mothering of Johnny and Jim felt left out on a limb in their relationship. She now realises that due to the smothering effect of her love for Johnny and Sean Og she unconsciously neglected her husband. Even though Jim was many years her senior, he still was very young at heart and ached for the attention and love of a wife. As she thinks back over Geraldine's birth, flashbacks come rushing back of the memory of how she laboured for two day and two nights. The cruel treatment she received while in labour now brings tears to her eyes.

Johnny's birth followed a long difficult labour in the home and while she laboured with him, revisited memories of her first labour made her reluctant to push him out in the second stage of labour. Her body was filled with pain, her heart filled with joy but her mind was filled with guilt and fear. Guilt in thinking that her baby had died in the Magdalen Laundry because of her neglect, well that was for the nuns had made her believe. She remembers the labour pains that she experienced for two days and two nights. Geraldine was born two weeks early and because of that, the nun in charge thought that Peg was falsifying her pain and faking her discomfort. She was ordered to continue working in the washroom and there she remained until on the third day she gave birth to Geraldine as she washed the sheets in the large laundry sink. She herself didn't understand what was happening for nobody had taken the time to explain what birth or labour was about. She remembers the shouts and screams for help from the laundry girls that worked with her. She remembers the nun scolding her and slapping her across the face. She remembers the fear that surrounded that moment. She thought that her whole body was about to rupture and she was going to die.

As she sat there in silence she reflects on the moment the baby was born and how the attending nun pressed so hard on her stomach and how she fainted. When she woke up she found herself lying in a pool of blood in the bed with her baby crying in a nearby cot. When she called out for help, the attending nun scolded her for her antics and left her on no uncertain terms that she was a wicked and stupid girl. As her eyes focuses once again on Johnny's picture, she reflects on the moment of his birth and how different it was. The verse that the midwife had her say during her labour comes flashing back into her memories,

A Prayer for an Expectant Mum
God grant me stamina, courage and strength
While abiding and seeing my labour through
And bless the joy these pains will bring
When this little human life blossoms through

Guide me through my mothering instinct
When I listen to the cries of joy and woe
And lead us through the pathway of life
That will allow our love to flourish and grow

When it came to Johnny's birth, she had the choice of going to hospital or remaining in her own home. She opted for a homebirth and from the moment she went into labour she had a midwife by her side. The midwife was helpful and caring and was willing to explain everything as the labour progressed. She remembers the attending doctor and how worried he was when the moment of birth arrived and when she was reluctant to push Johnny out and how he feared that he might lose both of them. The midwife, who had a great understanding of life, could see that Peg had a emotional problem and not a physical one and in her professionalism encouraged Peg to talk out her worries and woes. Peg shared her fears and the memories of the birth of her first child with both of them. The midwife was brought to tears on hearing Peg's story and reassured her that this time all would be grand. The doctor present just simply sat quietly as she told her story and on holding her hand, he encouraged her to continue with the birth.

She remembers the moment Johnny was born and how the doctor looked on with an anxious expression across his brow as the midwife handed her the little baby boy. He could tell that Johnny was a Down's syndrome child. But this didn't trouble Peg. He was her little baby who was born with a caul. This pleased her as it was a sign of good fortune and as the old saying goes, a person who is born with the caul will never meet death by drowning and that is one of the reasons why many sailors and fishermen carry a small piece of caul with them to sea.

She reflects back on the two days of love she shared with Geraldine and how she had a special connection with her when she met again while in service with Fr. Murphy. She could feel the bond she felt with her come rushing back again the moment she held Johnny just a few short moments after his birth. She reflects on the moments when it came to cutting Johnny's umbilical cord, the midwife and doctor allowed her to partake in that privilege and honour. She smiles at the thought of how protective she was of him. Even when the doctor advised that Johnny be taken to the nearby hospital, as he was very wheezy she refused to let him go in the fear that someone might take him away from her. She remembers how Jim couldn't understand why she was so insistent that the doctor should take care of them both in her home bed.

For two years, she never left him out of her sight. Nobody was allowed to see the child unless she was present. She remembers Jim telling the midwife how he couldn't understand Peg's obsessive protective attitude towards Johnny. He would tell their friend that she had developed a broody hen syndrome and was capable of getting into a right tizzy if a person came too close to Johnny. She now smiles, on how Jim insisted that they name their baby boy, John, after the American President John F Kennedy as Jim had a silent admiration of his strong courageous attitude when it came to standing up for people's rights. Thinking back on gone by years, she now sees how Jim felt ignored and how he put all his efforts into his job and into trying to please others. She can still hear the cynical whispers and jokes in local pub that were the sources of gossip of how Jim was only half a man to have fathered such a child as Johnny. But that didn't trouble Jim, for he was always very loving and proud of Johnny and took him everywhere with him.

The more she thinks about Johnny growing up, the more she smiles to herself at his strong streak of stubbornness running through the backbone of his willpower just like that of his Dad. From a very young age, he thought what he wanted to think and he would do what he wanted to do. Once he got a mental grip, on something, he wouldn't let go and he would often go into his hermit crab mood and remain there for days with a stiff upper lip. She reflects on the times when passers-by would compliment her on caring for him "ya'll be blessed in Heaven for all ya do for that wee handicapped child," they would say. But sadly, all they focused on was the handicap and not the child. For Peg, caring and loving Johnny was no different from the unconditional love that any mother would give her children. In Peg's eyes, Johnny was a child with a handicap and not a handicapped child. And only a parent of a child with a handicap could understand that she thought to herself. For in reality, it was that special handicap that had complimented his uniqueness and identity. And truth behold, if more of us could focus on the person and not the handicap, then we would be more aware of the person's ability to cope with their handicap.

As the hours slip by, the silence of the night is harmonised with the sound of the crickets coming from the back of the fireplace, the purring of Cuddy the great big house cat and the ticking of the old grandfather clock in the porch. The more she sat there thinking of Johnny growing up, the more she wondered about Geraldine and what her temperament would be like. Would she have a similar temperament to that of her brother or would she have developed a personality of her own? And, the more she thought about birth and life the more she understood and identify with the verse on the mantelpiece.

The Miracle of Birth

The womb embodying the unborn child
Resembles the chalice embodying the Spirit of the Christ
Each revealing sacred messages of their own

To love and cherish the behold

A mother's love is a blessing
Graced by wonders of the unborn child
But the miracle of birth is the blessing
That is passed on to us from the Divine

Nine sacred months we dwell in utero
Awaiting the coming of the day
Just as Christ nestled in his mother's womb
While finding safety on his way

From a tiny embryo a Human Being grows
Encountering many miracles on the way
But the miracle of birth will always unfold us
As we travel though life from day to day.

Peg stayed in bed a little longer the following morning to once again quietly reflect on her good news. The house is quiet and as she snuggles up listening to Cuddy purring away at her feet, the excitement that she feels in her heart is that of a little girl who has just received her long anticipated present from Santa Claus. It's about ten minutes to mid-day when Peg asks Sean Og to take care of Johnny for the afternoon as she intends to take Jim to the strand for she has something special to tell him.

When they arrived at the strand, she couldn't hold on to the suspense of keeping the wonderful news to herself any longer and it wasn't long before her tongue gushes the words forth like a river bursting its banks.

"What, Peg, let me get me head around what ya're telling me. Ya'r little baby girl didn't die, she happens to be Geraldine, Fr. Murphy's niece in America. His sister Kate adopted her and the nuns told ya that ya killed the baby, but in actual fact they'd given her to Fr. Murphy's sister Kate to adopt. Are ya tellin' me now, that Fr. Murphy knew this all along? And all these years he has left ya suffer mentally, thinkin' that ya'r baby had died 'cause of ya'r neglect?"

raged Jim totally bewildered as he tries to make sense of it all.

Peg could now see that things aren't going the way she had planned and hoped for. Jim isn't taking the news in the same spirit as she herself had taken it. She tries to calm him down and reassure him that all will be okay as she becomes more aware of the frustration and annoyance in his tone of voice.

"Jim… please….. don't be annoyed," she pleaded holding out her wind-chilled hand and touching him gently on his left cheek.

"Peg, I'm more than fuck'in annoyed, I'm fuck'in flippin' and flamin' disappointed with ya so-called friend, Fr. Murphy, for concealin' this from ya. He knew what ya'd suffered. We both trusted him and seemly all along he was keepin' us fuck'in sweet while leadin' us up the garden path. I just don't understand why he wouldn't come clean about this," demanded Jim pulling away and running his fingers through his raven black curly hair in his frustration and dismay.

"Would ya've done any different in his shoes, Jim?" she asked walking after him and catching a hold of his left arm.

"Achhhh Peg, to heck with that, fuck that for a deck of cards. I ain't goin' down that road of thought. He was fuck'in deceitful and there's no two ways of puttin' it. What ails that fellow anyway, what happened to ya in that fuck'in Industrial School and in that dreadful Magdalen Laundry in Cork has affected our lives, our marriage, our relationship and so much more and he of all people was aware of that," yelled Jim now pulling away from her grasp and pounding his clenched right fist into the palm of his left hand.

Peg hadn't seen him in this state of frustration and rage before but insists on taking a hold of him by the arms and looking straight into his eyes, she yelled.

"But…. be honest with ya'rself….would ya've told me?"

"But I ain't in his fuck'in shoes, am I?" snarled Jim squirming at her as he clenches his teeth and his brow now engraved with lines of anguish.

"But….if….ya were…..would ya've told me?" insisted Peg taking a tighter grasp of his arms and shaking him as if to bring him to his senses. At this stage she could feel a slight weakness overcome her body.

Jim stood there in silence for a moment or so staking with temper.

"No….I guess not," he scorned biting into his lower lip. "I… guess… not."

"Anyway Jim, we don't have time for anger or findin' blame 'cause we've too much livin' and lovin' to get on with. I can't lose me baby again 'cause of resentment and anger regardin' the horrible circumstances around me past. I don't have the energy to go out on a witch-hunt wonderin' why Fr. Murphy chose to keep it from me. But I guess he'd Kate and Geraldine's well-bein' in mind and for now, that's a good enough reason for me. Jim, ya must understand, I've so much to catch up on. Yerra Jaysus, I just want to hold her in me arms and be grateful to God for givin' me a second chance. We've a daughter and Johnny has a new sister and ach shur, all in fairneeees, ain't that wonderful news. We must prepare for Geraldine, she's….. comin'….. to Ireland," sobbed Peg embracing Jim and kissing him on his forehead.

"Wow," sighed Jim holding her close and as he holds her in his arms he is aware that her body had lost so much weight. "Ya'll never cease to amaze me, ya've such a wonderful outlook in life. Yerra Christ, ya're right, we can't waste time blamin' people and certainly not Fr. Murphy, he's a good friend and I guess truth behold, we've a lot to thank him for. Ach, Geraldine will love ya. Ach shur, she even has the look of ya and Johnny about her. She'll fit right into our clan like a finger into a glove. Let's get back and tell Johnny and Sean Og all about her…."

"Yeah," nodded Peg. "Yeah, lets head back yonder…"

"Yeah, lets go home darlin'," embraced Jim.

And with that, they both set on their way arm-in-arm across the wind swept strand.

Chapter Twenty-Eight

Jim And Fr. Murphy Meet Up On Ballybunion Strand

It's a misty October afternoon and Jim takes a drive out to meet up with Fr. Murphy to tell him about Peg's illness. They arrange to meet up in Ballybunion Strand. It's a place where one can be close to nature enjoying the sea breeze while having a private chat with a flask of tea and a few sandwiches. Fr. Murphy is taken back with the news and the fact that Peg hasn't spoken to him about her cancer. He was aware that she wasn't feeling her best the last time they met up, but he had put that down to a woman's issue! Jim explains to him that because of Peg's rejection of the local church when her time comes, she doesn't wish to have her remains transferred to that church before the burial. Her wish is that prayers and blessings would take place in the home and that Fr. Murphy would partake in the ceremony for her. Fr. Murphy is honoured that she thinks so highly of him and promises to grant her, her wish.

"How's she taking all of this?" he asked.

"Ahhhhhh God love her, she is handlin' it better that meself and now that ya've united her with the thought that her daughter is alive and well and God willin' they'll meet up in the near future has somehow eased the burden of the fear of the passin' on," Jim replied in a tearful voice. "Strange the affects illness and death have on a person. We've now learned to appreciate each day and cherish each moment we've together. Yerra Christ Father, believe it or not, we actually get on better now than before…."

"Illness has it's own way of making sense of life," shrugged Fr. Murphy as he looks out yonder to sea.

The beach is at peace, but that is to be expected for this time of the year. Other than for a few locals sitting in their cars and a number of hungry gullies on the rocks who were enjoying the isolation of the strand, one couldn't be blamed for thinking that the world had deserted Ballybunion. This town is like a leaf out of the book of nature, in winter everything seemed to hibernate and die off and yet come summer everything blossoms into life once again.

The two men get engrossed in deep discussion about life as they sit shoulder-to-shoulder on a small hand spun wool rug looking out to sea, happily sipped away at their mugs of tea. The tide is on the turn and has left a prominent mark along the sand. There is a strong smell of seaweed coming from the far end of the strand and throughout the grey sand there is a good scattering of broken shells that has left an artistic impression on the beach. The ghosts of children past have left their presence throughout the whole area. This place would be a heavenly haven for Johnny with his little bucket and spade, thought Jim to himself enjoying his moments of oneness in the company of a good friend.

"Jim, my dear man, every day we wake up to a new dawning, the first day of the rest of our lives. Each day is a new beginning and a new challenge. For many of us, it's another opportunity to live life, to offer our talents and abilities to life with a chance to recognise the good in others," muttered Fr. Murphy wiping the wind blown sand off the rug and covering the sandwiches with his Sunday newspaper.

"Peg's of the opinion that life doesn't fail us, people do. Yet, we spend the greater part of our daily lives blamin' life for our misfortunes," sighed Jim looking up at the fight of gullies overhead. "Wouldya agree Father?"

"How right she is," nodded Fr. Murphy pouring out a cup of tea. "Is it any wonder life passes us by, when on too many occasions we've turned our backs on it?"

"Truth behold, that's certainly true. We become totally oblivious of the beauty that surrounds us. We even neglect the foundation of our well-being," said Jim cutting a slice of apple tart and handing it to Fr. Murphy. "Wouldya agree?"

"You're right," nodded Fr. Murphy tucking it the apple tart. "One day we'll wake up to find out that we, 7don't need all that money and those materialistic objects that we accumulate in life...."

"Emm," replied Jim picking up a handful of sand and letting it sieve through his fingers.

"Jim, my good man, we need to live by the understanding that our lives should be a balance of work and play, family and loved ones, together with a self-recognition for all mankind. Give time to what's really the essence of living, such as enjoying your family and the simple pleasures in life. Don't take life for granted or it'll pass you by like that sand going through your fingers. But if there's one valuable lesson that I've learned on the Missions in Africa, and that is, we become what we live by. Our thoughts speak our words. Our words exhibit our actions. Our actions form our habits. Our habits become the foundation stone of our character. Our character is the pathway to our destiny," insisted Fr. Murphy buttering two more slices of the boiled teacake that Jim had brought with him.

"Peg always sets a day a month away for herself she calls it her WTF Day. It stands for What The Feck Day. On the day she refuses to do any housework, she just enjoys what she enjoys as she is a firm believer that people should take time out when they're well and not wait 'til they're sick. I guess because she has done this since I've met her she feels quite happy to accept her illness and live everyday as if it was her last. She loves life and yet I feel that life wasn't very fair to her. When ya take into account her past and that of Sean Og's, it's amazin' that they both have such energy for fun and happiness in their lives. They turn their struggles into challenges. That's ain't to say they don't have their down days, but somehow when they do have them, they don't mope about like many of us tend to do. They just get on with life and make the best of it," sighed

Jim as he attention is drawn towards another flight of gullies overhead. "I'm a lucky man to have them both in me life. Yerra shur Father, it'd be great if we could go on livin' forever with our loved ones. Wouldn't.....it?""

Fr. Murphy laughs.

Good for her, she's a very special woman and I always had a fondness for her. Even as far back to the first time, she came into my life. I could see that there was something unique about her. Ahhhhh Jim, in life we just borrow our loved ones and walk with them for a very short time. We might be linked together in marriage but we never own each other, we just borrow each other. We must all let go at some stage in our lives. Always remember loved ones are a gift from God......"

"Do ya believe that Heaven and Hell are places we travel to when we leave this earthly world of ours?" asked Jim picking up another handful of sand and slowly allowing it to sieve through his fingers once again.

"Heaven and Hell are with us here on this earthly zone, day in and day out. The sufferings that Hell brings are in the wars that are fought because of human greed, the torture that men, women, children and animals go through. Also ignorance, famines and poverty are all forms of Hell on this earth. It's important to remember, it ain't God who inflicts a state of hell on people. People themselves do that. Heaven on the other hand, stems from the joy, happiness and love we experience as we travel the pathway of life. Suffering is a part of our existence on this earth. Where there's birth, ageing, pain, illness and death, there'll always be a degree of suffering. Coming through our sufferings makes us strong in mind, body and soul."

"Strange enough Father, I believe that too often we inflict sufferin' on ourselves. Many of us allow our possessions to posses us. There's great fear in the loss of them and in many cases these possessions become our identity and to me that's another form of experiencin' Hell on earth. When we feel more comfortable with ourselves and accept our uniqueness, our possessions become a part of our livin' but never take from our identity. We become happy with the necessities of life and our wants don't exceed our needs….."

"Jim, my dear friend, being in touch with the here and now often allows us to be free of unnecessary future desires that lead to unnecessary worry and problems. When we listen to life and our inner voice, we're more ready to understand and accept what's in store for us and challenge the challenges that life delivers at our doorsteps," sighed Fr. Murphy as he shakes the crumbs from the rug and scatters them for the hungry gullies to feed on.

"Do ya fear death, Father? And what do ya think really happens when we die?" asked Jim drawing a circle on the sand with his index finger and making the imprint of the cross in the centre.

"Fear death, my dear friend?" muttered Fr. Murphy folding the rug. "Good God no, I certainly don't. I welcome it as a part of my life. And because I've learned to do so, over the years I've happily prepared for it…"

"Peg believes in reincarnation, what's ya'r opinion on it? I'm comin' around to the idea that reincarnation makes a lot of sense and maybe that's wan of the reasons why certain people in our lives play such a major influencing roll….."

"The Catholic Church may not believe in it, but references are made to it in the Old Testament and also in the new one. Between the years 553 and 556 A.D. the Church felt that the power of the belief of reincarnation would interfere with their power of manning souls and lessen their power over people, so they referred reincarnation as unorthodox and to believe in such a belief was classified as a mortal sin. The Church enslaved people into religion rather than granting them the right to become masters of their own spirituality. Enslaving people into religion was a profitable business and it kept the Church in its materialistic glory…"

"Truth behold," muttered Jim. "Was that so?"

"Yeah, truth behold. Deep in my heart, I also believe in reincarnation. You see Jim, all people aren't born equal for we're born with many different gifts and talents, but as we advance through our different lives and become more God like, we strive to become equal and achieve self-excellence within our Godly attitudes and ways. We become God like when we forgive those that cause injustices to us, we love unconditionally, we share our knowledge with those in need of it and we accept others that choose to live different lives to us. We must not judge others for that privilege is allotted to God only. We must rid ourselves of our earthly greed and repay our emotional and spiritual debts, if we fail to do so, we'll have to do so in the next phase of our lives. We all have lived many lives and will continue to live many others 'til we've become God like...."

"Yeah.... 'til we..... become God like," sighed Jim.

"I often ask myself why is it that plants and animals can lives in harmony yet humans have failed to do so. We destroy not only nature but also people. We fail to live in balance with nature. Life is about balance, not only with oneself but also with people, animals and plants. God won't destroy the world for we're the ones who're doing so day by day. Plants and animals will live on in harmony when we're long gone. We need to learn the wisdom of the essence of balanced living and 'til we do so, human lives will continue to be destroyed. Much of this destruction is brought about by human greed," replied Fr. Murphy taking off his white collar and slipping it into his jacket pocket.

"Areya happy in ya'r priesthood callin'?" Jim asked as he watches Fr. Murphy unbutton his black shirt.

"Indeed I am, most of the time," chuckled Fr. Murphy a little taken back by Jim question. "The life of a priest is often a very lonely one. I guess it's like the loneliness of a long distance runner. You've to befriend yourself to overcome this inner loneliness that grabs you every now again. You see Jim my good friend, there's loneliness in the thought of returning to your bedroom night-after-night, knowing that there's no loved one waiting for you, no loved one to share your joys and cherish you through your woes. You've to find an inner contentment and not always depend on your inner security from the company of others. Once you've accomplished that, then there's great harmony not loneliness in one's aloneness. I've come to understand in the harmony of my aloneness that the true way forward in life is recognition of peace, freedom, humanity and a deep belief and faith in one's own spirituality. There was a time in my youth when I felt I could come and go when I wanted but now that I've donated my life to the priesthood and handed my life's reins over to God there're times when He leads me into places I may not want to go. But once I place my trust in Him, I feel I find the strength to cope with whatever challenges He places in my care....."

"I understand, I've great admiration for ya, but the priesthood was never a pathway for me," said Jim looking at Fr. Murphy and you could see in his eyes that he had developed a great love and admiration for this man.

"Well, I suppose each to their own, each to their own, my good friend. Your calling was to be that of husbandhood and fatherhood and you've done them proud on both accounts."

"Ya're a very holy man, ya seem to find great resilience in religion," said Jim walking down the beach to throw a handful of pebbles into the sea.

"I'd like to think, I'm a holy man," Fr. Murphy chuckled to himself. "But my resilience comes from my spirituality rather than religion. You see, over the years from working in the Missions, I've realised that the Catholic Church just like many other churches is a business in a political arena embodied by religion. Maybe, if we were more spiritual and less religious, the world would've a greater understanding of injustices and become less materialistic. When people follow a religion, they get themselves entwined in a documented doctrine. But when they follow spiritually, they befriend God and all that's wholesome and good in life. They don't need to strive for wealth to find happiness for they germinate happiness from their own spirituality...."

"Truth behold, that's very true," nodded Jim happily throwing the pebbles into the waves.

"Sadly though my dear friend, for many of us our lure to God is lust rather than love. We love God because He's there to fulfil our desires or listen to our tales of woe. Once our desires are fulfilled, we happily go along with our lives only to call on Him again when we've another one of our earthly requests. Now to me that's lust and not love. Yet time and time again, it doesn't seem to matter to God for He created us out of love, His love, unconditional love and this unconditional love he gives to us in abundance. When was the last time we prayed for God's intentions or simply asked Him, how are you getting on today God? Now, that's what you'd do for a loved one or a friend, ain't it? To truly live in a spiritual manner we need to act justly, love tenderly and walk humbly with our God. To reach a state of tranquillity in our lives we need to learn to cultivate ourselves as human beings while distancing ourselves from hatred, greed, resentment and self-obsessive thoughts. To have a carefree life, we need to eliminate longings and desires from our minds and then our Spirit will be free from the destructive power of greed. When we allow our longings and desires to drive us, we become imprisoned in a greedy mind. When we aren't bound by greed we're free to see the world with our eyes as well as our hearts and the seeds of empathy will grow. You see Jim my dear friend, Heaven and Hell are with us here on earth. They're....apart of how... we feel.... react.... and think."

"Begorra ya right," replied Jim totally amazed by the spiritual wisdom of his friend.

"You see, my friend, we'll never find peace of mind or experience true tranquillity if our minds are clouded with desires, hatred, resentment and ignorance. Because many of us are driven by materialistic desires, we fail to see the beauty and simplicity of the world around us. To cherish what we have is a way of acknowledging our blessings. Poverty is only relevant to a given situation. We only discover it when others have a better standard of living than us. The people I worked with on the missions weren't controlled by their inner desires or feelings of greed and for that reason alone, suffering never controlled them. They had little......but in their eyes......they had many blessings," sighed Fr Murphy shaking the sand out of his shoes.

"How right ya are," nodded Jim and as he watches Fr. Murphy make his way bare-footed across the wet sand he feels humbled yet honoured to walk in this man's footprints. For he has now come to truly realise that it's through the companionship of this holy man that he has allowed himself the privilege of befriending God while discovering and understanding his own spirituality.

Late evening is setting in and the moon is beginning to make its presence known when they bid farewell and Fr. Murphy promises Jim that Peg will meet with her daughter to share precious moments together before God relieves her of her illness and rcunites her with her mother in the after life.

Chapter Twenty-Nine

Peg Accepts Her Destiny

Each night before she falls asleep she prays to God to give her the strength to know when to let go. But, as long as she has life she asks Him to allow her to live each moment and feel alive. Over the past few months, Peg and God have become well acquainted and she often wonders how He ever had time for anyone else since she seemed to take up so much of the day and evening asking for his help and guidance. Their friendship grows and somehow God has become such a dear friend and an important part of her daily life that she wonders why she waited until now to befriend him. The one thing that relieves the unknown fear of dying is that she knows deep in her soul and heart that she has a direct line to God and her Angels and they are always ready to listen to her questions, joys, woes and sins in an non-judgemental way. This is so important to her for at this stage in her life, it isn't judgement she needs, for that she capable of doing herself. The love, confidence and ability she now has acquired for living whatever life she is blessed with, gives her the strength to die in harmony with her wellness to live.

One very stormy night, she is awoken by a strange ghostly presence. Inwardly she hears a voice, which she believes to be the voice of her mother. A great sensation of warmth and stillness fills the room. She alerts Jim and he too is stunted by the unusual sensation and flickering of the candle on the bedside locker. The sensation he experiences is strange yet it holds no great fear for him. Then as if nothing had happened it dissolved into the dimness of the night.

"Didya…feel that?" whispered Peg.

"Yeah…but… in the name of Jaysus…what was it?" stuttered Jim sitting up in the bed.

"It was….me mother…..I'm sure….of that. She was lettin' me know that it's time to let go. I know that sounds crazy. But it seems so right. Now I feel so alive. Jim, I'm ain't afraid. I know that it's a sign to let me know that I'll always be able to watch over ya and Johnny from the other side. Ya see, I've prayed to God to let me know when it's time and to give me the strength to let go. And he has done so…."

" Yeah….really," exclaimed Jim.

"Yeah Jim. Lookin' back over me life, yerra ya could say that I was to Hell and back, but I feel in some strange way that while doin' so I was touched by the blessin' and graces of Heaven," whispered Peg sitting up and looking around the dim lit bedroom.

Jim looks at her within the shadows of the glowing candle and feels so at one with her as he takes her into his arms and embraces the life within her. Deep within his heart for the first time, he is ready to let go of her.

"Peg…darlin'…ohhhhhh…Peg," whispered Jim holding her close and gently kissing her on the cheek.

"Dearest….Jim," yawned Peg now feeling comfort in the core of her being. "Willya….promise me….that ya'll do wanthin'…. for me….when I've passed on?"

"Whatever ya ask of me Peg, Course I'll do it for ya," whispered Jim tightening his embrace of her as she nudges closer into his arms.

"Jim darlin', in me memory, will ya allow ya'rself the pleasure to walk hand-in-hand with ya'r Spirit Guide into each day of ya'r life while enjoyin' wan step at a time with ya'r Guardian Angels and ya'll never walk alone," whispered Peg kissing him on forehead. "Promise….ya do that….for me?"

"Indeed I will…love ya…so much darlin'," sighed Jim choking back the tears.

"Will ya give Geraldine the framed picture of the rose and the poem that stands on the table beside the night candle? That rose was in memory of her birth. I picked two roses when I left the Magdalen Laundry. Wan I gave to a special nun and the other is the wan in the hallway. Also, I've a little package for her and Johnny in the little patchwork box on top of the wardrobe. Will ya make sure that they'll get them, please Jim?"

"I will….of course….I will. Just rest now and don't be troublin' ya'rself darlin'," whispered Jim and he could feel a tightness emerge from his throat.

"Will ya thank Doc, Fr. Murphy and Patrick for their friendship to me as well?" she asked now wiping her tears with the corner of the sheet.

"Shhhhhhh…shhhhh…just rest darlin'," whispered Jim kissing her on the cheek.

Having snuggled up closer into the warmth of each other's bodies for ten minutes or so. Peg turns her warm slender body in towards Jim's and asks him to make love to her. He tells her that he has a confession to make. But Peg isn't having any of it for deep in her heart she knows that he is trying to tell her about Mary O' Sullivan. She isn't interested in the details of the affair. She tells him that she has been aware of his out of marriage relationship and says that she forgave him as it suited her at that period in time, as she wasn't willing to confront her own demons.

"Ya see Jim, yarra 'twas only ya'r flesh ya shared with that wan. With me ya've shared ya'r heart, ya'r soul and ya'r spirit. Sr. Dominic who was wan of the nuns in the Magdalen Laundry in Cork made me realise that we've the privilege to forget and the right to forgive and the choice is up to us. She told me that's a choice no wan can take away from us. And Jim darlin', I forgave ya. Ya see, I believe in ya'r own way ya suffered. Ya had the burden and inner torment of carryin' around this hauntin' secret with ya. I guess that was in some strange way ya'r penance for ya'r wrongdoin'. That umbrella of silent and guilt that ya'd to shade under made ya the wan that really suffered in the long run 'cause I've never allowed it to overtake me life....."

"Peg darlin' ya're a very wise, forgivin' and lovin' person and I'm so glad that we've shared so many good years together," whispered Jim as he sniffled back the tears and as he did so, he could feel the softness of her hair on his cheek.

"Shur Jim, we ain't got any more years, maybe we ain't even got any more months but with the blessin' of God we'll have many moments to share and care for each other. So as long as I've life in me marrow, please grant me the permission to live it," whispered Peg snuggling up to him.

"Peg...darlin'," was all Jim could whisper as he wept quietly. Embracing her he feels free and at ease with the closeness of her body in his arms.

Moment by moment as they both dissolve into each other, time doesn't seem to exist for now they are both just one. Jim is for the first time in his marriage to discover what the unity of matrimony really means. As he makes love to his wife for really the first and last time! An experience, he never embraced before and would cherish in his heart forever more. For it is the first time in his life that he understands what it's like to share the glory of love while embracing it in the spirituality of the sexuality of matrimony.

As his wife, falls asleep in his arms he looks on at the beauty in her pale thin worn out face and prays that her daughter will return so that his wife can rest in peace in the arms of her own mother in Heaven and continue sharing the love from her robbed childhood days.

Chapter Thirty

The Homecoming

It's wet windy Sunday morning in early November and Jim has spent the past few days getting the house ready for the homecoming of Geraldine. Peg is feeling very weak in herself as her strength and energy are sluggish and inwardly she is weeping for all those lost mothering years, but she thanks God for the return of her daughter. What she is finding so hard to come to terms with is the fact that the nuns had accused her of the death of her child. A crime she had carried in her heart and soul all these years. A crime that was imposed on her by religious people, who claimed they were carrying out the work of God but above all, who claimed to be brides of Christ. Peg's plight to prove to others but more so to herself had now ended.

It's late into the afternoon when Fr. Murphy's red car pulls into the yard and Peg hears the American accent of her daughter. Fr. Murphy stays in the car while Geraldine makes her way into the sitting room where Peg is sitting by the fire wrapped in a hand woven wool rug.

"I'm…here…mother," said Geraldine holding out her arms, kneeling down and kissing Peg on the cheek.

"Ohhhhh….me….little…Blathin…..ya've…..come home to me. Good God, ain't ya the prettiest girl I've ever laid me eyes on. I can't believe it. Ohhhhh…..Holy….God, here ya're, after so many years, me little precious baby girl," sobbed Peg as she embraces Geraldine.

After all these years, the proof of her innocence is now in her arms. Geraldine's warmth and lavender scented perfume eases her long life inner pain and torment. Anger is overcome with love and her emotional pain dissolves into hugs and embraces. As she holds her daughter at arms length, she could see a beautiful young girl that reminds her of herself at that age, but when she looks into her eyes she could see the baby she held in her arms all those years ago. And even though they were apart for so many years, the umbilical love remained as strong as the day their eyes first met. Geraldine also reminded Peg of her own mother. Her carrot red hair, her pale blue eyes but above all the puzzled frowned expression on her brow added to the charisma of her overall beauty. She is reminded of the memories of her endless questions that she plagued Fr. Murphy with regarding why the little girl that she met in the priest's house so many years ago looked so different from her parents. She now wonders why did the nuns transfer her into service with Fr. Murphy. Was there a message here to be learned or was it just some strange fluke of fate?

Johnny is overjoyed with his new sister and is anxious to show her around the farm and introduce her to all the animals.

"Wha's ur ame?" chirped Johnny as they wandered off around the farm.

"I'm Geraldine but you can call me Sis, that's short for sister. I'll call you Bro, that's short for brother. It's nice having a brother and especially one as nice and as special as you," smiled Geraldine.

Johnny smiles and embraces her.

"Uve yu Sis," he muttered shyly to her.

Geraldine just looks at him in admiration and cuddles him back for deep in her heart she feels a special bond with him.

"I've always prayed for a sister or a brother," she chuckled as they set on their way. "Now I've a very special brother, one that I can love and call my own. Johnny, you and I ain't only going to be bro and sis, we're going to be great friends as well…."

"Dends yaaah," cheered Johnny feeling more at ease with her presence.

"You're special Bro, very special. I've missed out on about 3500 days of your previous smiles and that's a lot of smiles to catch up on," cheered Geraldine smiling down at his bonny smiling face as they continue to stroll around the farmyard hand-in-hand. "Come on Bro, show me all your friends in your animal wonderland. I want to be introduced to each and everyone of them."
Johnny didn't reply and didn't need to for the smile that graced his face said it all.

When they return from their stroll around the farm Fr. Murphy had left for home and Jim had supper ready. Peg, Jim and Geraldine talk late into the night about the past and the goings and comings in New York. Peg tells her daughter about how she had prayed for her. The more Jim looks at Geraldine the more he can see Peg in her. Jim tells Geraldine about the terrible abuse that Peg suffered at the hands of the nuns in the Industrial Schools and how she came to be adopted by her mum, Kate. Geraldine is very interested to hear of her birthright and is eager to learn as much as possible about Peg's family ancestry.

"Jim, my Mum did her own research into the abuse in the Industrial Schools and seemly it happened in America and Australia as well," explained Geraldine as she cleared up the vessels after the supper.

"Ach truth behold....they were terrible times....for many young lads and lassies. Yerra in the name of Jaysus, no excuses should ever be made or tolerated for the horrific happens that went on," yawned Peg wrapping the rug around her shoulders as she slowly makes her way up the stairs to bed. Before she goes to bed she once again lights the candle on the landing window and says a prayer of gratitude to God for the return of her daughter.

"I'll brin' ya up a hot water bottle and a nice sup of coco darlin'," called out Jim from the kitchen.

"Thanks. I'm feelin' all worn out but I'm so happy and excited that our family is complete and here under one roof tonight," yawned Peg touching Geraldine on the cheek with the back of her cold hand. "Begorra I feel I've Heaven in me hands. At this moment in time, I could contently die from happiness."

"Good… night…Mother," embraced Geraldine.

"Niiiiteeeeni Maaaaa," yelled out Johnny from the kitchen who is contently settling down to having a feed on the big New York rock of candy that Geraldine had brought him from America.

"Night, night son, leave some of that nice candy rock for tomorrow," grinned Peg knowing in her heart that was an impossible task for Johnny to do.

"Yaaah Ma," Johnny spluttered back with a mouth full of candy rock.

"I've a letter here for you, Mother," said Geraldine handing a small white envelope to Peg. "It's from Mum. She asked me to give it to you. There's also a small gift for you as well."

Before Jim and Geraldine retire for the night they get deeply involved in a discussion about American politics, as Jim has always had a keen interest in American politics since the assassination of John F Kennedy.

"What do, ye Americans think of Nixon as a president?" asked Jim.

"Well, Mum always said that Nixon is a president with the ability of an intellectual salesman and he is able to entice and engulf the people of America with his salesmanship. Time and time again even though they mightn't like or approve of his policies they'll still vote for him," replied Geraldine with raised eyebrows.

"My American hero would certainly have to be John F Kennedy. A…great….man….he was," emmed Jim in a reflective tone of voice. "He had Ireland in his marrow but America in his heart And he'd have ya know that a country reveals itself not only by the men it produces but also by the men it honours, the men it remembers…"

"Mum had a great admiration for that man as well."

"Ach shur, we Irish folk were very proud of the son of Ireland who ye Americans proudly claimed as ye'r president."

Before Peg settles in for the night Jim reads Kate's letter to her. In the letter Kate thanks Peg for giving her a child that brought so much joy and happiness to her husband and herself and now hopes that Peg will experience the same joy and love, now that this special child is back in the arms of her rightful mother.

Over the days and weeks Peg health and illness is taking its toll but somehow she is inspired with a new release of energy since Geraldine's arrival. She is now living while she is dying, not dying while she is living and now Jim fully understand what Doc was trying to explain to him that day in the forest.

A week before her death, Peg requests a family day out to Kells Strand and there she has a heart-to-heart talk with Johnny about the future. She explains to him that she is dying and there will come a time very soon when she will not be there in body but will be there in spirit and whenever he needs someone to talk to, she'll be there to listen to him from Holy-God's house.

"Sometime in the near future, I'm gonna be livin' in the house of God and baby Jaysus and I won't be livin' with ya and ya'r Da anymore, do ya understand what I'm tryin' to tell ya darlin'?" asked Peg taking a gentle hold of Johnny by the chin to get his full attention and looking him straight in the eye.

"Da tay meee tat tooooo. Da tay, Desus hume is ike Tir-na-Nog, yuv ave no dickness," mumbled Johnny peering up at her over his specs and sniffles back the sea breeze in his usual manner.

Peg chuckles to herself and thought what a wonderful son I've given birth to, for even in times of sadness and difficulty he is able to bring such simplicity to the moment and who was she to question his understanding of dying. If he had reasoned it out in his own mind that dying was like a trip to Tir- na-Nog or in other words the Land of Eternal Youth, then so be it. Over the years from listening to Sean Og telling him stories about fairies, leprechauns and about legends of Ireland where Oisin went to live in Tir-na-Nog, Johnny had created a vision of this special place in his own mind and every now and again he would allow his mind to wander off and visit this special imaginary haven.

"Johnny ya'll need to be wary of people ya don't trust, but above all, I want ya to be a good friend to Sean Og and to ya'r sister Geraldine. Please, be a good son for ya'r Da and remember to say hallo to Holy God in ya'r prayers," whispered Peg sitting on the rocks looking out yonder to sea with her arm around Johnny's shoulder.

"Yaaaah…..meeee beee…..gud for Da….yuv in Deses hume," yawned Johnny as he hunches up into his mother's warm coat.

"I want ya to be a true friend to ya'rself," hushed Peg explaining to him that he would never be lonely if he could accept that there are three persons in everyone one of us.

"Ma, wooooo dey?" asked Johnny with a puzzled frown as he wipes his nose on the sleeve of his jacket.

"Me, meself and I," whispered Peg, holding Johnny tight.

"Me, meeeelf and Iiii" stuttered Johnny kissing her on her wind chilled cheek.

"Yeaaaah, so each day Johnny darlin', talk to these three special people and ya'll never be without a friend. Talk to ya'r two Angels, who're always by ya'r side just awaiting ya'r friendship. Tell them ya'r joys and woes and they'll help ya to find contentment when ya're feelin' sad. And always say ya'r prayers at night. I'll say them with ya from me own special bed in Holy-God's house. I'll be with ya'r Grandma. Ya'd have loved her and she'd have cherished ya. Sean Og will tell ya more about her when ya're older…"

"Yaaaa Maaaa," sighed Johnny entwining Peg's hair around his little thumbs, something he was accustomed to doing when he sat on her lap in times of deep thought.

As they sit on the rocks looking out yonder to sea, the raindrops begin to fall just in time to camouflage and engulf Peg's tears. She embraces Johnny and as she does so, she prays that God will pass on to Johnny the same strength that He gave to her as she lived her life overcoming and coping with confronting challenges that fate had faced her with over the years.

Chapter Thirty One

Confidential Matters

On her deathbed Peg gives Jim two letters. She asks him to read the letters out at the graves of the people named. One is to be read at her mother's grave and the other at her abuser's grave. She requests that the letters be kept confidential and wants both them burned at the gravesides. Jim is a little apprehensive but promises to carry out her final wishes. She also tells him that she has written out a list of instructions regarding the day-to-day caring of Johnny and what to do should emergencies arise. She asks Geraldine to keep in contact with the family and to look out for her brother. She gives Geraldine a special poem, a poem that any loving mother would love to give a daughter.

"Geraldine me dear, this is for ya. It tells ya, what I need to say to ya about life. Take it to ya'r heart and every time ya read it, remember that a mother who never gave up lovin' ya from the moment ya were born, wrote it. Live life, love life and life will love ya back, me little darlin'," said Peg handing the verse to Geraldine and stretching out her arms to embrace her.

"Thanks Mother, I'll treasure this and will always go on loving you," whispered Geraldine as the tears flow down her cheeks.

Special Daughter
For healthy luscious lips, speak no evil.
For bright sparkly eyes, look for the good in others.
Often badness is only goodness gone astray.

For a keen sense of hearing, refuse to listen to gossip or scorn.
For a graceful healthy body, be willing to share, your food and knowledge with others.
For beautiful hair, let the wind blow it's magic through it once a day
For inner confidence and a positive self-concept, believe in yourself and never give up.
Allow your Spirit guide to show you the way.
And you'll never walk alone.
Allow for mistakes. People are human.
Never throw out a Human Being,
Reclaim, restore or renew the Human
And the Being will return
If someone needs a helping hand, remember you have two.
One is for helping yourself.
The other is for the person in need of a helping hand.
As you grow from childhood to adulthood, discover that Heaven is a place on earth.
Allow yourself the pleasure of enjoying the simple things in life.
Respect Mother Nature. She will outlive you and your kin.
Measure your success not by money but by happiness.
Believe in yourself and live by the truth alone.
Don't be a passenger in your life.
Be captain of your own destiny.
Above all, grant yourself permission to live life
And never fear death for it's the Divine Path to life everlasting....

Then Peg turns to Johnny who is sitting on the edge of the bed sucking his thumb and cuddling into his teddy bear.

"Johnny darlin', I've something special for ya as well. It's a short verse to tell ya what ya mean to ya'r Da and meself. Sean Og put a frame on it for ya. It's to say that we'll always love ya and can never thank ya enough for all the wonderful moments ya've given us since ya chose us to be ya'r Ma and Da. We're so fortunate to have ya in our lives," yawned Peg.

The tears that she had held back for a number of days couldn't be suppressed any longer. As they rippled down her pale cheeks onto the starched white sheets, she somehow feels at ease.

Innocence

Your birth so stormy but delicate
Wilful cries expressing your joy
Your features so different yet beautiful
You are our little Down syndrome boy

Your innocence so special and clear
Embedding simplicity so wise and true
Receiving messages of love smiling through
Your little slanting eyes so blue

A child of this world you choose to became
Bringing change to all our lives
Each moment you live without a care
Knowing, it's your love that energises our joys

A new pathway in life you have shown us
While you enlighten us to the errors of our ways.
It's the grace of your innocence that guides us
While our unconditional love embraces your days

"Ta'ta Ma," Johnny muttered as he grabs the verse and cuddles into his mother.

"Okay children, I'd like to spend a little time with ya'r Da now, so would ya mind makin' a cup of tea for Sean Og and I'll have a cuppa with ya'r Da," sighed Peg and with that Geraldine and Johnny contently scramble off down the stair.

Peg insists once again that Fr. Murphy is the priest who will say the prayers at her graveside. She once again requests not to have her body transferred to the local church for a removal service when she dies. She wants the ceremony to be in the home. She requests a simple service. She wants it to be a celebration of her life and not a sad weepy day. For after all, it's a new beginning for her, a reincarnation into another stage of her development of her spiritual life and that should be reason enough for celebration. She talks about the nuns in the Industrial School and Magdalen Laundry that wronged her and tells Jim that she has forgiven them for when one looks beyond the crime you will discover a human being.

After having a few sups of tea and her medication Peg sleeps the night away while Jim and Sean Og sit by her bedside both praying to God that her passing will be easy and peaceful. And as they sit there in silence, Jim think to himself how right Doc was with his words of wisdom that he shared with Johnny and himself, the day they met up in the forest. In fact, Peg had completed the cycle of life, she entered this earthly world of ours as a baby and was to leave it with the needs and cares of a baby. Over the past three weeks since Geraldine had returned to her rightful mother, she had attended to Peg the way a mother would attend her baby. She fed, clothed and bathed Peg in the same manner Peg cared for her in the first few days of life. Their umbilical love strengthened over these few weeks and one might say that each moment that they were in each other's company made up for every moment and hour they lost out on over the years. He had come to realise also that it was the return of Geraldine that really eased the burden of dying for Peg, but more importantly, it had given her the gift of living while she was dying.

During the night Johnny makes his way into the bedroom and cuddles up beside his mother and sleeps cosy and contently until he is awoken in the morning by the crowing of George, the farmyard rooster.

Chapter Thirty-Two

The Passing

As Jim looks out onto the November night sky, the stars that blink and flicker seem much larger to the eye and this makes him aware that it's a sure sign that stormy windy wet weather is on the way. Earlier that evening he had lit all the fires in the house and also lit a few extra candles as somehow he felt that the electricity mightn't hold the night as Doc had told him earlier on during the day that some of the lines were down around the Killorgin and Glenbeigh areas. Geraldine had made supper and helped get Johnny to bed. Peg was resting and not saying much. All day she held her rosary beads close to her bosom and around her neck is a medal of the Holy Family that Fr. Murphy had given her when she was in service so many years ago. At the head of the bed is a framed picture of The Lord of Mercy that Geraldine had brought with her from America. It's like Peg knows that her time is near. She would just smile at the mention of her name and slowly raise her hand to you.

Fr. Murphy is staying at Doc's for the night, he had dropped on Peg during the day, and with his help, she had made her peace with God and with herself. Down in the kitchen, Sean Og sat quietly by the turf fire praying from his little prayer book. All day, Sally sat quietly at Peg's bedroom door but every now and again, she would take a ramble into the room as if to check on her. All around the room the flickering from the candles created their own mystic shadows on the walls. Get-well cards and pictures of the saints are to be found in every corner of the room.

Cuddy is stretched out purring contently on a pillow at the foot of Peg's bed. On a little bedside locker is a small porcelain bowl with a wet flannel that Geraldine used to wipe Peg's brow during the day. There is a glass of cool water beside the bowl, but at this stage, Peg is only taking sips. Jim arranges a chair for himself beside the bed and sits in silence while Peg sleeps. The labouring of her breathing comforts him, as it is a sign that she is still with him in body and spirit. Every now and again Geraldine would cuddle into Peg and whisper.

"Wait a little longer dear mother, sweet Jesus please don't take her yet."

And when she did so, Jim could feel the lump in his throat grow and grow as he tried to hold back the tears.

It's well into the early hours of the following morning when Jim is abruptly awoken by the crowing of George out in the farmyard. Sally the dog is anxiously licking at his face and whining, she was determined to wake him. Startled by the suddenness of the moment, it takes him a second or so to get his bearings. The flames of the candles are flickering on their last wicks and the light from the dawn gleams through the moth eaten curtains. As he focuses his attention on the bed where he had rested his head when he dosed off, he could see three heads. There in the bed in front of him are Johnny and Geraldine fast asleep and in the centre with her arms around them is the love of his life.

"Peg darlin'," Jim whispered as he reaches over Johnny to kiss her on her cheek.

But the stillness of her face and the coldness of her cheek soon let him know that she is only present in body. Her Spirit had passed on during the night hours. His eyes fill up with tears, tears of sadness and tears of joy. Sadness of knowing that she is lying there dead but the joy of knowing that she passed on during the night with the two of her most dearest in her arms. For him, this moment is both a relief and a strange blessing in itself. Gently removing her arm from around Johnny's neck and lifting him to the nearby chair, he covers him with a blanket and leaves him to rest. Then as he looks up Geraldine had awoken and as she frowns at Jim she realises that her mother has passed on and is on her way to God in Heaven.

"'Tis gand, just grand Geraldine, God has called ya mother home," whispered Jim.

"Oh Mother, I love you so much, I promise I'll look after Jim and Johnny. Mother dear, you can rest in Heaven now. All will be well, you see, I'll make you proud of me," sobbed Geraldine cuddling into Peg. The more she cuddled the more she tries to get a response from Peg. It's as if she is trying to convince herself that Peg hasn't gone.

At this stage, Johnny is awoken by the crying and approaches the bed in his own solemn way. Leaping up onto the bed, he kisses Peg on the forehead and with a look of uneasiness he mutters to Jim.

"Ma gon to Desus……. Ma gon to Desus…..beeee doka Da….. no kie……beeeee doka Da…."

Smiling shyly he reaches out to touch his father on the cheek. He then holds his arms out to Geraldine and cuddles into her. This comforts Geraldine and as she looks at Johnny with eyes filled with tears, she weeps softly.

"I'm so happy to have you as a brother. Johnny I'll never leave you…"

Jim just looks on for what he had to say was little, as he had said it all to his darling Peg over the years when they share their lives together. But he did thank God for allowing her into his life and for allowing her to feel so complete and wholesome as a mother, a wife and as a woman on her deathbed. Bringing Geraldine back into her life had returned the missing gem that was stolen from her all those years ago. As he looks around the room, he notices Fr. Murphy's bible on the bedside locker and somehow this surprises him, as it wasn't there earlier on during the night. When he goes down to the kitchen to tell Sean Og of Peg's passing who should be stretched out on a blanket in front of the smothering fire fast asleep, but Fr. Murphy.

"Father," whispered Jim, "Father, Peg has passed over."

With that, Fr. Murphy jumps up.

"I know my friend, that she has, that she has indeed. I got the urge to come during the night and she breathed her last just as I finished the Lord's Prayer and gave her a farewell blessing. I didn't like to disturb the moment that felt so right and fitting. She slipped away into the night with the four people she dearly loved asleep by her side. I opened the window to let her Spirit go free...."

"Thanks Father," replied Jim helping Fr. Murphy to his feet. The two men embrace in their moment of grief. Just then, Sean Og comes into the kitchen.

"Yerra, poor Peg has moved on Jim, hasn't she?" he asked and you could tell from the redness of his eyes that he had been crying.

"Indeed she has Sean Og and a lovely peaceful one it was. She glided out of her life like a cloud in the sky," said Fr. Murphy.

"Thanks be to God for that, she deserved a good passin'. May God bless her and keep her safe in the arms of me mother in Heaven," sighed Sean Og and the tears started to flow down his cheeks. He then makes his way up the stairs into Peg's bedroom with a sod of earth that he had dug out from the garden during the early hours of the morning. The country folk believed that by placing a sod of earth under the dead person's bed the sins that weren't wiped away by the act of contrition would be absorbed into the sod of earth and the soul would pass over without a care. After doing so, he knelt by the bed and said a quiet prayer for Peg in her moment of rest, peace and rebirth.

Throughout the day, the locals were coming and going saying prayers and bidding their final farewells. In the afternoon, the old Parish Priest's car pulls into the yard and as he approaches Jim, he puts out his hand.

"I'm here to apologise for I've done you both a grave injustice. My parishioners told me about the young lassie from America, Peg's daughter..."

"Father, ya're welcome. Now's the time to put grievances aside for there's too much grievin' to be done. Some of ya'r parishioners are in the kitchen. Go through

Father and have a cuppa with them. Yerra shur they'll be pleased to see ya. Do look in on Peg. Ach shur, she'll be glad to see ya also, no doubt she sent out the invitation to ya from Above," smiled Jim as he guides the elderly Priest into the kitchen. The priest just smiles and gently taps Jim on the back.

The following day after a short homely house Mass, Peg is finally laid to rest in the coffin. She is laid out in her cream wedding dress. A dress she was so proud of because for her it was symbolic of a new beginning. She had cut the end of it to make a christening dress for Johnny. When Johnny heard this he went to his bedroom, returned with his little christening dress, and placed it in the coffin beside her.

"Ma....u've......dall ud diss....fur desus," he whispered kissing his mother on the forehead. But as he does so, he is a little taken aback by the stillness of her body.

Geraldine places a small rag doll in the coffin just as it's about to be closed.

"Mother, you gave me this when we first met all those years ago in the Priests' house in Cahirciveen and when I'd ask Mum who you were, she'd always rely, someone very precious. I'll never, never forget you and the moments we shared since we found each other again. Rest in peace and I'll take care of Jim, Johnny and Sean Og for you. Love you Mother. Goodbye," mumbled Geraldine trying so hard to gag back the gulfs of tears. She is conscious that Johnny is a little uneasy and she doesn't want to upset him any further.

Once the coffin is closed, it isn't long before the funeral is on its way to Cahirciveen to the final resting place for Peg. She had request to be laid to rest in Jim's family grave in Cahirciveen. As the funeral makes its way, from Glenbeigh to Cahirciveen the road ahead is quiet and other than the odd wandering mountain sheep one might say the whole countryside was in mourning.

The funeral parade drives slowly into Cahirciveen and stops for a minute or so just at the entrance to the lane that leads up to the Priest's house and the Convent. This is to share a moment for the happy times that Peg experienced while in service with Fr. Murphy so many years ago. Then it continues on its way down passed the old castle ruins, over the bridge and up along the windy road to Killovarnogue burial ground. There she is laid to rest in the family plot where Jim's parents and grandparents are buried. The locals gather around the graveside to say their final farewells. Just as the final prayers are completed, Fr. Murphy puts aside his prayer book, steps forward and commands the attention of the mourners in a deep determined voice.

"A blanket of silence engulfed in a bed of denial, In the 30s, 40s, 50s and 60s the Irish State entrusted in the care of the Religious Order many young girls and boys. The understanding was that the Religious Orders were to foster these children, educate them in the Industrial Schools and offer each child a secure childhood. But truth behold, that wasn't to be, these little girls and boys were sentenced to long hours of childhood slavery. And a big leather strap replaced the love of a family. The one thing many of these children had in common was that they were found guilty in the Courts of this Land of having no one to love or care for them…"

The mourners just huddled up with heads bent low and nodded.

"To this very day, the memories of the horrific happenings in those Industrial Schools still live on in the minds and lives of the pupils that attended them. For those who died while in care, horrific secrets went to the graves with them. Many long forgotten and many others misrepresented on the death certificates."

He pauses for a moment to catch his breath from the chilling breeze and then continues aloud.

"Many of us took the Pharisees attitude to what was happening, we looked on, passed by and did nothing about it. It was the era when Religious Orders had a monopoly over mankind. They made you into God-fearing people. They became masters of your souls. But times have changed. We now have come to understand and accept that the God that you so innocently feared is a God full of love, forgiveness and strength. Therefore, if, we continue to take the Pharisees' attitude regarding abuse we're licensing the abuser to abuse. We also become perpetrators of abuse ourselves. We must have zero tolerance for all forms of abuse. We must blow the whistle on abusers. Abusers need help. As long as we've abusers, we'll always have victims. As long as abusers walk free amidst our communities, our children will never be safe. There's great strength in the truth but there's amazing strength in the power of prayer.

So today, I ask you to pray for Peg and for all the children who died in the Industrial Schools throughout Ireland so that they too may Rest in Peace. Pray for each other so that you may find the wisdom to follow the guidance of your Spirit Guides and our Angels. I ask you all to pray that each one of us will find the inner confidence not to tolerate injustices but above all, to do…. something…. about it."

Once again, he pauses for a moment and looks around at the mourners who are huddled close, each and every one of them harbouring on his every word. He looks at Jim and Sean Og and gives a nod of recognition to them both. Then he continues addressing the mourners once again.

"My message for Religious Orders is, that I strongly call on you to stop hiding beneath your shroud of silence and conspiracy. Stop denying, covering up and ignoring your horrific sins of the past regarding the evil rituals that consisted of raping and plundering the childhood dignity of innocent young children that took place in the Industrial Schools and elsewhere. Step forth, in the name of Christ and all that's true and put your wrongdoings to right. Stop keeping those boys and girls chalet to the chains of victim-hood. As long as you keep doing this, you continue to master the lives of innocent people and all you've just done is change your modem of abuse from sex abuse to emotional abuse. By taking responsibility for your actions, you'll help victims of abuse like Sean Og and many others to rebuild their lives. Giving them the opportunity to rediscover their lost identity and reclaim their stolen dignities. If the Religious Orders continue to obstruct the course of justice, the long-term effect will be detrimental. Our communities will never be free from the infestation of the abuser's plague. It'll wangle its way into the next generation only to eat through the core of humanity and kill of the spirit of every man, woman and child that is affected by it. I'll not be shunted off by red tape, bureaucracy or by bullyboy tactics that are placed in my way in order to obstruct the course of justice. I'll continue up rooting injustice, out root abusers and help victims to reclaim and rebuild their lives. I, hopefully with the help of other people will lay the foundation stone that'll allow our children to be safe from the abusers grip. Should any of my words have offended anyone here present, I make no apology for I firmly believe that nothing can stand in the way of the truth and nothing should stop us decent citizens of Ireland protecting our nation's most precious asset, our youngsters."

Once again he pauses for a moment and with a deep sigh continues to speak aloud.

"My prayer for all of you today, is that you'll find inner contentment so that you'll find the ability to enjoy the simple things of life. Just like Peg had the ability to do so. May God bless you all and may Peg be reunited with her mother, finding her peace and just reward in Heaven. And hopefully her strong faith in life and God will stand out in everyone's memory of her. For, your faith shouldn't only influence your living but it should also prepare you for a wholesome death. In doing so, you can live not only in harmony with God and yourself but also in harmony with life and others. When we achieve harmony in life, we've no reason to fear life or death for we are blessed with inner freedom. Bless you all and in memory of Peg please offer each other a handshake of peace and goodwill."

With that, the crowd shared good wishes with each other and join in prayer once more, as Geraldine recites the Lord's Prayer in Irish.

"Ár nAthair atá ar neamh, Go naofar d'ainim, Go dtaga do ríocht, Go ndéantar do thoil ar an talamh mar a dhéantar ar neamh. Ár n-arán laethúil tabhair dúinn inniu, agus maith dúinn ár bhfiachamar a mhaithimidne dár bhféichiúna féin Ach ná lig sinn i gcathú, ach saor sinn ó olc, Amen."

The crowd are taking back by her strong American accent for they were used to hearing the prayer been recited in the traditional brogue. Sean Og was quietly standing beside Geraldine all this time, steps forward, takes out his tin whistle and plays Peg's favourite hymn, Hail Queen of Heaven, and before he could finish the mourners sang aloud and throughout the town of Cahirciveen Peg's farewell hymn could be heard far and wide.

Everyone remained silent until the final shovel of clay is laid carefully and respectively on her grave. After replacing caps and pocketing their rosary beads, the mourners leave singing praises of Peg and making each other aware of how better off each and everyone were from coming to know her.

Patrick stood shoulder-to-shoulder with the Fianna Fail Councillor at the edge of the grave throughout the service. But before wondering off to his own parent's resting place, to say a quiet prayer and share an intimate thought with them, he makes it his business to have a quick word with the old Parish Priest from Glenbeigh who is standing alone looking on at the proceedings.

"Good to see you came, Father," said Patrick.

"I made my peace with Jim and Peg," replied the old Parish Priest with head bowed low.

"That's good Father, for grievances not only worry the soul but they also age the body," said Patrick holding out his hand to him. And respectively the two men shake hands and as their eyes meet they both knew in their hearts they had just laid the seed to a fresh beginning.

Meanwhile, some of the other mourners also wondered off to say a quiet prayer at the graves of loved ones. Sean Og and Jim remain by the graveside to say their own solemn private prayers and as they both embrace and share tears of grief and gratitude, joy and companionship now knowing in each other's heart when it comes to love, there is no cost. Deep in their hearts, they both now understand the meaning of the saying; you don't know what you've really got, 'til it's gone.

A robin perches on the handle of the gravedigger's shovel that stands in the yellow clay nearby and sings its little heart out as if in its own special way is saying farewell and thanks to Peg for her kindness towards nature and for leaving this world a better place. Meanwhile, Doc and Fr. Murphy have headed off with Geraldine and Johnny to the nearby hotel awaiting the return of Jim and Sean Og.

By the time Jim and Sean Og return to the hotel, the crowd had gathered and were drinking to the memory of Peg's life. After spending some time chatting with the locals, Jim is anxious to get away and spend some personal time with himself.

"Doc, would ya mind takin' Geraldine and Johnny home with Sean Og for there's somethin' I must attend to?" asked Jim taking off his overcoat on his way out to his car that is parked in front of the old cinema door.

"Yerra that'll be no bother. Indeed, I'll do that for you. Will you be alright now, Jim?" asked Doc and he could see that Jim is anxiously trying to get away from the sympathising crowd huddled around outside the hotel.

"Yeah….grant. Ach…I'll…be…grand," mumbled Jim in a tearful tone.

"Are you sure?" insisted Doc taking a hold of Jim's arm. "Maybe you'd like Fr. Murphy to go with you?"

"No. This is somethin' I've to face on me own," sighed Jim wiping his tears on the sleeve of his jumper while looking up at the heavy clouds.

"Right so, mind yourself and drive carefully," Doc replied tapping on the roof of Jim's car.

"Thanks," said Jim focusing his rear view mirror and with that, he starts up the ignition and drives off in the direction of Glenbeigh.

"Will….he…..be alright, Doc?" asked Fr. Murphy wondering what private matter Jim intended to attend to.

The suicide that Jim had attempted just over a year ago did cross his mind. Would he be thinking of trying it again? As he now had to cope with a greater sorrow and personal loss and this time his loss was so great for he had not only lost a wife, a lover, a partner but above all, a wonderful friend.

"Indeed he will," replied Doc placing his hand on Fr. Murphy's shoulder. "He has come a long way since last year and I'm sure he has the strength to come to terms with his suffering and sorrow now."

The road out of Cahirciveen to Kells and onto Doulus Head is quiet and as Jim pulls into a gap on the roadside that leads into the fields overlooking the cliffs, he feels a tight sensation deep within his throat and a cold shiver up the base of his spine. He pauses for a while and with an anxious feeling in the pit of his stomach, he walks slowly through the fields struggling against the strong November wind that is coming in from the sea. As he struggles over the rough patches of terrain, he closes his coat to ease the force of the wind gusting against his body. The place is deserted and the long tufts of grasses are scorched by winter tidal winds. The gorse and bracken that brightened up the landscape during the summer months are now bare and undressed of their glory. The rusty wire on small stone fences had the evidence of the presence of sheep and other than, for a scattered blanket of droppings from the gullies on the side of the cliffs and the nearby rocks one might say that nature had reclaimed full ownership of this patch of headland.

As he approaches the cliffs, he notices a weather beaten envelope stuck in the nearby rushes and overgrown grasses. Picking it up, his heart throbs for to his amazement it's the letter that he held in his hand just over a year ago. As he stands there in a moment of reflection and reading it over and over, the memory of that anguishing moment of his intention of taking his own life on that November afternoon comes flashing back. The feelings he now experiences eat to the core of his existence and an over whelping shrinking feeling of horror brings him to his knees. As he looks around at the bleakness of the countryside and the vastness of the ocean beyond the cliffs together with the force of the sound of the waves lashing up against the rocks beneath, his mind drifts off into reciting the Lord's Prayer. And as he continues to pray, he thanks God for protecting him from his potential fatal intention. Little did he realise on that day, that a year later he would be so grateful for a second chance.

Leaning back onto his heels his thoughts drift back over the year that was. He now realises that Peg and himself lived so much life within that year and hand-in-hand together they climbed so many of their emotional mountains while bringing life back into the core of each other's marrow. Maybe, God did have a purpose in life for him after all. Maybe it was to help Peg find peace and solace in her heart before she was taken from this earthly world. But, whatever it was, he now found a sense of inner peace and gratitude within the sorrow and grief of his personal loss. But one thing, he had now come to accept and had a greater understanding of, is that we are all accompanied by a Spirit Guide and two Guardian Angels as we travel through life and if we listen to the guidance of our inner voice and follow our own gut feelings, we will have a greater understanding of what life has in store for us. As we come through life, we all experience inner torment and challenging moments and often fate is such that we've no control over these unexpected events, but one thing we do have, is the choice to choose how we intend to deal with them.

The more he knelt in his moment of isolation and aloneness, the more he understands that regardless of race, culture or creed there is one common language and emotional thread that links mankind together and which gives us a unity within our individuality and that is the language of feelings and the familiar way we experience pain, grief, sorrow and joy. No matter, how we ache to be different, we all experience the feelings of those emotions in the very same way. As he knelt there, he asks himself, why is it that it takes a moment of loss to truly understand the sense of appreciation of the blessings that surround us as we travel through life?

A year ago, he stood in this very place and thought that there was nothing to live for, yet today even in his moment of great sorrow he feels that he has everything. Was Peg sent into his life for him to understand the true meaning of life? Maybe that was one question he would never find the answer to, but one thing for sure he now knew in his heart and soul that we all meet up with people in our lives for a purpose and it may take a life time to truly understand and recognise that purpose. The more he thinks about life, the more he accepts that God does work in mysterious ways, for today of all days, he feels a greater bond with God as the Spirit of Peg touches his heart. As he arises from his knees, he makes the sign of the cross on his forehead and slowly makes his way back to his car. His senses and vision of the world now seem much clearer and he has come to accept and appreciate that life is for living and giving. It's not all about taking but sadly, many of us only realise this when we are confronted with death. He feels honoured but humbled to be chosen by God to partake in the trip of life, a privilege that is granted to each and every one of us but sadly it's a privilege too few of us truly understand or appreciate.

Tonight the candle once again flickers on the windowsill but this time it's in memory of Peg. A woman who challenged the challenges that fate had granted her and who lived the final years of her life standing by the strength of her inner conviction and belief. And who died in peace with the conviction of her belief in her arms.

As Jim turns out the light, a loving familiar voice calls out from the back bedroom.

"Nit'nit Da, nit'nit Dedine, gud nite Ma, tisss onny ere."

Jim grins to himself and calls back.

"Good night son…" and as the tears ease their way into his eyes he once again thanks God in his prayers from rescuing him from making the wrong decision a year ago.

After all, who would have looked after Johnny if fate had allowed him to carry his fatal intention through?

It's a few minutes after midnight when Sally makes her way up the stairs into the bedroom and insists on leaping up onto the bed to rest beside Jim. As she rests her head on Peg's pillow, her watchful eye focuses on Jim. Every now and again, their glances connect and she would acknowledge his smile with a wag of her tail. As he laid there in the stillness of the night and as his eyes focuses on the shadows of the flickering candle on the wall, a poem by John Wilson that he had learned during his school going days as a young lad comes back to him and now for the first time, it all makes sense.

The air of death breathes through our souls,
The dead all round us lie;
By day and night the death-bell tolls,
And says, "Prepare to die."

The loved ones we loved the best,
Like music all are gone!
And the wan moonlight bathes in rest.
Their monumental stones!.

But not until the death prayer is said,
The life of life departs
And the body in the grave is laid,
It's beauty in our hearts.

At holy midnight voices sweet
Like fragrance fill the room
And happy ghosts with noiseless feet
Come bright ning from the tomb

And as he repeats the lines over and over in his head his exhausted, forlorn, lamenting body drifts off into a night's sleep with the ghost of his loving wife now living his heart.

Chapter Thirty-Three

The Letter Of Disclosure

A week later, the postman drops off a registered letter for Jim. To his surprise, it's a letter from one of the nuns that Peg came to know in the Magdalen Laundry in Cork all those years ago. In the letter is a very old worn faded pressed rose. Peg gave the rose to one of the nuns when she left the Laundry. Finally, the truth comes to light.

Dear Jim

My name is Sr. Dominic. I'm one of the nuns that was at the Magdalen Laundry in Cork where you loving wife Peg spent her final days in care. It's not easy for me to write this letter for it brings back so many buried memories, some good, some I'm ashamed of and many more I'll have to answer to my Maker for. And I fear that day is creeping up on me as my life has turned over its final chapter.

Fr. Murphy made contact with me during the summer to tell me about the terrible injustices that your wife endured. He feels so responsible, as so do I. I now know that we're just as guilty as the ones that inhumanly inflicted the punishments on the innocent. We stood by, looked on and did nothing.

The gospel tells the story about the Good Samaritan and the Pharisee but I tell you here and now, there were many Pharisees and too few Samaritans in the House of God on this earth. We were weak in flesh and soul and did very little to comfort the wounds of the wounded. We engulfed ourselves in our earthly comforts while the real brides of Christ, the young girls placed in our care were punished and suffered for sins they didn't commit. They were truly taunted angels in the flesh.

I remember the day Mother Superior robbed the baby from Peg's bedside. I can still hear her harsh words convincing Peg that the baby died. I was the nun who held Peg in my arms as she wept for her dead baby. I hypocritically soothed her, yet knowing the truth.

The days that followed, I kept a keen eye over your good wife, as I feared she might choose to pass on to the next life by her own makings. Her Spirit was low and her grief for a crime she never committed ate away at the marrow in her bones. Night after night, she soothed herself to sleep with the taste of her grieving tears. I guess it was my own prayers of guilt that got her to give life a second chance.

When I heard that Peg was due for a transfer from the laundry due to the fact that the nuns couldn't break or tame her free-spirited nature and knowing that Fr. Murphy's sister and brother in law from America were the adopting parents of Peg's little baby, I made enquiries maybe more out of guilt rather than honour. It was from those enquiries that fate allowed Peg to go into service with our good friend Fr. Murphy. This arranged transfer was a secret I've kept in my heart for years and never had the strength to tell the truth. I've made my contrition asking God for forgiveness for my silence on the matter and for the suffering, my unspoken words have caused your loving wife and probably your good self for so many years.

Fr. Murphy tells me that justice was served before Peg's passing and she and her child were reunited. My faith in prayer is now restored. You might say this is an unusual announcement for a Sister of Christ, but we too are only human.

The day that Peg left the Laundry she picked a yellow rose and gave it to me. I kept the rose in my prayer book to remember her as I've prayed for her and so many like her over the years. I sent you this rose as a symbol of my joy that justice was finally served and can only say thank you for looking after her. ... Peg, the red haired girl of strong character and whose loving nature was toughen by hardship. She was a rose in real life but whose innocence was wounded by so many thorns.

Please remember me in your prayers for I'll continue to remember you and yours in mine.
May the peace and blessings of Christ be always with you...
Sincerely
Sr. Dominic.
P.S. Maybe one day you'll allow your heart to understand that good people sometimes do very wrong things!

Enclosed in the envelope is also a little card that the rose is attached and hand written in red ink was,
Dearest Peg,
As the stars shine so bright around you
There's one wish I have for you
That in the joys and happiness of Heaven
May your reclaim your stolen
"CHILDHOOD DIGNITY"

That evening, Jim makes a little wooden frame for this special rose and forever more this rose will have a special place of honour over the West gable window, where a candle will flicker into the darkness of the night in memory of Peg and the challenges that life challenged her with.

Chapter Thirty-Four

Jim Carries Out Peg's Deathbed Wishes

The following afternoon, Jim carries out Peg's final wishes. The graveyard is deserted and a few late autumn withered leaves whirl around amongst the gravestones like children skipping around a May poll. Even though, a haunting dimness penetrates the atmosphere there is somehow a feeling of peacefulness within the moment. As Jim approaches the grave of Peg's mother, he is once again overcome with sadness of the departure of his wife. As he kneels at the graveside, he prays that she will find peace and harmony in the arms of her mother. Taking out his handkerchief to wipe away the tears, he proceeds to read Peg's letter in silence.

Dear Mammy,

I've asked Jim to read out this letter for me, as I'm unable to visit your graveside today. I've bid my last farewells to this world. I'm on my way to meet with my Maker who will judge me for my earthly life just as you had to answer for yours.

Where do I start Mammy, at the beginning or maybe at the time when things went so badly wrong? You know that I never stopped loving you, how could I, after all I was your flesh and blood. Mammy, I was so angry with you for so many years. I now ask you to forgive me for wronging you. But Mammy, why didn't you tell me that you were so sick all those years ago? If you did, I wouldn't have waited day after day looking out that school gate for you to come and collect me. Wasn't that what you promised when you kissed us good-bye. Now I know the truth. My heart broke in that school and my childish spirit died. Those has-been hags, who posed as Brides of Christ that were meant to care for me, robbed me of my childhood. But I don't really need to tell you what really happened all those years ago. I guess you were well aware of the earthly happenings as you roamed around your spiritual eternity.

My final prayer and wish is that God will allow both of us to build a spiritual bond with each other in a future life to help overcome the earthly bond that I feel I was so wrongly robbed of.

One last request, please look out for Johnny, my son, your grandson. The grandson I know you'd be proud of. Please don't forget to watch my little Blathin now known as Geraldine. I will tell you more about her when we meet. Sean Og is doing well and Jim is still a pillar of strength.
See you soon Mammy for I'm on my way.
RIP
Your ever-loving daughter,
Peg.

"Please look after me dear Peg and tell her that I miss her so much," sobbed Jim placing a bunch of flowers at the graveside.

Then he lights a little candle and with the flame he burns the note just as Peg had requested. As it wafted off into the November winds he makes a final wish that he would be as good a father to Geraldine and Johnny as Peg was a mother. Replacing his cap he makes his way across to Mr Keating's grave at the far side of the graveyard. Once again he kneels down at the graveside and reads the letter silently.

Mr. Keating
I've asked my husband to read this letter to you. He is fully aware of the horrific wrongdoings you imposed on me as a young girl. During my final moments on this earth I've released the hatred that I've carried in my heart

towards you but I've tried in my soul to forgive you for that's what the Bible teaches us. But I would only be a hypocrite if I say I forgave you. I simply can't and I'll never grant you that forgiveness so that you may RIP. How can you expect me to forgive you? My memories of you are of horrible dark moments where you engulfed me in your greedily bodily manly pleasures that were both unchristian and inhuman. I tried to forget what you said, I even tried to forget what you did, but I could never forget how you made me feel. So, how can you expect me to forgive you for raping and plundering my girlish innocence and robbing me of my dignity?

I've spent a lifetime trying to recapture my true identity while restoring treads of my lost dignity. I'm only truly grateful to God that He allowed Jim into my life, a kind understanding man, who never forced his manly ways on me. I never knew what it was to love a person through bodily sexual expression for that was a tainted experience of the memories of you. I do however ask God to forgive you for your sins and pray that I'll never meet with you in paradise for if I do I'll offer no goodwill towards you.
From
Peg, (The Industrial School girl... the mother of your child. The child you never knew. She is one of life's joys I stole from you. I couldn't let her know that dark secret of her past. After all, why should your tainted memory have the right to infest her as it has infested me. May God forgive you Sir, for I simply can't.)

Having read the letter, he feels a little uneasy and recites the Lord's Prayer to put his mind to rest. As he kneels quietly at the grave, the day at the strand all those months ago when Peg first told him about the abuse that she suffered at this man's hands flashes through his mind and he couldn't help feeling angry and wonders why in the name of Christ would someone want to abuse an innocent young child. Standing up, he takes a box of matches from his pocket and having lit one he burns the note and as he focuses on the burning paper he makes another wish but this time it is that all victims of abuse find peace and contentment in their lives. Now he feels relieved that he has carried out the final wishes of his loving wife. As he makes his way back across the graveyard to the car, his attention is alerted to the invigorating flame that comes from the candle at Peg's mother's grave. A gutting feeling nags him and nudges him back to Mr Keating's grave and he is inspired to light a candle for him. Jim couldn't reason out the reason why, but something in him probed him to do so. He thought, maybe it's Peg, for somehow maybe in her rightful and blessed place in Heaven and living in the midst of the grace of God, she now found it in her Spirit to forgive her abuser, a task she couldn't commit herself to while living on this earth.

On the way home he calls in to see Doc, as he is in desperate need of a friendly shoulder to cry on.

"Jim howya getting on, my good man?" asked Doc shaking hands with Jim and directing him into the kitchen.

"Ach shur, only fair to middlin', fair to middlin'. Ach truth behold, I'm not great Doc. I'm findin' it very hard to let go. Fr Murphy told me a few weeks back that each and everywan of us have a special friend who has a spiritual meanin' for us and I guess Peg over the years became mine," replied Jim.

"I've no doubt that you'll find it very hard, Jim. You know yourself, I always had a special fondness for your wife. She reminded me so much of my own Betty. Please God, let them both rest in peace. Somehow, both of them had that special mystic magnetic aura about them. Something you don't find in many women and once you fall in love with that special type of woman, it's very hard to let her go," sighed Doc putting on the kettle to make a cup of tea. He knew in his heart that Jim didn't come to see a doctor but was looking for the ear of a friend to listen and hear him out as he put his inner thoughts into words.

"Was over yonder at the graveyard in Tralee to say hello to Peg's mother and sort out some unfinished business for Peg. God, I miss her so much. I guess over the years she became me Gallia. Always there to fight for what she thought was right and just," mumbled Jim with tear filled eyes.

"Graveyards are strange places, so full of sorrow yet in that very same sorrow there's so much comfort. I go there myself to visit my Betty, looking for answers to my unsolved problems. And in the silence of her grave, the unanswered questions just seem to sort themselves out," muttered Doc handing Jim a cup of sweet tea with a noggin of whiskey in it.

"Doc, I find meself callin' Peg only to be startled into the fact that she is dead when I don't get a response. I put a cup and saucer out for her when I boil the kettle. Today, I told Nora in the Post Office that I'd tell Peg about next ICA outin'. In me head, I know she is dead, but it's like me heart refuses to accept it. It's like me mind and heart aren't in tune. Last night, I went out yonder into the farmyard and shouted for her to come in as I felt it was too cold a night to be out. I can't talk to Sean Og about her 'cause he's so upset. I feel I've lost me sense of ability. When I turned over in the bed last night I found meself stretchin' out to cuddle into her. Yerra Doc. am I goin' stark ravin' mad or can this happen to somewan when a loved wan dies? Truth behold, if Geraldine wasn't here to look after Johnny I don't know how I'd cope. I want to bawl me eyes out and yell at God but I find meself resistin' and scoldin' meself. Today I went to Peg's mother's grave as Peg had requested it of me and as I knelt there in silence I started to get annoyed with Peg for leavin' Johnny to cope without her," sobbed Jim as he sips the warm whisky tea and wipes the tears that flow down his cheeks with the sleeve of his jacket.

"Jim my good man, what you're feeling is normal I've been there. Life has a way of going on even though our loved ones ain't around. It's very difficult, it may seem to get easier as time passes but every now and again a memory, a little picture or even a smell will remind you of your grief and loss. From the loss of my own Betty and our little baby so many years ago and from walking side-by-side with other people's grief, I now know that the loss of a loved one, will certainly leave it's mark."

"Ya see Doc, what upsets me the most, is that Peg never got over the abuse she suffered in that Industrial School. Somehow, she did come to term with the situation around Geraldine and the terrible injustice she had to live with. But the sexual abuse, she never got over. She said, she could never forgive her abuser for how he had made her feel. I think that's a terrible cross to carry and so sad that wan should be burdened with such an emotional scar throughout their whole life….."

"That doesn't surprise me one bit," replied Doc, pouring out another cup of tea for Jim and himself.

"Doc, now that I think about it, lookin' back over the years when I was a wee lad, probably no more than six or seven, me mother would religiously warn me to stay away from a certain man. Ach shur, ya know ya'rself as a child ya'd listen into the adult conversations and I'd hear them say that this man had a savage hunger for children. At the time, it didn't make much sense, but thinkin' back on it now, shur he probably was a paedophile. Child sex abusers were rampant in all walks of society and not just in the Industrial Schools," sighed Jim shaking his head.

"How right you are, the lurking predators is what I call them. They're knifing, lurking predators that go through a calculated process of seducing young innocent children. They slowly reel in the child by building up their trust by seducing them until the child feels trapped in an environment of shame and guilt. One in four children will have experienced sex abuse at the hands of those predators by the time they've reached the age of adulthood. A very frightening thought but a reality we as a nation need to face up to."

"Do….children…..realise….that….they're….bein' abused?" frowned Jim.

"Believe it or not, many children are totally unaware that they're being abused. Most of the time, they never tell anyone. Often they're both physically and psychologically dependent upon the offender. The offender most likely to be a close acquaintance of the family, a member of the family or a stranger who has instilled fear into the child. Often it's difficult for a parent or guardian to recognise the abuse, as physical force may not have been present. Signs are often more subtle and innocent victims are enticed into the abuse rather than forced. The offender often rewards the victim, although threats and breaking down the victim's self-confidence ain't unusual. The offender is very crafty and sly about keeping the offence a secret between the offender and the victim," insisted Doc shaking his head in disgust.

"Doc, how'd ya know if a young child was bein' abused, take for instance Johnny, there must be times when parents are unaware that their child is in danger?" asked Jim taking the cup of tea from Doc and dunking his biscuit into it.

"Jim, The physical signs of sex abuse are an eye opener. One should be on the look out for signs such as any redness, irritation, bruising, lacerations, bleeding or discharge around the genital or anal area. A young victim of sex abuse, may exhibit unacceptable behaviours such as inappropriate self-touching of genital parts. Unacceptable bruising around different parts of the body may be present. Young children may demonstrate unacceptable gagging when chewing food. Pregnancy in very young teenagers shouldn't be ruled out," replied Doc getting up and walking to the back window that looks out onto the overgrown bramble garden.

"It must leave a horrific mark on a child. Ach shur, 'tis well I know that from Sean Og and Peg. They lived the emotional pain day in and day out and as ya know ya'rself I was unaware of that pain for they suffered it in silence," sighed Jim following Doc over to the back window.

"Jim my good friend, no child is psychologically prepared to cope with repeated sexual abuse. Even a three year old child, who can't know that sexual abuse is wrong will develop problems resulting from the inability to cope with the over stimulation of the body. Young children may suffer recurring nightmares or become very clingy and insecure. They may start bedwetting or even soiling between bowel motions. It ain't unusual for them to revert into an infantile state of behaviour or show an aggressive rebellious behaviour pattern. They often have an introvert disposition and fail to thrive physically. In older children, depression ain't unusual. These children may suffer from a poor self-concept and often turn to substance abuse as a form of escape. The victims may have difficulty in building up relationships and friendships with their peers. School performance may also suffer," said Doc and as he looks at Jim, he notices that the white of his eyes had become bloodshot from the strain of his sorrow.

"How'd ya go about helpin' a child such as Johnny, who comes to ya and tells ya that he's bein' abused?" asked Jim eager to find out as much as possible to protect Johnny.

"If you suspect that a child is being abused always approach the situation in a calm open-minded manner. Above all, listen, understand and recognize the problem. Every complaint should be taken seriously. If a child approaches you with the problem, give the child the privacy he or she requires to confide in you. Believe….them. Don't suggest to them……. what might have happened. The child will have to explain in his or her own words what happened. Keep the discussion time short so as not to cause any further emotional strain on the child. Reassure the child that it's okay to look for help and seek out help for the child. Most importantly, protect the child from the sex offender," insisted Doc as he places his hand on Jim's arm to ease his concern.

"It's a very frightenin' thought to think that there're abusers just lurkin' out there and children are at risk. But it's more frightenin' to think that the majority of abusers aren't strangers but acquaintances of the child. In the honour of Jaysus……..I simply…..don't know……what the world…… is comin' to at all."

"Well it's like this Jim, we as a nation must learn from the injustices of the past. We need to have zero tolerance when it comes to abuse so that our children can live in a safe healthy environment. We need to seek out the abusers so they too can find help. We mustn't relax our vigilance regarding the children of Ireland. All parents have a duty to protect their children. And as Fr. Murphy said at Peg's graveside, our children will never be safe while untreated sex offenders are allowed to walk the streets and live freely amidst our country's most precious inhabitants…"

"Doc, will the victims of the abuse that occurred in those Industrial Schools ever get an apology from their abusers?"

"Well I don't know, but I'll count on it that the Christian Brothers will silence their members who're implicated in the abuse of innocent children and they'll never be allowed to make that apology. You see, if they apologise, they're admitting to the abuse and will then have to come out of their world of denial and of hiding behind their legal teams. Any Christian Brother who is man enough to come forward and put his hand up in acknowledgement of his wrongdoings will have to defrock himself first and then he'll have to live with the consequences of his isolation from his brotherhood. I'm telling you now, not too many of them have the courage to do that. After all, it takes a brave and Christian man to admit to his wrongdoings and it's well known that it takes a coward to hide behind them. But, one thing that victims of abuse can reassure themselves by, is that the abusers may fool the law courts of this land but when they meet with God on their deathbeds, they'll have to face the book of justice," said Doc as Jim puts on his coat and gets ready to leave for home.

"Christttt, maybe so," replied Jim buttoning up his overcoat.

"One thing for sure, the members of Religious Orders that abused innocent children placed in their care by the Irish State may not be too troubled by illnesses of the flesh as they grow older but they'll be certainly troubled by illnesses of the soul if they'll continue to live in denial…"

"By Christttt, ya'r right," nodded Jim biting into his lower lip.

"I'll call around to see you tomorrow," Doc called out as he watches Jim drive out of the yard.

It's a few minutes to four when Patrick calls around to see Jim and to drop off some food he bought in the local village on his way back from a County Council meeting. While he is there the two men get chatting about the events that overtook the past year.

"Howya coping Jim?" asked Patrick.

"Can't hold back the tears. I miss her so much," replied Jim in a tearful voice. "They say it'll get easier but I'm not too sure. Peg was wan of a kind. Her time on this earth was short. Ach shur Patrick, 'twas really just over a score and a baker's dozen of years in all..."

"Sorrow is like a river, it takes on its own flow. Don't hold back the tears, let them flow for they're a source of healing. Sadness shouldn't be depressed, it needs to be expressed as it's a natural development of humanity. You see Jim, God gives and God takes away and when, where, how and why is the will of God himself," replied Patrick tapping Jim on the shoulder.

"Peg was an amazin' woman and regardless of all her hardships she'd a wonderful outlook in life. She lived her life by the wisdom that a problem was a pessimist view of a challenge and a challenge was an optimist view of a problem," smiled Jim wiping his eyes with the corner of his jacket sleeve.

"It certainly was a daunting year for yourself. You must have great inner strength to come through it," said Patrick and you could tell from the tone in his voice that he had great respect and admiration for Jim, "I dare say you'll be slow to forget 1972..."

"I don't know Patrick, for just there over a year ago as ya well know yarself I was ready to throw the towel in on me own life. But when life gave me a second chance, little did I realise that so many ghosts of times past would visit me and challenge me to confront the truth and conquer demons," muttered Jim as the two men sit shoulder-to-shoulder on the bonnet of Patrick's car. "I guess ya're right, 1972 was certainly a challengin' year for us all."

"Suicide is the reality of a desperate and lonely emotional plea for help, one that we need to be more understanding of. Mental health is the corner stone of well-being, but sadly our health services fail to recognise this. There'll come a time when we'll have more death by the hand of suicide than deaths caused by road accidents or heart disease. And when that time comes, maybe then our health services will start putting more resources into our mental health services and help those in need of rescue from their confused emotional state of minds," said Patrick handing Jim a bag of grapes for Johnny and Geraldine.

"Thanks Patrick, Geraldine is very fond of the grapes, strange Peg was the same," chuckled Jim nibbling at one of the grapes. "Doc and meself were chatting about the Industrial Schools earlier on. Do ya reckon the Irish Government will ever apologise to the boys and girls of Ireland who were abused while placed in care in those schools by the state?"

"I guess in years to come they will," Patrick replied fixing the aerial on his car.

"Will it just be a hypocritical wan, do ya think?" questioned Jim with a doubtful tone in his voice.

"Certainly not, just an administrational one," replied Patrick stretching across the bonnet of his car and looking down the boreen.

"I guess ya might be right, yeah, just an administrational wan. But, will it brin' peace of mind to the victims though?" asked Jim resting his elbows on the roof of Patrick's car.

"Yerra shur Jim, no apology will bring peace of mind if they haven't found contentment in their souls."

"But maybe it might brin' them a step closer to that contentment?"

"Hopefully it will, But I doubt that we'll ever find answers to why so many innocent children got locked into the organised insanity of the Religious Orders in charge of the Industrial Schools during the 40s, 50s and 60s but it'd be honourable of the Religious Orders responsible for the abuse to step forward and help to heal the wounds and sins of history. But even if they ain't willing to do so, there's one thing we as a nation need to make sure of, is that it'll never be allowed to happen again. It'd be nice to think that the day would come when victims of abuse could stop living life in the rear view mirror and find contentment in the present while preparing for the future. I think an apology from their abusers might help them to do just that."

"Yerra Jaysus ya'r right.."

"But there's one other issue that certainly needs investigation.."

"What that?"

"That's, why were so many doctors allowed to break the Hippocratic Oath by not protecting the children in their care that they knowingly knew were abused time and time again by the Religious Orders in those Industrial Schools in Ireland and elsewhere," insisted Patrick shaking his head in disgust.

"Yeah..... ya'r right."

"I.... know.... I'm right."

"Patrick, I keep askin' meself why did it happen, how could members of the Religious Orders abuse innocent kids?"

"Well, my gut feeling is that the Religious Orders got too secure in their quest for respect and power and as result of that, empathy was misplaced and for that reason alone they were unable to understand the hurt and torment that a defenceless child feels…"

"Emmm," nodded Jim.

" You see Jim, when empathy is nonexistent, evil flourishes. Evil originates and flourishes in a polluted mind. The principal of universal evolution is based on cause and effect. Because there's birth there'll be death and whoever commits evil acts and sets out to hurt others will eventually receive the bitterness and the sting of such evil…."

"Do ya think there were any good Christian Brothers in those Industrial Schools?"

"Yerra Jim, some might say there were probably a few, but in my opinion if that's so, they were as rare as hens' teeth…"

"Byjoe indeed they were, as rare as hen teeth indeed."

"And by Christ, if you did come across a good one, I guess he'd try and convince you that it was the fear of aloneness and of being boycotted by their own, silenced him and clouded his goodness and judgement. But no excuses should be made for those men. After all, they were intelligent grown men who knew right from wrong," replied Patrick letting out a long deep sigh.

"Be Jaysus, ya'r right."

"But truth behold, no matter what the Christian Brothers did or didn't do, the real culprit for the abuse that went on in those Industrial Schools of Ireland was the Irish State, for it didn't look after its children and it continued to off load its children into those school where they knowing knew that abuse was rampant. But like many injustices in this life, the whole truth may never unfold for it only takes a few inmates from the Industrial Schools to lie about the full extend of abuse they suffered and by doing so, they'll ruin it for others who've a honest to God story to tell…"

"Emmm," nodded Jim.

"In time, I'd dare say, we'll have some form of an investigation into the happenings at those schools. I'd like to think it'd be a fair one though. A fair investigation not only searches out the truth but it also roots out the truth about the facts. If I may be the devil's advocate for a moment Jim, when the truth does unfold regarding the abuse that went on in those Industrial Schools of Ireland and elsewhere and should there be a possibility that the State and Religious Orders confess to the abuse and compensation is offered to the victims, no doubt you'd certainly have so-called victims with their hearsay stories coming out of the closets like woodworm trying to claim that they were abused. Greed for money will lead to inmates lying and innocent people may end up wronged for something they didn't do. Now, that to me is abuse in itself.

But one thing for sure we mustn't let the hatred of others allow us to lose sight of the truth. I say it now and will continue to say it, that innocent people working in those schools mustn't be accused of crimes they didn't commit.

"Yeah, I guess that's the truth and there's no doubt about it. By the way Fr. Murphy told me this mornin' that Kate is thinkin' of returnin' to Ireland with her husband. He's a doctor and he's intendin' to set up general practice here in Kerry. They'd like Geraldine to complete her education here in Ireland and get to know Johnny better. And to crown it all, they're goin' to put the name Blathin on Geraldine's birth certificate."

Patrick could tell that Jim was very happy with this, as there was a spark coming back into the tone of his voice.

"That's great news, what about Fr. Murphy?"

"He's goin' to return to the Congo before Christmas. He feels that his true callin' is there, amidst the people who humbled him and who gave him a true understandin' of Christianity. In the short while that I've come to know that man, I've learned so much about life and religion. Wan thin' that I've come to accept and understand is that religion ain't all about parrot phrasin' on bended knee or prayin' with ya'r arse cocked up to the sun and moon, it's much more than that, it's about the way ya choose to live ya'r life, " replied Jim picking up a twig and throwing it across the yard for Sally to fetch.

"I see, I guess God had a purpose for him and that was one of the reasons why he fell ill. I guess his mission was to return to Ireland to put right an injustice and now that his mission is completed, it's only right and fitting he follows his true calling."

"I've no doubt that God works in mysterious ways. He has a purpose for all of us," replied Jim as he pulls the twig from Sally's mouth and sends her off on the chase once again, as he throws it high into the air.

"As the old saying goes, for the want of a nail the shoe was lost, for the want of a shoe the horse was lost and for the want of a horse the rider was lost," hummed Patrick tapping on the roof of his car. "And when it came to those

Industrial Schools in Ireland it could be said, for the want of humanity, proper care was lost and for the want of proper care many childhood dignities were lost. Sad, and shameful but it was the reality of the situation. You see Jim, in Roman times, Christian slaves were the appetising bounty for the ravaging lions in the Colosseum and from what I've discovered regarding those Industrial Schools in Ireland and elsewhere it might be true to say that many young innocent children were detained and enslaved into these schools and while there, they were plundered of their dignities by been forced to became the sexual bounty that fed the satanic appetite of many evil people… "

"Almighty Christ….shameful…sad….but true. But as ya said in ya'r letter regardin' the Industrial Schools young innocent children were sentenced into the belly of the beast durin' the decades between the forties and the sixties," replied Jim as he gazed up into the late evening sky that forecast a cold night. "Do ya think that evil will continue to infest the members of our Religious Orders?"

"To tell you the truth, I don't Jim, but like any organisation or congregation you'll always have the parasitic minority that are always ready to suck the energy out of good willed people. But there's one thing for sure and that is, if the filth that has impregnated our Religious Orders ain't gutted out, the Catholic Church will lose all creditability and its followers will dwindle away. But come to think of it, maybe that mightn't be so bad for our next generation will question their Faith and won't follow a blindfold religion like our parents and ancestors have done to date. Maybe it's time for a new ere and our mission should be to build a church on Christianity and not on rigid Catholic regimes alone."

"Maybe so," sighed Jim knocking off the cobwebs from the side mirror of Patrick's car.

And as the two men silently thought about the mystic wonders of life and as they gazed on into the peacefulness of the evening watching Geraldine and Johnny ramble off arm-in-arm down the boreen with Sally and Nancy the goat scrambling along in their footsteps.

Both of these youngsters born unto Peg had experienced true contentment with life and yet they were conceived into this world under very different circumstances.

As they drifted off into the dimness of the evening, the scene captured and embraced one of life's greatest messages...*Where there is love and support the seeds of contentment will grow.*

THE END

Translation of Irish words and slang

Aul	-	old
Ayezee	-	Easy
Bean-an-ti	-	woman of the house
Bail ó Dhia ort	-	The blessing of God on you.
Caorans	-	small pieces of turf or peat
Caid	-	football game
Fan linn	-	wait a moment
Garda	-	police man
Gardai	-	police men
Gra	-	love
Gra geal mo chroi	-	love of my heart
Garsun	-	boy
Mic	-	son
Póg mo thóin	-	kiss my arse
Rath Dé orthu	-	The grace of God be with you all
Sciotans or fineogs	-	insects
Sugan	-	straw- rope chair
Tuirseach	-	weary
Wan	-	one

Lightning Source UK Ltd.
Milton Keynes UK
22 June 2010
155946UK00001B/69/P